Edgar Rice Burroughs
The Bibliography

Edgar Rice Burroughs

The Exhaustive Scholar's and Collector's Descriptive Bibliography of American Periodical, Hardcover, Paperback, and Reprint Editions

by ROBERT B. ZEUSCHNER

with a foreword by PHILIP JOSÉ FARMER

McFarland & Company, Inc., Publishers
Jefferson, North Carolina, and London

The present work is a reprint of the library bound edition of
Edgar Rice Burroughs: The Exhaustive Scholar's and Collector's
Descriptive Bibliography of American Periodical, Hardcover,
Paperback, and Reprint Editions, *first published in 1996 by McFarland.*

Frontispiece: ERB in 1912 when *Tarzan* was first published
(© 1975 Edgar Rice Burroughs, Inc.)

LIBRARY OF CONGRESS CATALOGUING-IN-PUBLICATION DATA

Zeuschner, Robert B., 1941–
  Edgar Rice Burroughs : the exhaustive scholar's and collector's
descriptive bibliography of American periodical, hardcover,
paperback, and reprint editions / by Robert B. Zeuschner with
a foreword by Philip José Farmer.
    p.   cm.
  Includes index.
  ISBN-13: 978-0-7864-3113-7
  (softcover : 50# alk. paper) ∞

  1. Burroughs, Edgar Rice, 1875–1950—Bibliography. 2. Popular
literature—United States—Bibliography. 3. Fantastic fiction,
American—Bibliography. 4. Adventure stories, American—
Bibliography. 5. Science fiction, American—Bibliography.
I. Title.
Z8136.15.Z48   2007
[PS3503.U687]
016.813'52—dc20   96-273311

©1996 Robert B. Zeuschner. All rights reserved

*No part of this book may be reproduced or transmitted in any form
or by any means, electronic or mechanical, including photocopying
or recording, or by any information storage and retrieval system,
without permission in writing from the publisher.*

On the cover: Portrait of Burroughs given to Burroughs' mother-in-
law, ©1975 Edgar Rice Burroughs, Inc.; Lion ©2007 Pictures Now

Manufactured in the United States of America

McFarland & Company, Inc., Publishers
  Box 611, Jefferson, North Carolina 28640
    www.mcfarlandpub.com

Dedicated to
Lindy Landry Zeuschner

Acknowledgments

This book is not solely the work of one person. I have many people to thank. First, I must thank the memory of Edgar Rice Burroughs because he gifted me with John Carter and the incomparable Dejah Thoris; with Tars Tarkas and Woola; with Tarzan, Jane and La, Korak, Meriem and Akut; with David Innes and Dian the Beautiful; with Carson Napier, Duare, Norman of Torn, Waldo Emerson Smith-Jones and dozens of others; and because he provided me with a pastime that has given me more pleasurable hours than I could possibly count. My father, Raymond Zeuschner, owned many ERB books when he was a boy, and my grandmother, Clara Siggeman Zeuschner, sent two of them to me for my eleventh birthday. The very next week I was telephoning used book stores to try to find more stories about Tarzan and the moss-covered ochre sea bottoms of Mars. Thanks Dad, and thanks Grandma. Thanks to my wife, Lindy, who never complained about my obsession and even shared some of my enthusiasm. My special thanks also go to my children, Jennifer, David, Danae, and Scott, who patiently allowed me to read and reread aloud to them book after book by Edgar Rice Burroughs.

I have referred to Henry Heins' *Golden Anniversary Bibliography* constantly since I first purchased it in 1964, and my bibliography would not be possible were it not for Mr. Heins' work. That this work is indebted to George McWhorter's *Catalog* (House of Greystoke, 1991) for some of the detail offered herein is gratefully acknowledged. The information on the more obscure of the various artists, and details on various entries were supplied by art collector and scholar Robert R. Barrett, who very carefully read an earlier draft of this book and made numerous corrections and suggestions.

Bill Ross, Burroughs scholar and collector, graciously and carefully read an earlier draft of this book and made hundreds of suggestions and additions which improved it considerably. Those who find this book to be of value owe a special debt to Mr. Ross and his encyclopedic knowledge of the realm of Burroughs collectibles. Michael Conran read an earlier draft and assisted as well.

Acknowledgments

Also, this book would not exist were it not for the decades of devotion to Burroughs bibliography of people like the late Vernell Coriell (premier Burroughs fan, creator of the BURROUGHS BIBLIOPHILES and editor of the first ERB fan magazine, the BURROUGHS BULLETIN), Camille "Caz" Cazedessus, Jr., editor of the stellar fanzine ERB-DOM, and George T. McWhorter, the new editor of the resurrected BURROUGHS BULLETIN, who is both carrying on and enriching the Coriell tradition. Countless contributors whose work appeared in these and other fanzines have informed this reference book as well.

Thanks to John Anthony Miller, who read an earlier draft of this book and added additional facts about dust jackets based upon his own extensive collection. In addition, Mitchell Harrison of Chicago read an earlier draft and provided photographs and much additional information about some of the more unusual items in his extraordinary collection. Collector Joe Lukes graciously shared with me the results of his own research on Grosset & Dunlap variants. Bill Morse and J. G. Huckenpöhler contributed to the section on Burroughs pastiches. Laurence Dunn shared his knowledge of unpublished ERB manuscripts, and Frank Westwood helped me to sort out the various British editions of the second part of *The Mucker*. Clarence B. Hyde, president of the Burroughs Bibliophiles, graciously read a late draft and provided additional details on several titles. Thanks also to Danton Burroughs, and ERB, Inc., for providing the photographs of Edgar Rice Burroughs.

Special thanks are due Brian Kirby, a very special and best friend with whom I have shared three decades of mutual interests. Mr. Kirby, a legend as an editor and an expert on rare books, not only supplied many wonderful items for my collection but, in addition, carefully went over the final manuscript and improved it in a thousand different ways.

This bibliography would not be as accurate if it were not for these giants upon whose shoulders I have stood during its creation. However, despite all the assistance I received, all errors and omissions are, of course, solely the responsibility of the author.

ROBERT B. ZEUSCHNER
January 1996

Table of Contents

Acknowledgments — vii
Foreword by Philip José Farmer — 1
Preface — 3
Edgar Rice Burroughs: His Life and His Work — 7
"Edgar Rice Burroughs Tells All" — 21

PART I. BIBLIOGRAPHY OF BOOKS BY EDGAR RICE BURROUGHS
(ALPHABETICAL BY TITLE)

APACHE DEVIL	26
AT THE EARTH'S CORE	28
BACK TO THE STONE AGE	32
THE BANDIT OF HELL'S BEND	33
THE BEASTS OF TARZAN	35
BEYOND THE FARTHEST STAR	39
BEYOND THIRTY	40
CARSON OF VENUS	41
THE CAVE GIRL	43
THE CHESSMEN OF MARS	46
THE DEPUTY SHERIFF OF COMANCHE COUNTY	49
THE EFFICIENCY EXPERT	52
ESCAPE ON VENUS	53
THE ETERNAL LOVER	55
A FIGHTING MAN OF MARS	59
THE GIRL FROM FARRIS'S	61
THE GIRL FROM HOLLYWOOD	63
THE GODS OF MARS	67
I AM A BARBARIAN	69
THE ILLUSTRATED TARZAN BOOK NO. 1	70
JOHN CARTER OF MARS	73
JUNGLE GIRL	75
JUNGLE TALES OF TARZAN	77
THE LAD AND THE LION	80
LAND OF TERROR	83
THE LAND THAT TIME FORGOT	84
LLANA OF GATHOL	88
LOST ON VENUS	90
THE MAD KING	93
THE MAN-EATER	95
MARCIA OF THE DOORSTEP	97
THE MASTER MIND OF MARS	97
THE MONSTER MEN	100
THE MOON MAID	103
THE MUCKER	106
THE OAKDALE AFFAIR	108
THE OUTLAW OF TORN	110

Pellucidar	111
Pirate Blood	115
Pirates of Venus	116
A Princess of Mars	118
The Resurrection of Jimber-Jaw	123
The Return of Tarzan	124
The Rider	130
Savage Pellucidar	131
The Scientists Revolt	132
The Son of Tarzan	133
Swords of Mars	138
Synthetic Men of Mars	140
Tales of Three Planets	141
Tanar of Pellucidar	142
Tarzan and the Ant Men	143
Tarzan and the Castaways	147
Tarzan and the City of Gold	149
Tarzan and the Forbidden City	151
Tarzan and "The Foreign Legion"	154
Tarzan and the Golden Lion	155
Tarzan and the Jewels of Opar	158
Tarzan and the Leopard Men	163
Tarzan and the Lion Man	166
Tarzan and the Lost Empire	168
Tarzan and the Madman	171
Tarzan and the Tarzan Twins	172
Tarzan at the Earth's Core	176
Tarzan Clans of America	179
Tarzan Jr.	180
Tarzan, Lord of the Jungle	181
Tarzan of the Apes	184
Tarzan the Invincible	195
Tarzan: The Lost Adventure	196
Tarzan the Magnificent	198
Tarzan the Terrible	199
Tarzan the Untamed	203
Tarzan Triumphant	207
Tarzan's Quest	209
Thuvia, Maid of Mars	210
The War Chief	214
The Warlord of Mars	215
The Wizard of Venus	218
You Lucky Girl!	220

Part II.   Other Bibliographies

Unpublished and Miscellaneous Short Works by Burroughs (Alphabetical by title)	222
Big Little Books Based on Burroughs' Plots or Characters (Chronological by publisher or series)	226
Published and Unpublished Books Based on Burroughs' Plots or Characters (Alphabetical by author)	233

Table of Contents

A Selected Bibliography of Works About Burroughs
  (Alphabetical by author) — 238
A Selected Bibliography of Works About
  Burroughs Artists (Alphabetical by artist) — 249
A Selected List of Burroughs Fanzines (Alphabetical by title) — 252

Appendices
  A. Values of Burroughs First Editions — 255
  B. Chronological List (by Publication Date)
      of Burroughs Hardback First Editions — 257
  C. Companies That Published Burroughs First Editions — 258
  D. The Two Most Popular Burroughs Reprint Publishers — 260
  E. McClurg Print Run Records — 261
  F. The House of Greystoke Publications — 262
  G. Chronological List (by Date of Authorship)
      of Burroughs' Stories — 265

  Index — 269

Foreword

Herein is a book prepared by a lover of the works of Edgar Rice Burroughs, the creator of Tarzan, John Carter of Mars, David Innes of Pellucidar, Red Hawk, and many other shining heroes. It is a labor of love, written by one who fell in love with these semimythical beings at an early age. Bob Zeuschner did not write this for money. He wrote it because he felt, quite rightly, that there was a need for this book and because he had fun doing it.

Though the purpose of this work is utilitarian, we true fans of ERB will enjoy just reading it, even if we don't use it to collect rare editions. I know that when I go through it, and it'll be more than once, I'll recapture many of the golden moments I reveled in when these books first swam into my ken.

Philip José Farmer

Preface

This book is intended for collectors, libraries, rare book dealers, auction houses, and everyone else interested in the works of the extraordinary American author Edgar Rice Burroughs (September 1, 1875–March 19, 1950).

The emphasis of this book is on the American hardback editions. There is a complete description of every Burroughs first edition, and the *first state* of the first edition is clearly distinguished from the second state, the third state, all reprintings by first edition publishers, and all other American hardback reprints. This information can be found quickly because all of the titles of hardback and significant paperback editions published in North America through 1995 are listed in alphabetical order.

For the sake of completeness, there are brief entries for the two ERB books that are being published in 1997, *You Lucky Girl!* and *Marcia of the Doorstep*.

In this book Burroughs' major published works are set off by the use of boldface type, his short stories appearing with quotation marks and his novels in boldface italics.

Each listing begins with a description of the first magazine appearance of the story. Next, the hardback first edition is set apart from the rest of the entries and described in detail. Then the major American reprint editions are listed chronologically and differentiated. Finally, the earliest of the paperback printings are noted, followed by subsequent paperback reprintings which may be significant because of a change of cover artist, or for other related reasons.

The first entry of each listing situates the Burroughs story so that the reader will know approximately when it was written, and which novel or short story was written immediately before or after.

The information in the present work comes from several sources. The primary source is my own personal collection. My own knowledge and collection are not, however, sufficient to account for every listing in this book and I have therefore relied upon the expertise of many Burroughs scholars who have published articles in the hundreds of issues of Burroughs fanzines to which I have subscribed since the early 1950s. Many of these fine individuals are mentioned by name in the Acknowledgments.

Most importantly, this book is simultaneously an amplification and an abridgment of the two primary bibliographic sources:

> Henry Hardy Heins, *A Golden Anniversary Bibliography of Edgar Rice Burroughs*, Donald M. Grant, Rhode Island, 1964.

> George T. McWhorter, *Edgar Rice Burroughs Memorial Collection: A Catalog*, House of Greystoke (ERB Memorial Collection, University of Louisville, Louisville, Kentucky), 1991.

George T. McWhorter's *Catalog* is a comprehensive listing of library holdings up to 1991 of the Ekstrom Library at the University of Louisville, the world's largest collection of materials by and about Edgar Rice Burroughs. Profusely illustrated, it has a detailed and lengthy bibliographic essay by McWhorter which carefully describes the printing history of the first edition publishers and the reprint publishers of Burroughs' works.

Reflecting years of scholarly research in the Library of Congress and dozens of other original sources, Henry H. Heins' *Golden Anniversary Bibliography* lists precise details on all editions through 1964, with appendices, lists, and numerous illustrations. Heins also provides reproductions of the magazine art work of that great illustrator of Burroughs, J. Allen St. John. Unfortunately, Heins' *Bibliography* has been out of print since 1965, and is difficult and expensive to obtain.

In addition to the two books mentioned above, I have used valuable bibliographical information found in the remarkable biography of Burroughs written by Irwin Porges, *Edgar Rice Burroughs: The Man Who Created Tarzan* (1975).

For more information about the realms of Edgar Rice Burroughs, contact any of these Burroughs fanzines:

THE BURROUGHS BULLETIN (published for the Burroughs Bibliophiles)
c/o George McWhorter
Ekstrom Library—The Burroughs Memorial Collection
University of Louisville
Louisville, Kentucky 40492
Telephone (505) 852-8729

THE EDGAR RICE BURROUGHS NEWS DATELINE
c/o Mike Conran, Editor
1990 Pine Grove Dr.
Jenison, Michigan 49428
Telephone (616) 457-1446

PREFACE

ERBANIA
c/o D. Peter Ogden
8410 Lopez Drive
Tampa, Florida 33615
Telephone (813) 884-8144

ERB-COLLECTOR
Bill Ross, Editor
7315 Livingston Road
Oxon Hill, Maryland 20745
Telephone (301) 839-6666

ERB-DOM
c/o Camille "Caz" Cazedessus II
P.O. Box 2340
Pagosa Springs, Colorado 81147

ERB-FAN
Roland Schwegler, Editor
Eschenweg 5
D-85049 Ingoldstadt
Germany

ERB-NOTIZEN
Kurt S. Denkena, Editor
Rosentrasse 12
D-28755 Bremen
Germany

FANTASTIC WORLDS OF ERB
Frank Westwood, Editor
77 Pembroke Road
Seven Kings, Ilford
Essex, IG3 8PQ
England

LA TRIBUNE DES AMIS D'EDGAR
  RICE BURROUGHS
Michel DeCuyper, Editor
59 Rue de la Filature
59180 Cappelle la Grande
France

Edgar Rice Burroughs: His Life and His Work

No one's life should be summarized in just a few lines, least of all the life of Edgar Rice Burroughs. Born on September 1, 1875, in Chicago, young ERB was a creative, bright, and imaginative child. His father, George Tyler Burroughs, was a successful businessman and had been a Union cavalry officer during the Civil War; his son Edgar was always fascinated by his father's stories of war and battle. When he was fourteen (1889), his parents shipped young Edgar to a cattle ranch in Idaho run by his elder brothers. Two years later, he returned home. However, cleverness and a stubborn independence finally found young Edgar placed in a military school, where he had difficulty fitting into a highly structured atmosphere. Upon graduation, he applied to West Point but was not accepted. In May of 1896 he joined the army and was assigned to Fort Grant in Arizona, but was released in March of 1897 because a heart murmur was discovered.

He worked for his brothers for a few years, and then, at age 24, he married his childhood sweetheart, Emma, on January 31, 1900. However, Burroughs was unable to earn a decent living and could not support his wife and growing family, no matter what business he tried. He ran a stationery store in Pocatello, Idaho; he dredged for gold in Parma, Idaho, and he was a railroad policeman in Salt Lake City, Utah. Finally, flat broke, he and Emma auctioned off all their belongings and returned to Chicago. There he tried selling candy to drug stores, selling electric light bulbs to janitors, selling pencil sharpeners, and he even pretended to be an accountant. He was a salesman for a quack cure for alcoholism until the Food and Drug Administration closed the business down. More than once, Burroughs visited a pawn shop to raise enough money for food. Finally, at age 35, he transferred his frustrations and his daydreams to paper, and managed to escape from unpleasant reality. The result was the magazine publication of *A Princess of Mars* (1912). It was a romantic adventure set on the planet Mars, where the hero is transported to a dying world collapsing into barbarism and facing imminent extinction. It is a world where only the fittest survive, but there was a beautiful Martian princess and plenty of swordplay. It was ideal for the pulp magazine audience. Thomas Newell Metcalf, *All-Story* editor, paid him $400 for it. The serial was well received, and Burroughs tried writing another, a medieval romance inspired by *Ivanhoe* titled *The Outlaw of Torn*. At the time, nobody wanted to buy it. Frustrated, he almost gave up writing.

Writing allowed some catharsis, some place where things worked out the way he wanted. In his imagination, Burroughs freed himself from failure and frustration. He daydreamed of being free from business and petty bureaucrats, and living in a primeval jungle Eden. These daydreams provided another idea for a story, set in the jungle, away from the nastiness and defects of civilization. It is a place where we find the simple virtues of nature's creatures, all living free. Biographer Irwin Porges quotes Burroughs on how he came to write *Tarzan*:

> I suppose it was just because my daily life was full of business, system, and I wanted to get as far from that as possible. My mind, in relaxation, preferred to roam in scenes and situations I'd never known. I find I can write better about places I've never seen than those I have seen.[1]

A tiny child is raised by a tribe of apes, yet the child is the product of millions of years of higher evolution. Using only his own strength and human intelligence, he grows up to battle his way into the rank of lord of the jungle. ERB started writing his tale of ape-to-man in December, 1911, and worked on it for six months. The result was the enduring popular classic, *Tarzan of the Apes* (1912). Burroughs received $700 for this effort, at a time when a decent job paid $15–$25 per week.

Tarzan of the Apes was a genuine sensation in the pulp magazine world. It combined romance and adventure with a droll sense of humor. The letters columns of subsequent issues of its parent magazine *All-Story* were filled with requests for more Burroughs stories. Edgar Rice Burroughs' self-confidence began to soar. He wrote a sequel to his previous novel of Mars, *The Gods of Mars* (1913), one of his very best. He received $750 for this effort.

Next, Burroughs tried his hand at the short story form, writing two in 1912. Neither sold. Meanwhile, Metcalf, the *All-Story* editor, wanted Ed Burroughs to write a new story, reuniting Tarzan and Jane. Burroughs toyed around with many ideas, and finally responded with a sequel, *The*

ERB on his favorite horse, Colonel, at Tarzana Ranch, 1928 (© 1975 Edgar Rice Burroughs, Inc.).

Return of Tarzan. The editor rejected it. Disappointed and feeling betrayed, Ed Burroughs submitted it to a different pulp magazine, and it was purchased for $1,000. Realizing the power he had, he began negotiating better and better rates, until he became the reigning monarch of pulp fantasy fiction for the next thirty years, demanding and receiving the highest payment possible. In fact, he became so successful that he was able to move his family to southern California, and in 1919, he purchased the 540-acre ranch estate of Gen. Harrison Gray Otis in the San Fernando valley. The city which eventually grew around the ranch was given the name "Tarzana" in 1930.

In 1931, ERB formed his own publishing company, Edgar Rice Burroughs, Inc., and in addition to reprinting his earlier titles, published twenty-three new Burroughs books during his lifetime (and one title posthumously). From his office in Tarzana, Burroughs was able to use the business skills which had failed him so miserably two decades earlier, and built an empire based upon books, films, radio programs, newspaper comic strips, and many advertising campaigns featuring Tarzan.

Although some people tend to dismiss his novels as juvenile, Burroughs' primary audience was never children. The noble and keenly intelligent Tarzan whom Edgar Rice Burroughs had created in 1912 was transferred to film and became virtually unrecognizable in the many versions produced by the Hollywood film industry. The scriptwriters trashed the scenarios which Burroughs himself produced, and instead created a brain-damaged yet cunning Tarzan who pointed and grunted in monosyllables, "Tarzan, Jane." Ed Burroughs was frustrated because the Tarzan he had created was able to speak fluent English and French before the end of the first Tarzan novel. His Tarzan may be the ape-man, but he is also Lord Greystoke, who moves freely in the drawing rooms of London and Paris, although he prefers his jungle estate (in the novels, Tarzan and Jane never occupied a tree house).

The books which Ed wrote between 1912 and 1930 were usually quite good, and many are genuine classics in the history of American fiction. They have remained in print virtually continuously since their original publication.

Why do people like to read his stories? One answer is that each of them is a romance, and in almost all of them the beautiful damsel is rescued by a wonderful hero and true love conquers all. The pulps required this structure, and it fit perfectly into the author's own psychology. However, there is more to the fiction of Burroughs than this.

HIS LIFE AND HIS WORK

The romances are also adventures, and Burroughs was extraordinarily gifted when it came to describing action sequences. Each chapter arouses the imagination and stimulates the adrenalin. Long after their parents had told them to turn off the light and go to bed, many generations of readers of Burroughs' stories read late into the night, under the covers with a flashlight. Every book and story by Edgar Rice Burroughs offers escape. Ed knew this. In 1932, writing on "The Tarzan Theme" for *Writer's Digest* magazine, he mused:

> His appeal to an audience is so tremendous that it never ceases to be a source of amazement to me. This appeal, I believe, is based upon ... the constant urge to escape that is becoming stronger in all of us prisoners of civilization as civilization becomes more complex. We wish to escape not alone the narrow confines of the city streets for the freedom of the wilderness, but the restrictions of man-made laws, and the inhibitions that society has placed upon us.... We would each like to be Tarzan. At least I would; I admit it.

The prose is not always elegant, but the energy level is so high that we must turn the page and, after finishing one entire book, we need to buy and read the next in the series to find out what happens to the hero and heroine. Their lives and exploits continue to live in our minds beyond the covers of the book. When we read a book by Burroughs, we create images of the sea bottoms of Mars or hear the lion roaring in rage and frustration. In provoking our imagination, Burroughs makes us active participants and co-creators of universe after universe. When you've got a book by Edgar Rice Burroughs, you never say, "I'm bored; what shall we do?" However, there is more to the fiction of Edgar Rice Burroughs than this.

There are ideas in these books as well. The characters in Burroughs' books all live by a strong moral code. The heroes and heroines are profoundly moral; they know the difference between duty and desire, and always do what they believe to be correct. They value friendship above all, and understand honor. The hero is a gentleman. The heroine is a gentlelady. Neither of them give in to greed or lust, and those characters in the books who do succumb to the baser human instincts often wind up with their bones bleaching beneath the burning equatorial sun. In the jungle of ERB's imagination, Tarzan evolves from feral child to British lord, and he survives not only because he is strong and quick, but also because generations of noble ancestors have produced the foundation for

ERB in 1934.

a genetically noble human being. Whenever John Carter of Mars, born a Virginia gentleman, sees someone facing unfair odds, he rushes in to help. Instinctively, the Burroughs hero and heroine stand up against injustice, no matter what the cost. But this morality is not based on the divine commands of a deity or inspired by the love of a divine father. None of

Opposite page: ERB in Malibu, California, 1933 (both photos: © 1975, Edgar Rice Burroughs, Inc.).

EDGAR RICE BURROUGHS

Left: ERB in 1934.
Below: ERB at his large desk with his reference books.
(Both photos: © 1975, Edgar Rice Burroughs, Inc.)

his heroes is religious in the conventional sense of the word. Burroughs had a rather negative attitude towards all organized religions, and one often finds asides in his books that are profoundly critical of religious rituals and ceremonies, which are used to control blindly uncritical followers. In *The Gods of Mars*, Burroughs has a character describe the role of religion on Barsoom:

> The whole fabric of our religion is based on superstitious belief in lies that have been foisted upon us for ages by those directly above us, to whose personal profit and aggrandizement it was to have us continue to believe as they wished us to believe.[2]

Even if ERB was not religious,[3] neither was he a materialist. Perhaps we could call him "spiritual." Many of the passages in his books reverberate with a profound feeling of awe for nature, for the jungle, for the wild, prowling animals, for the distant planets and their moons which hurtle overhead illuminating dying civilizations, and for the mountains of the west caught in the alpenglow of the setting sun. Burroughs loved animals, and his deep and obvious affection for horses and dogs permeates many of his books. His asides in his novels often indicate that he held the natural virtues of wild animals in higher regard than the cruel behavior of so-called "civilized men." He loved and appreciated the wondrous beauty of what nature had wrought, but Darwin's explanation for human existence seemed to make more sense to him than the stories which most of us have been taught in childhood. The books that Burroughs wrote teach a clear moral code which helped to shape the ethical values of many of his readers, and this is combined with Burroughs' genuine gift for describing the wonders of nature.

One important theme which Burroughs explored over and over was the threat of death and its inevitability. His heroes are caught in mazes, trapped in dungeons, and they face death. They fight and they escape one more time, but they know that death cannot be avoided forever. Each Burroughs hero recognizes that fact, but none of them ever quits. Burroughs was trapped in the mazes of business and social institutions, but he was stubborn, and he had an imagination which far outstripped most of his contemporaries.

Ever since he was a young man, Burroughs was searching for a way out. He joined the army. He traveled in Arizona and dredged for gold in Idaho. He was constantly taking his family on elaborate camping trips.

But Burroughs could not escape by going to some physical place. Finally, he did escape by going inward—he put his pen to paper and he wrote.

Borne of deeply held ideals, a well-developed sense of humor, a healthy skepticism, and a rich imagination, many of the literary creations of Edgar Rice Burroughs achieve their enduring quality because they can tap into a universal unconscious. Tarzan of the Apes, the personal daydream of Edgar Rice Burroughs, is an archetype for every young person who ever wanted to be brave and strong, to be a hero, to stand face to face with death and rescue his loved ones from perilous conditions. Tarzan has moved from a hero in an adventure story to an icon of mythic proportions.

In a sense, Tarzan of the Apes is a Janus figure, simultaneously the missing link between ape and man, and also the next step in human evolution. Tarzan is what we hope to become when we grow up, brave, tall, straight, and strong. For the Burroughs hero, no situation is too terrible, no battle is ever hopeless. The hero never gives up. There is a way out. There is always a way out if only you try hard enough. The motto of John Carter of Mars, "I Still Live!" has inspired generation after generation of young men and women.

In the literary universe of Edgar Rice Burroughs, life is an adventure and death is its inevitable outcome, but each of us is alive now and that means that we must try again. Burroughs inspires us to wander the world and to study the heavens above, to explore the caves below, to use our own imaginations.

Burroughs may have been king of pulp fiction, but authors who wrote for the lowly pulps were given no respect within the literary community. Although outwardly denying that he was doing anything more than putting daydreams down on paper, inwardly Ed wanted to be thought of as a real *author*. He tried writing serious fiction and western novels, but they never attained anything like the success that his fantasies of the jungle and Mars did. In fact, rarely were they as good as his more imaginative tales; it was in the creation of alternative universes where his genuine talent and gift lay. His editors and fans wanted to read more adventures of Tarzan, and Burroughs found himself forced to continue writing stories of the ape-man long after his interest had waned. As had happened to others (like A. Conan Doyle), he became trapped by his own success. Although one of the most financially successful authors of the first three-quarters of the twentieth century, he always had large bills

ERB in 1935, dictating a novel (© 1975, Edgar Rice Burroughs, Inc.).

which needed to be paid, and he never had enough money saved to allow him to break away from what his fans demanded. So, he continued to write Tarzan stories year after year, about twenty-six of them in thirty-two years.

In the later Burroughs novels, the characters have a tendency to lose whatever psychological complexity they may have had in the earlier tales, and sometimes become delineated by cultural stereotypes, serving as pawns to the needs of the plot. Coincidences, always a strong element which ERB relied upon in his fiction, became more and more unbelievable, and the plot lines started to sound overly familiar. In several different books, Tarzan (or another hero) is bumped on the head, loses his memory, wanders off for two hundred pages until he is banged on the head once again, and then regains his memory just in time to save the beautiful heroine yet one more time.

Burroughs had expenses and a mortgage, and his writing was controlled by pulp editors who knew what their readers wanted. If a story was not set in Africa or on Barsoom, no editor wanted to pay the high rates Ed demanded and required. He tried writing in other genres, and several times submitted other stories under pseudonyms. When accepted, his "serious" stories were less desirable and he was paid at lower rates. The pieces which he submitted under pen names were always rejected.

Like his literary creations, Burroughs was not completely comfortable in social or emotional situations; he had difficulty making small talk, and he was not a "ladies' man." Although capable of a terse eloquence, by nature Tarzan is taciturn. John Carter is tongue-tied in the presence of his beautiful Martian princess, Dejah Thoris. David Innes of Pellucidar almost loses the woman he loves because he cannot tell her how he feels. This element is autobiographical. Although he loved his children, he was never as close to them as they wished. In the 1930s, his marriage foundered. Ed and Emma were divorced in 1934. He married a second time, to Florence Gilbert Dearholt, a beautiful woman who had been an actress and formerly married to a Hollywood film director. Unfortunately, the marriage did not endure, and was amicably dissolved seven years later.

When Ed was sixty-six, he and his son Hulbert were in Honolulu and witnessed the bombing of Pearl Harbor on December 7, 1941. Fiercely patriotic all of his life, Burroughs desperately wanted to be involved in the war effort. Despite his age, he managed to become an accredited war correspondent and produced a series of newspaper columns under the title, "Laugh It Off." The novel *Tarzan and "The Foreign Legion"* (written between June and September of 1944) reflects this period, with Tarzan ("Lord Greystoke") fighting on the side of the British during World War II. After the war ended, ERB returned to southern California, living in a modest home in Encino, California, near Tarzana.

In the novels, Tarzan found the secret of immortality, but Burroughs himself did not. He started one last Tarzan novel on September 7, 1946, but he did not have the energy to complete it. He left 83 typewritten pages. As he grew older his health became more precarious. On Sunday, March 19, 1950, after reading the funnies in the newspaper, Edgar Rice Burroughs had a heart attack and died. He was buried under a black walnut tree in Tarzana, in an unmarked grave as he wished.

Edgar Rice Burroughs did die, but Tarzan still swings through the upper terraces of the forest giants, leaping perilously from branch to branch, racing to rescue Jane or La of Opar from a hideous fate. John Carter still fights side by side with his great friend, Tars Tarkas, the green Thark chieftain, the clanging of their swords echoing beneath the twin moons of Mars. The creations of Edgar Rice Burroughs continue to live on in the imagination of his readers in a way that few authors ever achieved. No matter where you go in this world, everyone knows of Tarzan. The imagination of Edgar Rice Burroughs is with us today and endures.

NOTES

1. Irwin Porges, *Edgar Rice Burroughs: The Man Who Created Tarzan* (Provo, Utah: Brigham Young University Press, 1975), p. 133.

2. Edgar Rice Burroughs, *The Gods of Mars* (Chicago: A.C. McClurg, 1918), chapter 10, "The Prison Isle of Shador," p. 158.

3. In a January 24, 1916 letter to Robert Davis, who had been ERB's editor at *All-Story Cavalier* since 1914, ERB wrote: "Because I am not religious don't think that I couldn't write a religious story. It's just a matter of imagination, and I can easily imagine myself a religious bigot; and anyway I wouldn't make it [a proposed story on the theme of Cain and Abel] too religious." Quoted in Porges' *Edgar Rice Burroughs*, p. 278.

"Edgar Rice Burroughs Tells All"
An Autobiographical Sketch
by Edgar Rice Burroughs

This delightful example of Burroughs' humor was originally written for a small Hollywood publication of the 1930s entitled Rob Wagner's SCRIPT *published July 9, 1932 (© 1975, Edgar Rice Burroughs, Inc.).*

I am sorry that I have not led a more exciting existence, so that I might offer a more interesting biographical sketch; but I am one of those fellows who has few adventures and always gets to the fire after it is out.

I was born in Peking at the time that my father was military advisor to the Empress of China, and lived there, in the Forbidden City, until I was ten years old. An intimate knowledge of the Chinese language acquired during those years has often stood me in good stead since, especially in prosecuting two of my favorite studies, Chinese philosophy and Chinese ceramics.

Shortly after the family returned to the United States I was kidnapped by gypsies and held by them for almost three years. They were not unkind to me; and in many respects the life appealed to me, but eventually I escaped and returned to my parents.

*

Even today, after the lapse of many years, I distinctly recall the storm-torn night of my escape. Pedro, the king of the gypsies, always kept me in his tent at night where he and his wife could guard me. He was a very light sleeper, which had always presented a most effective obstacle to my eluding the clutches of my captors.

This night the rain and wind and thunder aided me. Waiting until Pedro and his wife were asleep, I started to crawl toward the tent flap. As I passed close beside the king one of my hands fell upon a hard metal object lying beside him; it was Pedro's dagger. At the same instant Pedro awoke. A vivid lightning flash illuminated the interior of the tent, and I saw Pedro's eyes fixed upon me.

Perhaps fright motivated me, or perhaps it was just anger against my abductors. My fingers closed upon the hilt of his dagger, and in the darkness that followed the lightning I plunged the slim steel blade deep into his heart. He was the first man I had ever killed; he died without a sound.

My parents were rejoiced by my return, as they had long since abandoned all hope of ever seeing me again. For a year we traveled in Europe, where under a tutor, I pursued my interrupted education to such good effect that I was able to enter Yale upon our return.

*

While at Yale I won a few athletic honors, annexing both the heavyweight boxing and wrestling championships; and in my senior year I captained the football team and the crew. Graduating *summa cum laude*, I spent two years at Oxford and then returned to the United States and enlisted in the army for a commission from the ranks.

At the end of two years I received my appointment as a second lieutenant and was attached to the 7th Cavalry. My first active service was with Custer at the battle of the Little Big Horn, of which I was the sole survivor.

My escape from death during the massacre was almost miraculous. My horse had been shot from under me, and I was fighting on foot with the remnant of my troop. I can only guess at what actually occurred; but I believe that the bullet that struck me in the head must have passed through the head of the man in front of me and, with its force spent, merely have stunned me.

I fell with my body between two small boulders; and later a horse was shot above me, his body falling on top of mine and concealing it from the eyes of the enemy, the two boulders preventing its weight from crushing me. Gaining consciousness after dark, I crawled from beneath the horse and made my escape.

*

After wandering for six weeks in an effort to elude the Indians and rejoin my people, I reached an army outpost, but when I attempted to rejoin my regiment I was told that I was dead. Insistence upon my rights resulted in my being arrested for impersonating an officer.

Every member of the court knew me and deeply deplored the action they were compelled to take; but I was officially dead, and army regulations are army regulations. I took the matter to Congress, but had no better success there; and finally I was compelled to change my name, adopting that which I now use, and start life all over again.

For several years I fought Apaches in Arizona; but the monotony of it palled upon me, and I was overjoyed when I received a telegram from the late Henry M. Stanley inviting me to join his expedition to Africa in search of Dr. Livingstone.

I accepted immediately and also put five hundred thousand dollars at his disposal, but with the understanding that my name or my connection with the expedition was not to be divulged, as I have always shrunk from publicity.

*

Shortly after entering Africa I became separated from the relief party and was captured by Tippoo Tib's Arabs. The night that they were going to put me to death I escaped, but a week later I fell into the hands of a tribe of cannibals. My long, golden hair and my flowing mustache and beard of the same hue filled them with such awe that they accorded me the fearful deference that they reserved for their primitive gods and demons.

They offered me no harm, but kept me a prisoner among them for three years. They also kept in captivity several large anthropoid apes of a species which I believe is entirely unknown to science. The animals were of huge size and of great intelligence; and during my captivity I learned their language, which was to stand me in such good stead when I decided, many years later, to record some of my experiences in the form of fiction.

I finally escaped from the cannibal village and made my way to the coast, where, penniless and friendless, I shipped before the mast on a wind-jammer bound for China. Wrecked off the coast of Asia, I eventually made my way overland to Russia, where I enlisted in the imperial cavalry. A year later it happened to be my good fortune to kill an anarchist as he was attempting the assassination of the Czar; for this service I was made a captain and attached to the imperial bodyguard.

*

It was while in his Majesty's Service that I met my wife, a lady-in-waiting to the Czarina; and when, shortly after we were married, my

A portrait of Burroughs given to Burroughs' mother-in-law (© 1975 Edgar Rice Burroughs, Inc.).

grandfather died and left me eight million dollars, we decided to come to America to live.

With my wife's fortune and mine, it was unnecessary for me to work; but I could not be idle; so I took up writing, more as a pastime than as a vocation.

We lived in Chicago for some years and then came to Southern California, where we have lived for more than thirteen years at that now famous watering place, Tarzana.

We have eleven children, seventeen grandchildren, and three great-grandchildren.

I have tasted fame—it is nothing. I find my greatest happiness in being alone with my violin.

–Finis–

© 1918, J. Allen St. John

I
Bibliography of Books by Edgar Rice Burroughs

I. BIBLIOGRAPHY OF BOOKS

Apache Devil

1. "The Apache Devil" (ARGOSY ALL-STORY WEEKLY, May 19, 26; June 2, 9, 16, 23, 1928)
On August 4, 1927, about two weeks after Burroughs finished writing *Tarzan, Lord of the Jungle*, he began to work on this western story. It is a sequel to **"The War Chief"** (which appeared in the May-June 1927 issues of ARGOSY). In the magazine serial, the hero is called "Black Bear," but in the hardback publication, he is called "Shoz Dijiji," the name used previously in **"The War Chief."** **"Apache Devil"** was serialized in six parts and sold for 10¢ each issue. Paul Stahr did the cover illustration for the first installment (May 19, 1928) and Roger B. Morrison (who signed his MUNSEY pulp illustrations "Mori") did one interior black-and-white drawing for each of the following five installments.

──────────── FIRST EDITION ────────────

2. *Apache Devil* (Tarzana: Edgar Rice Burroughs, Inc., February 15, 1933)
The first edition can be identified by the standard ERB, Inc. blue cloth binding with red lettering on the cover and spine. *Apache Devil* does *not* have "First Edition" on the copyright page. This is the fourth book published by ERB, Inc., and none of the first four ERB, Inc. books are labeled "First Edition." However, all ERB, Inc. books published after this do have "First Edition" on the copyright page. ERB, Inc. never reprinted this title. Studley O. Burroughs (Burroughs' nephew) did the colorful dust jacket (of the Apache on horseback waving a rifle over his head) and five black-and-white illustrations. Price: $2.00. 310 numbered pages.

3. *Apache Devil* (New York: Grosset & Dunlap, 1934)
The first American hardcover reprint edition has the usual Grosset & Dunlap red cloth binding with black lettering on the front cover and spine. The dust jacket and *four* (not five) black-and-white illustrations are by Studley Burroughs. The front jacket illustration is identical to the first edition jacket. There is at least one variant with a slightly different listing of advertisements at the end of the book; the ERB list of titles is identical. The jacket thought to be earliest does not have a price on the upper front flap; another jacket exists with the 75¢ price on the front flap, and a "new editions" message added to the lower right corner. Price: 75¢. 310 numbered pages.

4. *Apache Devil* (New York: Grosset & Dunlap, 1940)
Heins lists a 1940 reprinting in his bibliography but there is serious doubt that G&D reprinted this title in 1940. The author has been unable to locate a copy in any collection anywhere. Most probably, it does not exist. If it did exist, it would be distinguished by the fact that there would be no illustrations. The rest of the details would be the same as the 1934 G&D edition described above.

BY EDGAR RICE BURROUGHS

First edition jacket for *Apache Devil* (1933)

5. *Apache Devil* (New York: Ballantine Books, June 1964)
The first U.S. paperback edition has an illustration on the front cover by Ronnie M. Lessor. Stock No. U2046, price 50¢. 192 numbered pages.

6. *Apache Devil* (New York: Gregg, 1975)
This edition has a brown cloth binding, with dust jacket illustration reprinted from the Studley Burroughs cover. It has three of the Studley Burroughs interior illustrations. 316 numbered pages.

7. *Apache Devil* (New York: Ballantine Books, October 1975)
The second Ballantine edition has a new illustration on the front cover by Greg and Tim Hildebrandt. Stock No. 24605, price $1.25. 216 numbered pages.

At the Earth's Core

8. "At the Earth's Core" (ALL-STORY WEEKLY, April 4, 11, 18, 25, 1914)
This is the sixth story Burroughs wrote (begun in January 1913), and its working title was **"The Inner World."** Burroughs began work on this story directly after he finished *The Return of Tarzan*. It was printed as a four-part serial. Modest Stein painted the front cover illustration for the April 4th installment. Each installment was decorated with a black-and-white headpiece by an unknown artist, and each issue sold for 10¢.

―――――――――― FIRST EDITION ――――――――――
9. *At the Earth's Core* (Chicago: A.C. McClurg & Co., July 22, 1922)
The first edition of the fourteenth published hardback book by ERB is bound in gray cloth with black lettering on the front cover and spine. It originally sold for $1.75. The J. Allen St. John dust jacket is a stunning vision of a flying reptile attacking a woman and a man, who has just shot an arrow. There are nine sepia interior plates, also by J. Allen St. John. McClurg records reveal that McClurg published 17,000 copies of this first edition. Price: $1.75. 277 numbered pages.

10. *At the Earth's Core* (New York: Grosset & Dunlap, 1923)
This title was first printed by G&D in 1923, and then reprinted numerous times subsequently. The first printings are bound in red cloth with black letters, and list six titles by ERB in the advertisements at the back. The next printing lists 11 ERB titles (possibly 1924). After 1924, the cover is dark brick-red cloth with black lettering on the front cover and spine. A 1926 variant has 15 ERB titles in

the back, and another lists 23 titles (1928), then 28 titles (1930), then 29 titles (1931). There are only *eight* black-and-white interior plates by J. Allen St. John. The earliest dust jacket has the St. John cover, and on the back is a photo of ERB in an oval design, with eight ERB titles listed in black letters. Subsequent dust jackets have the ERB photo in a rectangular device, and list 12 ERB titles (after 1925), 16 ERB titles (after 1926), 18 titles (after 1927), and 24 titles (after 1927). Price: 75¢. 227 numbered pages.

11. **"Lost Inside the Earth"** (MODERN MECHANICS AND INVENTION, February-April 1929)

Burroughs sold the second serial rights to **"At the Earth's Core"** in 1928. It is a three-part abridged serialization. Each issue cost 25¢. The first part contains two red-and-black illustrations plus a photograph of ERB; part two has two red-and-white illustrations; part three has one red-and-black illustration and one black-and-white illustration. Although the illustrations are initialed "C.R.," the artist remains unidentified. The April 1929 issue was a double Burroughs issue because it also included part one of **"Carter of the Red Planet"** (*A Princess of Mars*). This entry is unusual because there were only a handful of Burroughs' stories which were *re*printed in magazines *after* the hardback books had been published (among the others were *Tarzan of the Apes, The Beasts of Tarzan, Tarzan and the Jewels of Opar, The Moon Maid, Land That Time Forgot* and *A Princess of Mars*). In addition, many of Burroughs' stories were reprinted in daily newspapers from time to time.

12. *At the Earth's Core* (New York: Grosset & Dunlap, 1940)

The 1940 G&D reprint is bound in red cloth with black lettering on the front cover and spine. The 1940 reprinting is distinguished from the earlier G&D reprints by the total absence of any interior illustrations. The dust jacket is by J. Allen St. John, and on the back there is a sketch of ERB against a yellow background. Price: 75¢. 277 numbered pages.

13. *At the Earth's Core* (New York: Ace Books, Inc., September 1962)

The first paperback edition has a Roy G. Krenkel cover and title page drawing. Stock No. F-156, price 40¢. 142 numbered pages.

14. *At the Earth's Core* (New York: Canaveral Press, Inc., October 24, 1962)

The Canaveral reprint is bound in tan cloth with black lettering on the front cover and spine. Mahlon Blaine provided the dust jacket art and seven black-and-white interior illustrations. Price: $2.75, raised to $2.95 in 1963. 159 numbered pages.

I. BIBLIOGRAPHY OF BOOKS

"At the Earth's Core" April 4, 1913

BY EDGAR RICE BURROUGHS

15. *At the Earth's Core / Pellucidar / Tanar of Pellucidar: Three Science Fiction Novels by Edgar Rice Burroughs* (New York: Dover Publications, Inc., December 1963)
    This Dover paperback collection has dark blue covers with yellow lettering on the front cover and spine. J. Allen St. John provides the cover art (from his art work for the book *Pellucidar*), and 12 black-and-white illustrations from the G&D editions; in addition there is one illustration by Paul F. Berdanier. The three stories are consecutively paginated. Price: $2.00. 433 numbered pages.

16. *At the Earth's Core / Pellucidar / Tanar of Pellucidar: Three Science Fiction Novels by Edgar Rice Burroughs* (New York: Peter Smith, 1963)
    This is a hardbound library binding whose inside is identical with the Dover paperback collection. Although this is a hardback, it did not have a dust jacket. The three stories are consecutively paginated. Price: $3.50. 433 numbered pages.

17. *At the Earth's Core* (New York: Ace Books, Inc.)
    The second Ace paperback edition has the same Roy G. Krenkel cover and title page drawing. Stock No. G-733. It sold for 50¢. 142 numbered pages.

18. *At the Earth's Core* (New York: Ace Books, Inc.)
    The third Ace paperback edition has the same Roy G. Krenkel cover and title page drawing. Stock No. 03321. 60¢. 142 numbered pages.

19. *At the Earth's Core* (New York: Ace Books, Inc.)
    The fourth Ace paperback edition has new cover art by Frank Frazetta. Stock No. 03322. It sold for 75¢. 159 numbered pages.

20. *At the Earth's Core* (New York: Ace Books, Inc., July 1976)
    This is a paperback printing tied to the motion picture of the same name. This edition has a cover illustration from the film but no interior illustrations. 210 numbered pages. Stock No. 03325, price $1.75.

21. *At the Earth's Core* (New York: Doubleday, November 1976)
    This Science-Fiction Book Club hardback is bound in black boards with silver lettering on the spine. The dust jacket illustration takes its inspiration from the film version. There are eight black-and-white still photographs featuring the film's stars: Doug McClure, Peter Cushing, and Caroline Munro. 152 numbered pages.

22. *At the Earth's Core* (New York: Ballantine–Del Rey, May 1990)
    This new reprinting has new cover art by David B. Mattingly. Stock # 36668. Price $3.95. 181 numbered pages.

23. *A Princess of Mars* and *At the Earth's Core* (Norwalk, CT: The Easton Press, 1996)

This is a quality leather bound edition with an introduction by L. Sprague de Camp, illustrations by Ron Miller, and is available by subscribing to the "Masterpieces of Science Fiction" series. Price $38.50. 318 (+xvi) numbered pages.

Back to the Stone Age

24. "Seven Worlds to Conquer" (ARGOSY WEEKLY, January 9, 16, 23, 30; February 6, 13, 1937)

When Burroughs finished *Tarzan's Quest* in January of 1935, he turned his attention to this tale of the realm inside the hollow earth, whose working title was "**Back to the Stone Age: A Romance of the Inner World.**" It was initially published as a serial in six parts. The cover illustration on the January 9th issue is by Emmett Watson, with one black-and-white interior drawing by Samuel Cahan in each installment. Each issue sold for 10¢. There is a foreword in the first issue which was omitted in the book publication.

─────────────── FIRST EDITION ───────────────

25. *Back to the Stone Age* (Tarzana: Edgar Rice Burroughs, Inc., September 15, 1937)

The first edition of the forty-ninth published book of ERB is bound in blue cloth with red lettering on the front cover and spine, typical of almost all ERB, Inc. firsts. It says "First Edition" on the copyright page. The book has a very colorful wrap-around dust jacket of a world teeming with grotesque prehistoric animals. There are several varieties of dust jackets: (a) laminated with a ripple-like effect; (b) laminated without a ripple; (c) unlaminated. The laminated dust jackets have trimmed inner flaps. Burroughs' son, John Coleman Burroughs, did the dust jacket and seven black-and-white plates. The book sold for $2.00. 318 numbered pages.

26. *Back to the Stone Age* (Tarzana: Burroughs–Grosset & Dunlap, 1939)

In 1939, Burroughs remaindered the 1937 first editions to Grosset & Dunlap, who put their own Grosset & Dunlap dust jacket over the book (a "Mixed Edition"). The book itself is the ERB, Inc. first-edition blue cloth with red lettering on the front cover and spine. The wrap-around G&D dust jacket illustration and seven black-and-white plates are by John Coleman Burroughs. The reprint sold for 75¢. 318 numbered pages.

27. *Back to the Stone Age* (New York: Ace Books, Inc., November 1963)
The first paperback edition has cover art by Roy G. Krenkel with the assistance of Frank Frazetta, and a title page drawing by Roy G. Krenkel. Stock No. F-245, price 40¢. 221 pages.

28. *Back to the Stone Age* (New York: Canaveral Press, Inc., November 12, 1963)
This Canaveral reprint is bound in yellow cloth with red lettering on the front cover and spine. The dust jacket design by Sam Sigaloff is clearly based upon the original by John Coleman Burroughs, with a black-and-white photograph of ERB on the back cover. There are also seven black-and-white interior illustrations by John Coleman Burroughs. 318 pages.

29. *Back to the Stone Age* (New York: Ace Books, Inc.)
The second paperback edition has the same cover art by Roy G. Krenkel and Frank Frazetta, and a title page drawing by Roy G. Krenkel. Stock No. G-737, price 50¢. 221 pages.

30. *Back to the Stone Age* (New York: Ace Books, Inc.)
The third paperback edition has the same cover art by Krenkel and Frazetta, and the title page drawing by Krenkel. Stock No. 04631, price 60¢. 221 pages.

31. *Back to the Stone Age* (New York: Ace Books, Inc.)
The fourth paperback edition has new cover art by Frank Frazetta. Stock No. 04632, price 75¢. 251 pages.

32. *Back to the Stone Age* (New York: Ballantine–Del Rey)
The first Ballantine paperback edition has cover art by David B. Mattingly. Stock No. 36671, price $3.95. 230 pages.

The Bandit of Hell's Bend

33. "The Bandit of Hell's Bend" (ARGOSY ALL-STORY WEEKLY, September 13, 20, 27; October 4, 11, 18, 1924)
This western novel was the result of the October 1922 written suggestion of British publisher Sir Algernon Methuen. Burroughs began working on it in March of 1923. He toyed with two titles, "**The Black Coyote**" and "**Diana of the Bar Y.**" It was serialized in six parts with a front cover illustration on the September 13th issue by Modest Stein. Roger B. Morrison ("Mori") did one interior headpiece, in black-and-white, for each installment which sold for 10¢. One

I. BIBLIOGRAPHY OF BOOKS

month after Burroughs completed this story, he began work on *Tarzan and the Ant Men*.

FIRST EDITION
34. *The Bandit of Hell's Bend* (Chicago: A.C. McClurg & Co., June 4, 1925)

The twenty-second published hardback book by Edgar Rice Burroughs. The first edition is bound in blue cloth with black lettering on the front cover and spine, typical of the majority of the McClurg first editions of this period. The sepia frontispiece is the same illustration as the color dust jacket by Modest Stein. A.C. McClurg records indicate that only 5,000 copies of the first edition were printed. Original price: $2.00. 316 numbered pages.

---

35. *The Bandit of Hell's Bend* (New York: Grosset & Dunlap, 1926)

The first reprint is bound in the usual G&D red cloth with black lettering on the front cover and spine. It has a color dust wrapper and a black-and-white frontispiece by Modest Stein, the same as the first edition. On the back of the earliest version of the jacket we find a list of 12 ERB titles in blue letters. Later jackets list 16 titles, and then 18 titles. After 1927, we find 24 and then 28 ERB titles. Later reprintings of the book have page tops dyed yellow or green. Price: 75¢. 316 numbered pages.

36. *The Bandit of Hell's Bend* (New York: Grosset & Dunlap, 1940)

This 1940 reprint is bound in the usual G&D red cloth with black lettering on the front cover and spine. It can be distinguished from the earlier reprint by the absence of the frontispiece. It does have the color dust wrapper by Modest Stein. Price: 75¢. 316 numbered pages.

37. *The Bandit of Hell's Bend* (New York: Ace Books, Inc., January 1977)

First paperback edition with front cover art by Boris Vallejo. Stock No. 04745, price $1.75. 280 numbered pages.

38. *The Bandit of Hell's Bend* (New York: Gregg, 1979)

This Gregg hardback has the same frontispiece as the first edition and a dust jacket whose art is reprinted from the Modest Stein original. 316 numbered pages.

39. *The Bandit of Hell's Bend* (New York: Charter Books, 1979)

This Charter paperback has the same Boris Vallejo cover which was used on the earlier Ace Books edition, reduced in size with an aqua border. Stock No. 04746, price: $1.95. 280 numbered pages.

BY EDGAR RICE BURROUGHS

The Beasts of Tarzan

40. "The Beasts of Tarzan" (ALL-STORY CAVALIER WEEKLY, May 16, 23, 30; June 6, 13, 1914)

Three weeks after finishing "The Eternal Lover," Burroughs began work on his third Tarzan story in January of 1914 and finished it in one month. ALL-STORY WEEKLY changed its name to ALL-STORY CAVALIER WEEKLY with the May 16, 1914, issue. This tale was first published as a five-part serial with a front cover illustration on the May 16th issue by F. W. Small. A black-and-white copy of the cover painting functions as a headpiece for each installment. Each issue sold for 10¢. The magazine story is shorter than the book; ERB had to add new material near the end of the tale to make it book-length.

41. *The Beasts of Tarzan* (Chicago: A.C. McClurg & Co., prior to March 1916)

McClurg issued a paperback edition of *The Beasts of Tarzan*, just as it did with *Tarzan of the Apes, The Return of Tarzan, The Son of Tarzan* and *A Princess of Mars*. The original purpose of these is not completely clear. They were probably done to supply advance copies of the story so that reviews could be published to coincide with the date the book was released to bookstores. ERB referred to one of these as "advance sheets" of the book. The cover is the same as the St. John dust jacket, and the interior is the same as the first edition below. The price, $1.30, appears on the spine in a red box. 336 (+1) pages.

42. *The Beasts of Tarzan* (Chicago: A.C. McClurg & Co., prior to March 1916)

For several early titles, we know that McClurg produced something called a "printer's dummy." On the outside these books look like the first edition. However, on the inside of *The Beasts of Tarzan*, we find only about the first 30 pages of text and illustrations and the rest is completely blank. The St. John interior illustrations are all bunched together at the beginning of the book. The copy owned by Mitchell Harrison has a McClurg stamp on the unusually thick dust jacket (with blank end flaps) which is dated "3/1/16" and which says "unique salesman's copy," and so it seems that this is how McClurg referred to them. These "dummies" were probably printed by McClurg to help the publisher and editor see the book size and typeface, or used so a salesman could take advance orders for the book by demonstrating what the finished product was going to look like. The exact number of pages is unclear because most pages were unnumbered and unmarked. We know that other McClurg "printer's dummies" exist for *The Return of Tarzan, The Son of Tarzan, Cave Girl* and *The Eternal Lover*, and it is very possible that there were dummies produced for other McClurg ERB titles as well. A printer's dummy for the Volland edition of *The Tarzan Twins* exists.

I. BIBLIOGRAPHY OF BOOKS

Original McClurg first edition dust jacket for *The Beasts of Tarzan* (1916)

BY EDGAR RICE BURROUGHS

ERB, Inc. also produced some (*Jungle Girl, The Lad and the Lion,* and *The Deputy Sheriff of Comanche County* are known).

―――――――――― FIRST EDITION ――――――――――
43. *The Beasts of Tarzan* (Chicago: A.C. McClurg & Co., March 4, 1916)

This is the third Tarzan story, and also the third hardback novel published by Burroughs. He dedicated it to his daughter, Joan. The first edition is bound in an olive green cloth with bright gold lettering on the front cover and spine. The dust jacket has a wrap-around illustration by J. Allen St. John. Like the jacket for *Tarzan of the Apes*, this has a price on the spine of $1.30. This book is gorgeously and profusely illustrated with black-and-white line drawings by St. John. The title page and frontispiece form a magnificent two-page illustration of Tarzan and the beasts of Tarzan. McClurg records indicate that 19,500 copies were printed. 336 (+1) pages.

44. *The Beasts of Tarzan* (New York: A.L. Burt Company, 1917)

This, the first reprint, is one of the five titles published by A.L. Burt. It is bound in dark green cloth with *white* lettering on the front cover and spine. The dust jacket, frontispiece, decorated title page, numerous interior black-and-white drawings by J. Allen St. John are all present. Price: 60¢. 336 (+1) numbered pages.

45. *The Beasts of Tarzan* (New York: A.L. Burt Company, 1918)

The second reprinting is bound in dark green cloth and is identical to the first Burt reprint except that it has *black* lettering on the front cover and spine. A.L. Burt reprinted *The Beasts of Tarzan* in 1917, 1918, 1919, 1923, 1925, 1926 and 1927 (last reprinting), with variations in the green (also gray) binding. They can be dated by carefully checking the different advertisements for the latest books in the Burt catalog in the back. Each sold for 60¢.

46. *The Beasts of Tarzan* (New York: Grosset & Dunlap, 1927)

The first G&D reprint (ten years after the earliest Burt reprinting) is bound in the usual red cloth with black lettering on the front cover and spine. The illustrations remained the same: the dust jacket, frontispiece, title page decoration and black-and-white drawings by J. Allen St. John. The first G&D printing lists 15 ERB titles in the advertising pages at the back of the book. In 1928, there were 23 ERB titles listed, and subsequent printings increased the number to 28, 29, and 33 ERB titles listed in the back. The earliest dust jacket has 18 ERB titles listed inside the dust jacket. Price: 75¢. 336 (+1) numbered pages.

47. "Tarzan Returns" (TRIPLE-X MAGAZINE, November, December 1929; January, February 1930)

In this magazine reprinting, there are no cover illustrations, but each issue has a large headpiece and a small interior illustration. In the November and

December 1929 issues, Tarzan is portrayed with a beard and mustache (in Burroughs' original stories, Tarzan keeps himself clean-shaven). The artist who did the two interior illustrations for the November issue is possibly Charles E. Dameron. The December issue has a headpiece illustration and small interior illustration, by Charles E. Dameron. The artist who did the January and February 1930 issues (Tarzan without a beard) is unknown. Each issue sold for 25¢.

48. *The Beasts of Tarzan* (Racine, WI: Whitman Publishing Company, 1937)
This is one of the Big Little Books, a small but thick, fragile, illustrated children's book bound in paper boards. This series of books measures 3½" wide by 4⅜" high, and average about 1¼" in width. The cover illustration is by Hal Arbo, and there are 218 interior drawings by Rex Maxon adapted from his 1929 daily newspaper comic strips. Stock No. 1410. 432 pages.

49. *The Beasts of Tarzan* (New York: Grosset & Dunlap, 1940)
The 1940 reprinting is also bound in red cloth with black lettering on the front cover and spine. This has the same dust jacket cover illustration, title page design and interior black-and-white illustrations by J. Allen St. John, but lacks the frontispiece. The page tops are dyed green. 336 (+1) numbered pages.

50. *The Beasts of Tarzan* (New York: Grosset & Dunlap, 1943)
The very cheap WWII wartime edition is bound in inexpensive maroon cloth with black lettering on the front cover and spine. The dust jacket art is by J. Allen St. John. It is readily identified by (1) its thin size, (2) by the cheap paper which quickly becomes brown and brittle, (3) by the "Madison Square" label on the inside front flap of the dust wrapper, and (4) by the small blue diamond over the G&D imprint on the spine. The decorated title page and numerous interior black-and-white illustrations are by St. John. The original price was 50¢, lowered to 49¢ after 1945. 336 (+1) numbered pages.

51. *The Beasts of Tarzan* (New York: Ace Books, Inc., May 1963)
The first U.S. paperback edition has a front cover, back cover and title page illustration by Frank Frazetta. In addition, there are three more black-and-white interior illustrations by J. Allen St. John. This is the only Ace printing. As George McWhorter points out, instead of copyright information, the publishers state: "This Ace edition follows the text of the first hard-cover book edition, originally published in 1916." Stock No. F-203, price 40¢. 191 numbered pages.

52. *The Beasts of Tarzan* (New York: Ballantine Books, July 1963)
This is the second paperback edition but the first Ballantine printing. The front cover illustration is by Richard Powers, and there are no interior illustrations. Stock No. F 747, price 50¢. 159 numbered pages. The Ballantine reprint-

ings of the first ten Tarzan titles were so much in demand that they were reprinted in November 1963.

53. *The Beasts of Tarzan* (New York: Ballantine Books, April 1969)
The cover artist changed on this, the third Ballantine printing. The front cover illustration is by Robert Abbett, and there are no interior illustrations. Stock No. 01593, price 50¢. 159 numbered pages.

54. *The Beasts of Tarzan* (New York: Ballantine Books, April 1975)
This sixth paperback printing has a new front cover illustration by Neal Adams and there are no interior illustrations. Stock No. 24161, price $1.25. 159 numbered pages.

Beyond the Farthest Star

55. "Beyond the Farthest Star" (THE BLUE BOOK MAGAZINE, January 1942)
Written a week after he completed "**Men of the Bronze Age**" in October of 1940, (which became a part of *Savage Pellucidar*), ERB began work on a brand new adventure series, of which this was to be the first part. It is not a full novel, rather, it is the first half or third of a novel, a novelette of 11 chapters, with one double-page illustration by Grattan Condon. The issue sold for 25¢.

──────────── FIRST EDITION ────────────

56. *Tales of Three Planets* (New York: Canaveral Press, Inc., April 27, 1964)
The hardback first edition has a blue cloth binding with black lettering on the front cover and spine. The book says "First Edition" on the copyright page. The dust jacket illustration is by Roy G. Krenkel, with a photograph of ERB on the back cover. In addition to "**Beyond the Farthest Star**," the book also contains "**The Resurrection of Jimber-Jaw**," "**Tangor Returns**," and "**The Wizard of Venus**." The illustrated endpapers and black-and-white interior illustrations are by Roy G. Krenkel. The four stories are continuously paginated with 282 (+1) numbered pages.

57. *Beyond the Farthest Star* (New York: Ace Books, Inc., June 1964)
The first paperback edition of *Beyond the Farthest Star* has cover and title page art by Frank Frazetta. Stock No. F-282, price 40¢. 125 numbered pages.

58. *Beyond the Farthest Star* (New York: Ace Books, Inc., 1969)
The second printing by Ace is unchanged except for the price and number. Stock No. 05651, price 60¢.

59. *Beyond the Farthest Star* (New York: Ballantine–Del Rey, November 1992)
This is the first Ballantine paperback edition. The front cover illustration is by Michael Herring, and there are no interior illustrations. Stock No. 345-37836-9, price $3.95. 133 numbered pages.

Beyond Thirty

60. "Beyond Thirty" (THE EVENING WORLD Newspaper, November 15–20, 1915)
This story, which Burroughs began on July 8, 1915, and finished on August 10, 1915, received its first publication in a New York newspaper, without illustrations, after its rejection by the editor of ALL STORY and several other magazines. Two months later it was printed in the ALL AROUND MAGAZINE (see below). It was Burroughs' reaction to World War I, which had just started shortly before. It is his vision of a world divided by war, with Europe and Asia reverting to a barbaric civilization while the United States prospers. It then goes into the future (the year 2137 C.E.) and Burroughs makes an interesting (although completely incorrect) prognostication of the future of civilization. When he finished this, he began work on *Tarzan and the Jewels of Opar*.

61. "Beyond Thirty" (ALL AROUND MAGAZINE, February 1916)
This story was printed complete in one issue, and sold for 15¢. This magazine printing is the last authorized appearance of this story during Burroughs' lifetime (ERB died in 1950), although five copies were informally produced by Darrell C. Richardson in 1944, and given away to friends. It was not reprinted again until the Eshbach pirate edition in 1955 described below. There are no illustrations. The story is 61 pages long.

——————————— FIRST EDITION ———————————

62. *Beyond Thirty* (Lloyd A. Eshbach, 1955)
This ERB short story was published anonymously by Lloyd Arthur Eshbach (founder of Fantasy Press, a fan and a prolific author) in a 57-page typed offset edition, on 8½ x 11" paper in red paper covers. According to the publisher, 300 copies were printed. There are no illustrations. Even though this is not a book, some people consider it the *true* first edition.

BY EDGAR RICE BURROUGHS

63. *Beyond Thirty* and *The Man-Eater* (New York: Science-Fiction & Fantasy Publications, 1957)
This, the *only hardback* printing of this story, was done by Bradford M. Day. It has "First edition limited to 3,000 copies" on the copyright page. The cloth binding is red, with gold lettering on spine. The white dust jacket has a black-and-white cover illustration by Gilbert Kane. There are no interior illustrations. The two stories are continuously paginated. 229 numbered pages.

---

64. *The Lost Continent* (New York: Ace Books, Inc., October 1963)
The first Ace paperback edition of *Beyond Thirty* has been retitled *The Lost Continent*, perhaps so people would not think it referred to the generation gap celebrated in the rock songs of the 1960s. It has a front cover and title page illustration by Frank Frazetta. The paperback clearly states: "Original title: *Beyond Thirty*." Stock No. F-235, price 40¢. 123 numbered pages.

65. *The Lost Continent* (New York: Ace Books, Inc., October 1969)
The second Ace paperback edition has the same front cover and title page illustration by Frank Frazetta; however, the price has increased by 20¢. Stock No. 49291, price 60¢. 123 numbered pages.

66. *The Lost Continent* (New York: Ace Books, Inc., March 1973)
The third Ace paperback edition has a new larger format, with the same front cover art by Frank Frazetta. Stock No. 49292, price 75¢. 144 numbered pages.

67. *The Lost Continent* (New York: Ace Books, Inc., January 1979)
This, the seventh Ace paperback edition, has a new front cover illustration by Sanjulian, and the price is now $1.95. Stock No. 49296. 141 numbered pages.

68. *The Lost Continent* (New York: Ballantine–Del Rey, September 1992)
The first Ballantine paperback edition has a front cover illustration by Michael Herring. Stock No. 37834, price $3.99. 131 numbered pages.

Carson of Venus

69. "Carson of Venus" (ARGOSY WEEKLY, January 8, 15, 22, 29; February 5, 12, 1938)
In July of 1937, a few months after finishing *Tarzan the Magnificent* (in January of 1937), Burroughs turned to this, the third in the Venus series. It was originally published as a six-part serial with a cover illustration on the January 8th issue by Rudolph Belarski. In addition, each part has one black-and-white drawing by C. Brigham. Each issue sold for 10¢.

I. BIBLIOGRAPHY OF BOOKS

―――――――――― FIRST EDITION ――――――――――

70. *Carson of Venus* (Tarzana: Edgar Rice Burroughs, Inc., February 15, 1939)

The fifty-second hardback to be published, the first edition has the usual blue pebbled cloth with red lettering on the front cover and spine. As was common with ERB, Inc. editions, there is a red design on the spine directly underneath the title. The copyright page is imprinted *"First Edition."* The dust wrapper and six black-and-white interior plates are by John Coleman Burroughs, ERB's son. As with several other ERB books of this period, the dust jacket appears in two states: (1) laminated with trimmed corners; (2) unlaminated. The back side of the jacket has an advertisement for *Tarzan and the Forbidden City*. The book is dedicated to Florence Gilbert [Dearholt] Burroughs, ERB's second wife whom he married in 1935. Illustrated endpapers consist of map of Amtor (Venus) by ERB. Price: $2.00. 312 numbered pages.

71. *Carson of Venus* (Tarzana: Edgar Rice Burroughs, Inc., March 26, 1948)

The 1948 ERB, Inc. reprints are generally bound in buff-colored boards. This title has dark red lettering on front cover and spine. As in the first edition, there is the dark red design of Carson on spine directly under the title. The dust jacket design by John Coleman Burroughs is the same as the first edition; however the back side of the jacket has a drawing of ERB. There are no interior illustrations. This edition sold for $1.00 and has the same 312 numbered pages.

72. *Carson of Venus* (New York: Canaveral Press, Inc., November 15, 1963)

This Canaveral reprint is bound in light green cloth with dark green lettering on the front cover and spine. It uses the dust jacket illustration originally by John Coleman Burroughs for the first edition, redesigned by Sam Sigaloff. There is a photograph of ERB on the back cover. There are six black-and-white plates by John Coleman Burroughs; the endpapers are the original ones done by ERB himself. Heins reports the existence of a semi-opaque sticker masking the dedication on approximately the first 125 books printed; subsequent copies have an opaque green sticker. Price: $3.50. 312 numbered pages.

73. *Carson of Venus* (New York: Ace Books, Inc., December 1963)

The first American paperback edition has covers and a title page illustration by Frank Frazetta. Stock No. F-247, price 40¢. 192 numbered pages.

74. *Carson of Venus* (New York: Ace Books, Inc.)

The second American paperback edition has covers and a title page illustration by Frank Frazetta. Stock No. 09200, price 50¢. 192 numbered pages.

75. *Carson of Venus* (New York: Ace Books, Inc.)
The fourth American paperback edition has new cover art work by Frank Frazetta. Stock No. 09202, price 95¢. 192 numbered pages.

76. *Carson of Venus* (New York: Ballantine–Del Rey, July 1991)
The first Ballantine paperback edition has cover art by Richard Hescox. Stock No. 37010, price $3.95. 197 pages.

The Cave Girl

77. "**The Cave Girl**" (THE ALL-STORY, July, August, September, 1913)
The seventh story Burroughs wrote was started in February of 1913, immediately after he finished *At The Earth's Core*. It was published as a three-part serial with a front cover illustration for the July issue by Clinton Pettee. THE ALL-STORY used the same black-and-white headpiece by Fred W. Small for each installment. Each issue sold for 15¢.

78. "**The Cave Man**" (ALL-STORY WEEKLY, March 31; April 7, 14, 21, 1917)
Directly after he finished *Thuvia, Maid of Mars*, Burroughs wrote the sequel to "**The Cave Girl**" in 1914 (although it was not published until 1917). It has a front cover illustration for the March 31st issue by Fred W. Small, but no interior illustrations. Each issue cost 10¢.

79. *The Cave Girl* (Chicago: A.C. McClurg & Co., prior to March 1925)
For several early titles, we know that McClurg produced something called a "printer's dummy." On the outside these books look like the first edition. However, on the inside we find only sample pages of text and illustrations and the rest is completely blank. McClurg referred to them as "unique salesman's copy." These "dummies" were probably printed by McClurg to help the publisher visualize the binding, dust jacket, typeface, paper and illustrations. They could also help a salesman sell the book by demonstrating what the finished product was going to look like before the book was finally printed and bound. The exact number of pages is unclear because most pages were unnumbered and unmarked. We know that other McClurg "printer's dummies" exist for *The Return of Tarzan*, *The Beasts of Tarzan*, *The Son of Tarzan*, and *The Eternal Lover*, and it is possible that there were dummies produced for other McClurg ERB titles as well. A printer's dummy for the Volland edition of *The Tarzan Twins* exists. ERB, Inc. also produced some (*Jungle Girl*, *The Lad and the Lion*, and *The Deputy Sheriff of Comanche County* are known).

I. BIBLIOGRAPHY OF BOOKS

"The Cave Girl" July 1913

BY EDGAR RICE BURROUGHS

---FIRST EDITION---
80. *The Cave Girl* (Chicago: A.C. McClurg & Co., March 21, 1925)

The first edition of the twenty-first hardback has the typical McClurg blue cloth binding with dark green lettering on the front cover and spine; however, on the spine the title is just *Cave Girl*, omitting the word "*The*." The dust jacket design is by J. Allen St. John. The same illustration in sepia is used as a frontispiece. A.C. McClurg records reveal that only 5,000 copies of this title were printed. Price: $2.00. 323 numbered pages.

---

81. *The Cave Girl* (New York: Grosset & Dunlap, 1926)

The *first* Grosset & Dunlap reprint edition has a *blue* cloth cover and no ERB titles listed in the advertising pages at the end of the book. Like the first edition, this and all subsequent reprints omit *"The"* from the title on the spine. The dust jacket art and frontispiece are by J. Allen St. John. On the back of the earliest G&D dust jacket is a list of 12 ERB titles. Price: 75¢. 323 numbered pages.

82. *The Cave Girl* (New York: Grosset & Dunlap, between 1927 and 1939)

The subsequent Grosset & Dunlap reprints have the traditional red cloth binding with black letters on the front cover and the spine. The earliest red reprinting has 11 ERB titles listed in the advertising pages at the back of the book. Sometime after 1930, there were 29 ERB titles listed at the back. The dust jacket and frontispiece are the same artwork as in previous reprints. On the back of the dust jacket we find 16 or more ERB titles listed. Price: 75¢. 323 numbered pages.

83. *The Cave Girl* (New York: Grosset & Dunlap, 1940)

The 1940 Grosset & Dunlap reprint is distinguished from the previous reprints by the absence of the frontispiece. The dust jacket is the same as the previous reprints. Price: 75¢. 323 numbered pages.

84. *The Cave Girl* (New York: Dell, August, 1949)

The first American paperback edition is this 1949 Dell paperback which sold for 25¢. It has a front cover painting of a dancing cave girl by Jean des Vignes. On the back cover is a map by Ruth Bellew entitled: "Wild island home of Nadara the Cave Girl where violence and bloodshed rule." No interior illustrations. Dell catalog no. 320. 240 numbered pages.

85. *The Cave Girl* (New York: Canaveral Press, Inc., 1962)

The cover of the Canaveral hardback is brown. The dust jacket and six interior illustrations are by Roy G. Krenkel. Price: $2.75 and then raised to $2.95 in 1963. 323 pages.

I. Bibliography of Books

86. *The Cave Girl* (New York: Ace Books, Inc., February 1964)
The first Ace paperback edition is the second paperback printing of *The Cave Girl*. It has covers and title page art by Roy G. Krenkel. Stock No. F-258, price 40¢. 224 numbered pages.

87. *The Cave Girl* (New York: Ace Books, Inc.)
The second Ace paperback edition differs from the first only in the price and stock number. It has the same covers and title page art by Roy G. Krenkel. Stock No. 09281, price 60¢. 224 numbered pages.

88. *The Cave Girl* (New York: Ace Books, Inc.)
The third Ace paperback edition has borrowed cover art by Frank Frazetta which was originally used by Ace for their printing of *Savage Pellucidar*. Stock No. 09282, price 75¢. 224 numbered pages.

89. *The Cave Girl* (New York: Tempo Books, February 1981)
Tempo Books is a division of Grosset & Dunlap (as is Ace Books). The first Tempo publication uses the same cover art by Frank Frazetta which originally appeared on the early Ace printing of *Savage Pellucidar*. Stock No. 17176, price $1.95. 246 numbered pages.

90. *The Cave Girl* (New York: Ballantine–Del Rey, September 1992)
The first Ballantine paperback edition has a cover illustration by Michael Herring. Stock No. 345-37833-4, price $3.99. 249 numbered pages.

The Chessmen of Mars

91. "Chessmen of Mars" (Argosy All-Story Weekly, February 18, 25; March 4, 11, 18, 25; April 1, 1922)
In January of 1921, three weeks after completing *Tarzan the Terrible*, Burroughs turned his attention to writing what would become the fifth story of the Mars series. It was published as a seven-part serial with a P. J. Monahan front cover illustration on the February 18th issue. The headpiece illustrations by Roger B. Morrison for each installment are done in black-and-white. Each issue sold for 10¢. Four days after he finished writing this book, he began working on *The Girl from Hollywood*.

──────────── FIRST EDITION ────────────

92. *The Chessmen of Mars* (Chicago: A.C. McClurg & Co., November 29, 1922)

The fifteenth hardback by ERB is bound in red cloth with black lettering on the front cover and spine. The dust jacket cover and eight sepia plates are by the great Burroughs illustrator, J. Allen St. John. The back cover of the McClurg jacket has a stylized chess board, a brief description of the book, and the price ($1.90). There is a three page appendix (pp. 373–375) entitled: "Jetan, or Martian Chess." A.C. McClurg records indicate that it printed 12,500 copies of this first edition. 375 numbered pages.

93. *The Chessmen of Mars* (New York: Grosset & Dunlap, 1924)
This first reprint edition is the Grosset & Dunlap reprint bound in a dark red cloth cover with black lettering on the front cover and spine. The earliest G&D reprinting has six ERB titles listed in the advertisements in the back, and the next has 11 ERB titles in the back. The dust jacket front illustration and four (*not* eight) black-and-white plates are by J. Allen St. John. On the back of the earliest version of the dust jacket is ERB's photo in an oval device and lists eight ERB titles inside a fancy blue border. The next jacket uses a fancy red border. The copyright page has an M.A. Donohue printer's imprint. 75¢. 375 numbered pages.

94. *The Chessmen of Mars* (New York: Grosset & Dunlap, reprinted several times after 1924)
Later reprint editions are bound in the standard red cloth with black lettering on the front cover and spine. The dust jacket front illustration and four black-and-white plates are by J. Allen St. John. These are distinguished from the first reprintings by the *absence* of the M.A. Donohue imprint on the copyright page. The advertisements at the back list 23 or more ERB titles. The dust jacket has ERB's photo in a rectangular box in blue letters, and lists 24 ERB titles, and then 27 or 28 titles. Price: 75¢. 375 numbered pages.

95. *The Chessmen of Mars* (New York: Grosset & Dunlap, 1940)
The 1940 G&D reprint is bound in the standard red cloth with black lettering on the front cover and spine. It has the dust jacket front illustration by J. Allen St. John, but there are no interior illustrations. The copyright page lacks the M.A. Donohue printer's imprint. Price: 75¢. 375 numbered pages.

96. *The Chessmen of Mars* (Tarzana: Edgar Rice Burroughs, Inc., March 26, 1948)
The first ERB, Inc. reprint is bound in tan boards with red lettering on the front cover and spine. As with the previous editions, the dust jacket and frontispiece are by J. Allen St. John. Price: $1.00. 375 numbered pages.

97. *Three Martian Novels: Thuvia, Maid of Mars / The Chessmen of Mars / The Master Mind of Mars* (New York: Dover Publications, Inc., April 1962 and again at least eight different times)

I. BIBLIOGRAPHY OF BOOKS

This compilation volume was one of the very first Burroughs books available in the early 1960s, and presaged the Burroughs revival dominated by the Ace paperbacks and the Canaveral hardbacks. It is a thick paperback with cover and 16 interior black-and-white illustrations by J. Allen St. John. The stories are continuously paginated. Stock No. T39, price $1.75. There are 499 numbered pages.

98. *The Chessmen of Mars* (New York: Ace Books, Inc., December 1962)
The first Ace paperback edition of *The Chessmen of Mars* has cover and title page art by Roy G. Krenkel. Stock No. F-170, price 40¢. 256 numbered pages.

99. *Three Martian Novels: Thuvia, Maid of Mars / The Chessmen of Mars / The Master Mind of Mars* (New York: Peter Smith, 1963)
This is the Dover volume (listed above) bound in a red cloth hardback (with black lettering on the spine only) for the use of libraries. It has 16 St. John illustrations. The book sold for $3.75. 499 numbered pages.

100. *The Chessmen of Mars* (New York: Ballantine Books, October 1963)
The second paperback edition, and first Ballantine paperback edition has a front cover illustration by Robert Abbett. Stock No. F 776, price 50¢. 220 numbered pages.

101. *Thuvia, Maid of Mars* and *The Chessmen of Mars* (New York: Doubleday, 1972)
The Science-Fiction Book Club edition is bound in green boards with gold lettering on the spine. A beautiful wrap-around dust jacket illustration and six interior black-and-white illustrations are by Frank Frazetta. 341 numbered pages.

102. *The Chessmen of Mars* (New York: Ballantine Books, October 1973)
The third Ballantine paperback edition has a new front cover illustration by Gino D'Achille. Stock No. 23582, price $1.25. 220 numbered pages.

103. *The Chessmen of Mars* (New York: Ballantine–Del Rey, May 1979)
The tenth Ballantine paperback edition has new front cover art by Michael Whelan. Stock No. 27838, price $1.95. 220 numbered pages.

104. *Science Fiction Classics by Edgar Rice Burroughs* (Secaucus, NJ: Castle, 1982)
This anthology volume is bound in orange boards with black lettering on spine. The dust jacket design is inspired by the J. Allen St. John original, and the 26 interior black-and-white illustrations are photographs of the originals by St. John. In addition there is one black-and-white illustration by Paul F.

BY EDGAR RICE BURROUGHS

Berdanier. This volume contains five novels: *Pellucidar; Thuvia, Maid of Mars; Tanar of Pellucidar; The Chessmen of Mars;* and *The Master Mind of Mars.* The specific Castle printing can be determined from the numbers on the copyright page. The five novels are continuously paginated. ISBN 0-89009-582-5, 451 numbered pages.

105. *Science Fiction Classics by Edgar Rice Burroughs* (Secaucus, NJ: Castle, 1982)
The second printing of this anthology volume (bound in orange boards with black lettering on spine) has a new dust jacket illustration by Kevin Johnson. The interior illustrations are unchanged. This volume contains five novels: *Pellucidar; Thuvia, Maid of Mars; Tanar of Pellucidar; The Chessmen of Mars;* and *The Master Mind of Mars.* The specific Castle printing can be determined from the numbers on the copyright page. The five novels are continuously paginated. ISBN 0-89009-582-5, 451 numbered pages.

106. *Science Fiction Classics by Edgar Rice Burroughs* (Secaucus, NJ: Castle, 1982)
The third printing of this anthology volume is bound in maroon boards with gold lettering on spine. This volume contains five novels: *Pellucidar; Thuvia, Maid of Mars; Tanar of Pellucidar; The Chessmen of Mars;* and *The Master Mind of Mars.* The specific Castle printing can be determined from the numbers on the copyright page. The five novels are continuously paginated. ISBN 0-89009-582-5, 451 numbered pages.

107. *Three Martian Novels: Thuvia, Maid of Mars / The Chessmen of Mars / The Master Mind of Mars.* (New York: Dover Publications, Inc.)
This compilation volume was reprinted with a different cover by J. Allen St. John. It is a thick paperback with 16 interior black-and-white illustrations by J. Allen St. John. The stories are continuously paginated. Stock No. 486-20039-6. The price is $9.95 There are 499 numbered pages.

The Deputy Sheriff of Comanche County

108. "The Terrible Tenderfoot" (THRILLING ADVENTURES, March, April, May, 1940)
Begun one week after he finished *Tarzan the Invincible* in June of 1930, and inspired by ERB's own memories of experiences more than thirty years before,

First edition jacket for *The Deputy Sheriff of Comanche County* (1941)

this story was first published as a three-part serial with a cover illustration on the March installment by Arthur Mitchell, and numerous black-and-white interior illustrations by C.A. Murphy. It underwent several tentative working titles, including "**That Damn Dude**" and "**The Brass Heart.**" The magazine sold for 10¢ a copy.

109. *The Deputy Sheriff of Comanche County* (Tarzana: Edgar Rice Burroughs, Inc., April 23, 1940)

For at least three titles, we know that ERB, Inc. produced a "printer's dummy," as did A.C. McClurg. These are sample printings so that the publisher and author get to see samples of the binding, the typeface, the illustrations, and the paper. The ERB, Inc. printer's dummies have the standard front cover and spine (gray cloth and red lettering in this case), but the back cover is only 3½" wide. This has a sample title page, sample glossy page for the illustrations, sample dedication and contents page, and six loose pages laid in. The first loose page says "SAMPLE PAGES for EDGAR RICE BURROUGHS." The loose pages also include technical measurements, such as trim size, page size, text type, etc. In addition, three sample pages from the finished book are included. There is a dust jacket, but the only printing is on the front cover and spine; the back cover and end flaps are blank. We know that another ERB, Inc. printer's dummy exists for *Jungle Girl* and *The Lad and the Lion.*

———————————— FIRST EDITION ————————————

110. *The Deputy Sheriff of Comanche County* (Tarzana: Edgar Rice Burroughs, Inc., September 13, 1940)

The fifty-fifth hardback published, the first edition from ERB, Inc. is *not* in blue cloth but rather has a gray pebbled cover with red lettering on the front cover and spine. As with several other books of this period, the dust wrapper appears in both a laminated and unlaminated state. The dust jacket, frontispiece and 22 chapter headpieces are by John Coleman Burroughs (ERB's son). It has the usual ERB, Inc. "First Edition" imprint on the copyright page. It is dedicated to Mary Lucas Pflueger (the Pfluegers were friends during the years Burroughs spent in Honolulu). Some of the material in the original magazine version has been omitted from the hardback book. Price: $2.00. 312 numbered pages.

111. "**The Terrible Tenderfoot**" (Evergreen, Colorado, ERB-DOM #71-73, 1971)

This story was one of the rarest of the ERB, Inc. titles to find. The magazine version was reproduced beautifully in a fanzine offprint of the original pulp serial (by Camille "Caz" Cazedessus, Jr., editor of ERB-DOM). It was published in three installments, with color covers on each installment. The offprint includes all the original black-and-white illustrations.

112. *The Deputy Sheriff of Commanche* [sic] *County* (New York: Ace Books, Inc., September 1975)
The first paperback edition (which has misspelled the word "Comanche") has Boris Vallejo cover art. The frontispiece and black-and-white chapter headpieces are the originals by John Coleman Burroughs. The book appears to be a photographic reproduction of the original ERB, Inc. edition. Stock No. 14247, price $1.50. 312 numbered pages.

113. *The Deputy Sheriff of Comanche County* (New York: Charter, 1979)
This paperback edition by Charter has the cover illustration by Boris Vallejo inside a red frame. The John Coleman Burroughs frontispiece and chapter headings are also included. Stock No. 14248-6, price $1.95.

114. *The Deputy Sheriff of Comanche County* (New York: Gregg, 1979)
The Gregg hardback edition has a stylized reproduction of the John Coleman Burroughs original dust jacket. 312 pages.

The Efficiency Expert

115. "The Efficiency Expert" (ARGOSY ALL-STORY WEEKLY, October 8, 15, 22, 29, 1921)
Burroughs began work on this "realistic" short story in September of 1919, a week after he finished "**Tarzan and the Valley of Luna**" (a section from *Tarzan the Untamed*). "**The Efficiency Expert**" was first published as a four-part serial with a front cover illustration on the October 8th issue by Stockton Mulford. This was Mulford's first cover illustration of a story by Edgar Rice Burroughs. The story is based upon Burroughs' actual experiences in 1911 when he wrote and tried to sell booklets on expert salesmanship and how to run a business (ironic, since he was such a complete failure at running any business during those early years). There is one interior black-and-white headpiece, each installment, by Roger B. Morrison. Each issue was 10¢.

──────────────── FIRST EDITION ────────────────

116. *The Efficiency Expert* (Kansas City, MO: House of Greystoke, 1966)
This first edition was published by the consummate Burroughs fan, Vern Coriell, for subscribers to his BURROUGHS BULLETIN. It is professionally printed for the Burroughs Bibliophiles and measures 6¾" × 9¾". The front cover art is by Frank Frazetta. The same illustration serves as a frontispiece. In addition, there are four interior black-and-white illustrations by Roger B. Morrison. The

interior is a photographic reprint of the ARGOSY ALL-STORY WEEKLY magazine story with added materials by Vern Coriell. 84 unnumbered pages.

117. *The Efficiency Expert* (Kansas City, MO: House of Greystoke, BURROUGHS BULLETIN #57-58, 1976)
This title is a reworked printing of the 1966 first edition, and is a professionally printed wrapper edition distributed to subscribers of the BURROUGHS BULLETIN. It measures 8½" × 11". The front cover art is by Frank Frazetta. The same illustration serves as a frontispiece. In addition, there are four interior black-and-white illustrations by Roger B. Morrison. The interior is a condensed photographic reprint of the ARGOSY ALL-STORY WEEKLY magazine story with added materials by Vern Coriell. The 84 page earlier printing has been cleverly condensed into 40 unnumbered pages.

118. *The Efficiency Expert* (New York: Charter, June 1979)
This Charter paperback edition has cover art by John Rush. Stock No. 18900-8, price $1.95. 211 numbered pages.

Escape on Venus

119. "Slaves of the Fish Men" (FANTASTIC ADVENTURES, March 1941)
This short story, originally entitled "**Captured on Venus,**" was illustrated by J. Allen St. John for both the front cover and two full-page black-and-white illustrations. Each issue sold for 20¢. Burroughs began work on this Venus story in May of 1940, three months after completing *Tarzan and the Madman*.

120. "Goddess of Fire" (FANTASTIC ADVENTURES, July 1941)
This short story, originally entitled "**The Fire Goddess,**" was begun in September of 1940, and was later published in hardback as the second part of *Escape on Venus*. Burroughs scholar Robert Barrett relates an interesting story concerning the front cover art. The original by J. Allen St. John (the Venusian and background) included a nude woman. The editor suggested to St. John that he revise the cover by painting a robe on the woman, but he refused. It was at this point that the editors asked H.W. McCauley to repaint the girl. Interestingly, McCauley had been a student of St. John's. The story has two full-page black-and-white illustrations by St. John.

121. "Goddess of Fire" (FANTASTIC ADVENTURES QUARTERLY, vol. 1, no. 1, winter 1941)
Returned copies of FANTASTIC ADVENTURES were rebound in groups of

three, and called FANTASTIC ADVENTURES QUARTERLY. This issue has a cover by an unidentified artist; same two black-and-white interior illustrations by J. Allen St. John. Sold for 25¢.

122. "The Living Dead" (FANTASTIC ADVENTURES, November 1941)
Begun in October of 1940, this third short story later became the third part of *Escape on Venus*. The front cover art and two full-page black-and-white illustrations are by J. Allen St. John.

123. "The Living Dead" (FANTASTIC ADVENTURES QUARTERLY, vol. 1, no. 3, summer 1942)
Returned copies of FANTASTIC ADVENTURES were rebound in groups of three, and called FANTASTIC ADVENTURES QUARTERLY. This issue has a cover by Frank Durban and back cover by Jay Jackson. The interior uses the same two black-and-white illustrations by J. Allen St. John. Sold for 25¢.

124. "War on Venus" (FANTASTIC ADVENTURES, March 1942)
Written in five days of November 1940, this completed the fourth Venus tale by Edgar Rice Burroughs. The color painting on the front cover and two full-page black-and-white illustrations are by J. Allen St. John. Price: 20¢.

125. "War on Venus" (FANTASTIC ADVENTURES QUARTERLY, vol. 1, no. 4, fall 1942)
Returned copies of FANTASTIC ADVENTURES were rebound in groups of three, and called FANTASTIC ADVENTURES QUARTERLY. This issue has a cover by McCall, back cover by Julian S. Krupa; same two black-and-white illustrations by J. Allen St. John. 528 pages. Sold for 25¢.

──────────── FIRST EDITION ────────────

126. *Escape on Venus* (Tarzana: Edgar Rice Burroughs, Inc., October 15, 1946)
The first edition of this, the fifty-seventh hardback by ERB, is bound in two variations of the typical ERB, Inc. blue cloth with red lettering on the front cover and spine. The first is the standard blue pebbled binding and the second variant is a blue silky smooth textured cover. Priority has not been established. The copyright page has "First Edition." The dust jacket (unlaminated only) and five black-and-white illustrations are by John Coleman Burroughs. Illustrated endpapers of ERB's map of Amtor. Price: $2.00. 347 numbered pages.

127. *Escape on Venus* (New York: Canaveral Press, Inc., 1963)
The Canaveral hardback is bound in green, with a Sam Sigaloff adaptation of the first edition jacket. The five interior illustrations are those of John Coleman Burroughs. 347 pages.

128. *Escape on Venus* (New York: Ace Books, Inc., March 1964)
The first Ace paperback edition has Roy G. Krenkel cover art and title page illustration. Stock No. F-268, price 40¢. 254 numbered pages.

129. *Escape on Venus* (New York: Canaveral Press, Inc., 1975)
The second Canaveral hardback reprint is bound in green, with a Sam Sigaloff adaptation of the first edition jacket. The five interior illustrations are those of John Coleman Burroughs. 347 pages.

130. *Escape on Venus* (New York: Ace Books, Inc.)
The second Ace paperback edition has Roy G. Krenkel cover art and title page illustration. Stock No. 21560, price 50¢. 254 numbered pages.

131. *Escape on Venus* (New York: Ace Books, Inc.)
The third Ace paperback edition has the same Roy G. Krenkel cover art and title page illustration. Stock No. 21561, price 60¢. 254 numbered pages.

132. *Escape on Venus* (New York: Ace Books, Inc.)
The fourth Ace paperback edition is a new, larger size with a new Frank Frazetta front cover illustration. The Roy G. Krenkel frontispiece is also used. Stock No. 21562, price 95¢. 254 numbered pages.

133. *Escape on Venus* (New York: Ballantine Books, July 1991)
The first Ballantine paperback edition has Richard Hescox cover art. Stock No. 37011, price $3.95. 246 numbered pages.

The Eternal Lover

134. "The Eternal Lover" (ALL-STORY WEEKLY, March 7, 1914)
In November of 1913, when Burroughs finished writing *The Mad King*, he immediately began work on this, his fourteenth story. Tarzan appears in it, but only as a minor character. This short story became the first half of the hardback book with the same title, although the working title was "**Nu of the Niocene.**" The front cover illustration is by Modest Stein. There is one black-and-white headpiece by Fred W. Small. Price: 10¢ each issue.

135. "Sweetheart Primeval" (ALL-STORY CAVALIER WEEKLY, January 23, 30; February 6, 13, 1915)
This was published as a four-part sequel to "**The Eternal Lover**" with a lovely cover illustration on the January 23rd issue by P. J. Monahan. There are

I. BIBLIOGRAPHY OF BOOKS

"Sweetheart Primeval" (part II of *The Eternal Lover*), January 23, 1915

no interior illustrations. When this was reprinted in hardback form, the first chapter was slightly abbreviated. 10¢ each issue.

136. "The Eternal Lover" (IDLE HOUR MAGAZINE, November, December 1915)
The November issue of this magazine reprint includes chapter 1 through part of chapter 4. It has five illustrations by an unknown artist. The December issue includes the remainder of chapter 4 through part of chapter 6. There are no illustrations in the December issue. It is unknown whether there were any subsequent issues continuing the serialization.

137. *The Eternal Lover* (Chicago: A.C. McClurg & Co., prior to October 1925)
For several early titles, we know that McClurg produced something called a "printer's dummy." This is so different from those that it is not even clear whether it should be called a variant "printer's dummy." This book is really not at all like the forthcoming McClurg first edition, and certainly could not be used to show a prospective buyer what the finished product would look like. The binding is in red cloth (the first edition is bound in blue cloth), and it has only the title of the book on the cover ("by Edgar Rice Burroughs" is omitted). In addition, this book contains only the first signature (eight pages) of the book. It begins with a fly leaf, then eight pages, and then the end flyleaf. The covers are bent around the signature so there is no flat spine. The St. John cover illustration is glued to the inside front cover. We know that other McClurg printer's dummies exist (for *The Return of Tarzan*, *The Son of Tarzan*, and *The Beasts of Tarzan*), and it is probable that there were dummies produced for other McClurg ERB titles as well. ERB, Inc. also produced some printer's dummies.

———————————— FIRST EDITION ————————————
138. *The Eternal Lover* (Chicago: A.C. McClurg & Co., October 3, 1925)
This was the twenty-third hardback of ERB. The first edition is bound in the standard McClurg blue cloth with black lettering on the front cover and spine. The J. Allen St. John color dust jacket illustration is repeated as a sepia frontispiece. A.C. McClurg records indicate that only 5,000 copies were printed. Price: $2.00. 316 numbered pages.

139. *The Eternal Lover* (New York: Grosset & Dunlap, 1927)
The first reprint has the usual G&D red cloth binding with black lettering on the front cover and spine. The earliest reprinting lists 15 ERB titles in the advertising at the end of the book. The same dust jacket by J. Allen St. John with same black-and-white illustration as frontispiece. On the back of the earliest dust jacket is a photograph of Burroughs in an oval device, and a list of 16 ERB titles. Price: 75¢. 316 numbered pages.

I. BIBLIOGRAPHY OF BOOKS

Original McClurg first edition dust jacket for *The Eternal Lover* (1925)

BY EDGAR RICE BURROUGHS

140. *The Eternal Lover* (New York: Grosset & Dunlap, 1940)
This reprint is distinguished from the earlier reprintings by its total absence of the St. John frontispiece (like all the other 1940 G&D reprintings, there are *no* interior illustrations). It has the same color dust jacket illustration by J. Allen St. John. Price: 75¢. 316 numbered pages.

141. *The Eternal Savage* (New York: Ace Books, Inc., October 1963)
The first Ace paperback edition uses cover art and a title page drawing by Roy G. Krenkel. Stock No. F-234, price 40¢. To avoid confusion, the cover also states "Original title: *The Eternal Lover*." 191 numbered pages.

142. *The Eternal Savage* (New York: Ace Books, Inc.)
The second Ace paperback edition uses the same cover art and a title page drawing by Roy G. Krenkel. Stock No. 21801, price 50¢. 191 numbered pages.

143. *The Eternal Savage* (New York: Ace Books, Inc.)
The third Ace paperback edition uses cover art by Roy Krenkel. Stock No. 21802, price 75¢. 191 numbered pages.

144. *The Eternal Savage* (New York: Ballantine Books, November 1992)
The first Ballantine paperback edition uses cover art by Michael Herring. Stock No. 345-37835-0, price $3.99. 201 numbered pages.

A Fighting Man of Mars

145. "A Fighting Man of Mars" (THE BLUE BOOK MAGAZINE, April–September, 1930)
On February 28, 1929, two weeks after he finished *Tarzan at the Earth's Core*, Burroughs began work on his seventh novel of Barsoom. This story was first published as a six-part serial, and each issue cost 25¢. Each chapter has a title, but the titles were not used in the hardback publication. The typically colorful BLUE BOOK cover art is by Laurence Herndon for the first four installments and the sixth. Each installment has seven black-and-white drawings by Frank Hoban. There is a photograph of Burroughs with a brief biography in the September installment. Five months after he finished this he began work on *Jungle Girl*.

──────────── FIRST EDITION ────────────

146. *A Fighting Man of Mars* (New York: Metropolitan, May 15, 1931)
The first edition of this, the thirty-fifth book of ERB, has a heavily textured red cloth binding with green lettering on the front cover and spine. The

bright blue wraparound dust jacket and black-and-white frontispiece are by Hugh Hutton. Price: $2.00. 319 numbered pages.

147. *A Fighting Man of Mars* (Metropolitan and Grosset & Dunlap, 1932?)
This is a mixed edition with the Metropolitan title page and interior pages, encased in a Grosset & Dunlap binding and dust jacket. This sold for 75¢.

148. *A Fighting Man of Mars* (New York: Grosset & Dunlap, 1932)
The first reprint is a standard G&D red cloth with black lettering on the spine. The dust jacket cover and frontispiece are the same as the Metropolitan edition. Price: 75¢.

149. *A Fighting Man of Mars* (New York: Grosset & Dunlap, 1940)
The 1940 reprint differs from the 1932 reprint most clearly in the total absence of any interior illustrations. The jacket is like the Metropolitan edition.

150. *A Fighting Man of Mars* (Tarzana: Edgar Rice Burroughs, Inc., March 26, 1948)
This reprint edition has tan boards with dark red lettering on the front cover and spine. Dust jacket art and black-and-white frontispiece by Hugh Hutton are the same as the Metropolitan first edition. Price: $1.00. 319 numbered pages.

151. *A Fighting Man of Mars* (New York: Canaveral Press, Inc., May 17, 1962)
The Canaveral hardback reprint has a brown binding with dust jacket and seven interior illustrations by Mahlon Blaine. In 1962, the price was $2.75, but was raised to $2.95 in 1963. 249 pages.

152. *A Fighting Man of Mars* (New York: Ace Books, Inc., March 1963)
This first Ace paperback edition has Roy G. Krenkel (assisted by Frank Frazetta) front cover art and a title page drawing. Stock No. F-190, price 40¢. 253 numbered pages.

153. *A Fighting Man of Mars* (New York: Ballantine Books, January 1964)
The first Ballantine paperback edition used Robert Abbett for the front cover art. Stock No. U2037, price 50¢. 192 numbered pages.

154. *A Princess of Mars* and *A Fighting Man of Mars: Two Martian Novels by Edgar Rice Burroughs* (New York: Dover Publications, Inc., May 1964)

Large paperback edition with cover design by Frank E. Schoonover. Four black-and-white interior illustrations by Schoonover and one by Hugh Hutton. Consecutively paginated, 356 numbered pages.

155. *The Mastermind* [sic] *of Mars* and *A Fighting Man of Mars* (New York: Doubleday, 1973)
Although this Science-Fiction Book Club edition is dated 1973, H. Heins's research established the actual date of publication as January 1974. It is bound in dark blue cloth with gold lettering on the spine. The dust jacket and six black-and-white illustrations are by Frank Frazetta. Consecutively paginated, 348 numbered pages.

156. *A Fighting Man of Mars* (New York: Ballantine Books, October 1973)
This is the third Ballantine printing, with new cover art by Gino D'Achille. Stock No. 23584, price $1.25. 192 numbered pages.

157. *A Fighting Man of Mars* (New York: Ballantine-Del Rey, April 1979)
The third *revised* Ballantine printing has new cover art by Michael Whelan. Stock No. 27840, price $1.95. 239 numbered pages.

The Girl from Farris's

158. "The Girl from Farris's" (ALL-STORY WEEKLY, September 23, 30; October 7, 14, 1916)
This four-part serial (written from July 14, 1913, to March 19, 1914, directly after *The Warlord of Mars*) was originally entitled "**The Girl from Harris's.**" The cover illustration on the September 23rd issue is by C. D. Williams. There were no interior illustrations.

——————————— FIRST EDITION ———————————

159. *The Girl from Farris's* (Tacoma, Washington: The Wilma Company, 1959)
This tiny (3⅝" × 4⅜") book, published in an edition limited to 250 copies (each individually numbered), is generally considered the true first edition. Because of the laxity of the ERB, Inc. legal department, this title was allowed to fall out of copyright, and fan Eldon K. Everett and some others copied the

text from the ALL-STORY magazine, reduced it to one-sixth size, photo-offset and bound 150 copies in rust-colored marble boards with blue or green tape reinforcing the spine, as well as black leather (20 copies) and paper covers (80 copies) and sold it for $3.50. The text is so small that it is virtually unreadable. It has 48 (+1) pages: 47 numbered pages with the title page designated as "-A-". The individual copy number appears on page 47.

160. *The Girl from Farris's* (Kansas City, MO: House of Greystoke, August 1965)

This attractive edition was published by ardent Burroughs fan Vern Coriell, and was advertised as an "*authorized* first edition" from the Burroughs Bibliophiles. It is 6¾" x 9¾" and is bound in stiff yellow paper covers with cover art (repeated as frontispiece) by Frank Frazetta. This is an offprint of the serial described above (#1), but Coriell has included a "Pictorial Bibliography" of the story at the end, reproducing two drawings by Sam Armstrong from the newspaper serial published in the TACOMA TRIBUNE in 1920. It also contains information on the Wilma Company edition. In addition to the stiff yellow paper edition, Coriell had a few copies professionally bound in blue denim cloth hard covers which he shared with close friends. The title and the author's name were stamped in silver on the front cover. Coriell's own personal copy was bound in red leather with gold lettering. None of these had a dust jacket. 70 (+6) numbered pages.

161. *The Girl from Farris's* (Kansas City, MO: House of Greystoke, BURROUGHS BULLETIN No. #59-60, 1976)

This title is a reworked reprinting of the 1966 first edition and is a professionally printed edition distributed to subscribers of the BURROUGHS BULLETIN. This was larger, 8½" x 11". The cover art (repeated as a frontispiece) is by Frank Frazetta. In addition, there are four interior black-and-white illustrations by Roger B. Morrison. The interior is a condensed photographic reprint of the ARGOSY ALL-STORY WEEKLY magazine story with added materials by Vern Coriell. Coriell has included a "Pictorial Bibliography" of the story at the end, reproducing two drawings by Sam Armstrong from the newspaper serial published in the TACOMA TRIBUNE in 1920. It also contains information on the Wilma Company edition. 37 (+2) numbered pages.

162. *The Girl from Farris's* (New York: Charter, June 1979)

This is the first actual paperback printing, and is advertised as such. This edition has the same illustration by artist John Rush on both the front and back covers. There are no interior illustrations. Stock No. 28903-7. Price $1.95. 150 numbered pages.

BY EDGAR RICE BURROUGHS

The Girl from Hollywood

163. "The Girl from Hollywood" (MUNSEY'S MAGAZINE, June-November 1922)
On November 16, 1921, just a week after he finished *The Chessmen of Mars*, Burroughs began work on this "realistic" novel of life in Hollywood with the working title, "**The Penningtons.**" It was first published as a six-part serial in MUNSEY'S, a magazine which sold for 25¢ per issue, considerably more than the 10¢ per issue adventure pulps. It is probable that the story was aimed at the large audience of female readers who purchased women's magazines, rather than the more typical young males who preferred action stories published in the adventure magazine market. There are no illustrations. A month after completing this, Burroughs began writing *Tarzan and the Golden Lion*.

─────────────── FIRST EDITION ───────────────

164. *The Girl from Hollywood* (New York: The Macaulay Company, August 10, 1923)
There is some disagreement about the first edition of this, Burroughs' eighteenth published hardback. Heins' *Golden Anniversary Bibliography* lists the first state as bound in red cloth with a pronounced pebbling effect, with light green lettering and a design on the front cover; and light green lettering on the spine. However, following the research of Burroughs collector and scholar, Bill Ross, internal evidence of printing plate deterioration strongly suggests that this pebbled binding is a later reprinting. His research shows that the true first edition (reflecting the sharpest printing plates) has a rough horizontally woven grain texture (not pebbled or bubbled). In addition, Ross argues that the first edition frontispiece has "he said" as the last two words of the caption, but almost all subsequent printings omit the "he said" on the frontispiece and show various stages of wear on the original printing plates, especially noticeable on page 9 and 195. The dust jacket illustration is by P. J. Monahan (repeated in black-and-white for the frontispiece). The first edition dust jacket is different from the subsequent reprintings; on the bottom of the spine of the first edition jacket, we find a black rectangle with the corners trimmed (making a sort of modified octagon), with "The Macaulay Company/New York" inside the box. Each printing sold for $1.90. 320 numbered pages.

165. *The Girl from Hollywood* (New York: The Macaulay Company, 1923)
There are two points which mark this book as the second Macaulay printing: a difference on the frontispiece and a difference with the dust jacket. This variant is bound in the same *rough* red cloth with a woven horizontal pattern, and the same light green design and *green* lettering. The first distinction between

this and the one listed as the first state is that this edition omits the two words, "he said," at the end of the frontispiece caption. Lettering on the copyright page, page 9, and page 195, is all sharp and clearly unworn. The second difference is with the dust jacket. We find the same dust jacket illustration by P. J. Monahan, but on the bottom of the spine of the second printing dust jacket and all later jackets, we find a coat-of-arms or shield with a large letter "M" on the shield, a bird atop the shield, and the motto "CARPE DIEM" ("Seize the Day") enclosed on a banner device below the shield. The bottom of the spine has the single word "MACAULAY" in capital letters along the bottom.* Price: $1.90. 320 numbered pages.

166. *The Girl from Hollywood* (New York: The Macaulay Company, 1923)

Following Bill Ross' research, there are two differences between this Macaulay printing and the previous one. First, it is bound in *smooth* fine grain red cloth with green lettering. Second, there is a slight deterioration of the print plates noticeable on page 9, but the copyright page and page 195 are still sharp and clear. The frontispiece by P. J. Monahan is unchanged, the phrase "he said" is *not* found on the frontispiece caption. As noted above, the spine of the dust jacket is different from that of the first edition. On the bottom of the spine is a coat-of-arms or shield with a large letter "M" on the shield, a bird atop the shield, and the motto "CARPE DIEM" ("Seize the Day") enclosed on a banner device below the shield. The bottom of the spine has the single word "MACAULAY" in capital letters along the bottom. 320 numbered pages.

167. *The Girl from Hollywood* (New York: The Macaulay Company, 1923)

The book listed here as the fourth reprinting is an awkward anomaly for three reasons. First, unlike the other variants, this *does have* the two words, "he said," on the frontispiece caption, just like the one described as the first state edition. However, there is some visible deterioration of the printing plates on page 9, so it is more likely that it is a later reprinting. Third, it is bound in red cloth with a pronounced *pebbling* or *bubbling* effect, with light green lettering and a design on the front cover and light green lettering on the spine. If it were not for the fact that the original plates show wear on page 9, this would be a good candidate for being the first edition. The dust jacket illustration is by P. J. Monahan (repeated in black-and-white for the frontispiece), and on the bottom of the spine is the shield and the motto "CARPE DIEM" ("Seize the Day") enclosed on a banner device below the shield. The bottom of the spine has the single word "MACAULAY" in capital letters along the bottom. 320 numbered pages.

In addition to the shield logo, there are at least four additional variants of the reprint jackets, with the back cover of the jacket advertising different titles of books printed by Macaulay.

BY EDGAR RICE BURROUGHS

Original Macaulay Co. first edition dust jacket for *The Girl from Hollywood* (1923)

I. Bibliography of Books

168. *The Girl from Hollywood* (New York: The Macaulay Company, 1923)

The book listed here as the fifth reprinting is the one which Heins' *Bibliography* lists as the first edition. This version has two differences compared to the variant listed above. It does *not* have the two words, "he said," on the frontispiece caption. In addition to the slight visible deterioration of the printing plates on page 9, there is the beginning of deterioration on the copyright page (page 195 remains clear and sharp). Thus, the additional wear makes it more likely that this is later than the one described as the fourth. Like the fourth listed above, this is bound in red cloth with a pronounced *pebbling* or *bubbling* effect, with light green lettering and a design on the front cover and light green lettering on the spine. The dust jacket illustration is by P. J. Monahan (repeated in black-and-white for the frontispiece), and the spine has the shield and the motto "CARPE DIEM" ("Seize the Day") enclosed on a banner device below the shield. The bottom of the spine has the single word "MACAULAY" in capital letters along the bottom. 320 numbered pages.

169. *The Girl from Hollywood* (New York: The Macaulay Company, 1925)

This Macaulay printing (from 1925), unlike the earlier printings, is bound in a fine grained red cloth with *black* lettering and design. The copyright page and page 9 show clear deterioration, but page 195 is still sharp and clear. The words "he said" are *not* on the caption of the frontispiece. The dust jacket is the reprint jacket with the shield described above. 320 pages.

170. *The Girl from Hollywood* (New York: The Macaulay Company, 1925)

The next variant Macaulay printing (from 1925), like the previous one, is bound in a fine grained red cloth with *black* lettering and design. The copyright page and page 9 show clear deterioration, but now page 195 is showing signs of deterioration. The words "he said" are *not* on the caption of the frontispiece. The dust jacket is the reprint jacket with the shield described above. 320 pages.

171. *The Girl from Hollywood* (New York: The Macaulay Company, 1925)

This Macaulay printing, like number 7 and 8 above, is bound in red cloth with *black* lettering and design. There are two distinguishing points between this and the previous reprintings: (1) this printing completely *lacks* the frontispiece, and as a result, (2) the artist's name is omitted from the title page. The dust jacket is the reprint jacket with the shield described above. The price was lowered to 75¢. 320 pages.

172. *The Girl from Hollywood* (New York: Ace Books, Inc., January 1976)

The first paperback edition from Ace has cover art by Boris Vallejo. No interior illustrations. Stock No. 28911, price $1.75. 244 numbered pages.

173. *The Girl from Hollywood* (New York: Charter Books, June 1979)
The Charter paperback edition uses the same Boris Vallejo cover illustration found on the Ace Books paperback. The illustration has been reduced with a red border around it. This illustration and border are duplicated on the back cover. There are no interior illustrations. Stock No. 28912, price $1.95. 244 numbered pages.

The Gods of Mars

174. "The Gods of Mars" (THE ALL-STORY, January, February, March, April, May 1913)
This five-part serial of Burroughs' fourth written story was begun July 14, 1912, two months after Burroughs finished "**Tarzan of the Apes**." *The Gods of Mars* is regarded by many as one of ERB's finest stories. There are no cover illustrations, but there is one black-and-white headpiece repeated for each installment, designed by Fred W. Small. Each issue sold for 10¢. After completing this, his next novel was *The Return of Tarzan*.

────────── FIRST EDITION ──────────

175. *The Gods of Mars* (Chicago: A.C. McClurg & Co., September 28, 1918)
The seventh hardback to be published, the first edition of ERB's second tale of Barsoom is bound in dark red decorated cloth with black lettering on the front cover and spine. The Frank E. Schoonover color dust jacket illustration serves as the sepia frontispiece. The copyright page says "W. F. Hall Printing Company, Chicago" in very small type. A.C. McClurg records indicate that the combined printing of the first edition plus the second printing one year later was 10,000 copies. Price: $1.35. 348 numbered pages.

176. *The Gods of Mars* (Chicago: A.C. McClurg & Co., 1919)
This scarce McClurg reprint is clearly dated 1919 and is thereby easily distinguished from the 1918 true first. It is identical in all other respects including the W.F. Hall imprint. It sold for $1.35.

177. *The Gods of Mars* (New York: Grosset & Dunlap, 1919)
This, the first G&D reprint, does not have the red cloth covers of the later G&D reprints. The earliest G&D printing is thought to be the one bound in a

mustard-brown cover with black letters and a dark yellow arc. The next printing is believed to be in light green with black letters and an olive-green design of an arc. Both of these have a "W.F. Hall" printer's imprint. The dust jacket and identical frontispiece by Frank E. Schoonover are present; the earliest dust jacket does *not* have a photograph of Burroughs on the rear, and *A Princess of Mars* is the only ERB title listed on the reverse inside of the jacket. Price: 75¢. 348 numbered pages.

178. *The Gods of Mars* (New York: Grosset & Dunlap, 1920)
The third reprint. This is bound in a light yellow-green, tan, blue or red cloth with dark green (also brown) cover design and black lettering on both the front cover and spine. The dust jacket and identical frontispiece by Frank E. Schoonover are present. The rear of the 1920 jacket has a photo of Burroughs with three ERB titles listed. This G&D printing is clearly distinguished from the first reprint by the *absence* of the W.F. Hall imprint. There are subsequent printings (probably from 1925, 1927, 1929, and 1934) with cloth covers in gray with black letters and green arc, dark greenish gray with olive-green arc, green, blue and red cloth. For some reason, the price was raised to $1.00 for this 1920 printing, and reduced back to 75¢ in 1922. 348 numbered pages.

179. *The Gods of Mars* (New York: Grosset & Dunlap, 1940)
This is the next significant G&D reprint of this title. It is bound in a light green cloth with dark green cover design and black lettering on both the front cover and spine. The dust jacket is by Frank E. Schoonover. As was typical of the G&D reprintings of this period, it is easily distinguished from the earlier G&D reprints by the *absence* of the frontispiece. Price: 75¢. 348 numbered pages.

180. *The Gods of Mars* (Tarzana: Edgar Rice Burroughs, Inc., March 26, 1948)
The Burroughs, Inc. reprint says "Copyright 1940" on the copyright page, even though the actual date is 1948. The cover is the standard tan-gray boards. Price: $1.00. 348 numbered pages.

181. *The Gods of Mars* (New York: Canaveral Press, Inc., November 30, 1962)
A photographic reproduction of the original book plates, in blue cloth with black letters on the front cover and spine. Dust jacket, frontispiece and eight interior illustrations by Larry Ivie. The book sold for $2.75 until 1963, when the price was raised to $2.95. 348 numbered pages.

182. *The Gods of Mars* (New York: Ballantine Books, January 1963)
The first paperback reprint is by Ballantine. The front cover illustration is by Robert Abbett. Stock No. F 702, price 50¢. 190 numbered pages.

183. *The Gods of Mars* and *The Warlord of Mars* (New York: Doubleday, January 1971)
The Science-Fiction Book Club edition is bound in black cloth with silver lettering on spine. A striking dust jacket and six black-and-white illustrations are by Frank Frazetta. 336 numbered pages.

184. *The Gods of Mars* (New York: Ballantine Books, October 1973)
The fifth paperback reprint by Ballantine has two important differences when compared to the previous four. First, the new front cover illustration is by Gino D'Achille. Second, on the title page ERB's last name is misspelled "Burrows." This was corrected on the next printing. Stock No. 23579, price $1.25. 190 numbered pages.

185. *The Gods of Mars* (New York: Ballantine–Del Rey, May 1979)
The thirteenth paperback reprint by Ballantine has new front cover art by Michael Whelan. Stock No. 27835, price $1.95. 190 numbered pages.

I Am a Barbarian

———————— FIRST EDITION ————————

186. *I Am a Barbarian* (Tarzana: Edgar Rice Burroughs, Inc., September 1, 1967)
Burroughs was nearing the end of his writing career when he wrote this between April and September, 1941. This novel reflected his deep fascination with history, and he spent a great deal of time and effort researching the historical period. Shortly after he finished *I Am a Barbarian*, he wrote "**Skeleton Men of Jupiter**" and eventually produced one more full-length Tarzan novel, *Tarzan and "The Foreign Legion." I Am a Barbarian* was not published during Burroughs' lifetime. It appeared in hardback 17 years after his death, and only 2,000 copies were printed. It is the sixty-sixth hardback to be published, and it is the last hardback to be published by ERB, Inc. It is bound in a maroon cloth binding with gold lettering on the front cover and spine. The white dust jacket and frontispiece are by fantasy artist Jeff Jones. It is not known whether Burroughs made any attempt to sell it to any magazines. This novel was finished in September of 1941, and three months later, the United States became embroiled in World War II. ERB desperately wanted to participate in the war effort, in spite of the fact that he was 66 years old, and eventually he became a war correspondent. Apparently Burroughs either forgot about this novel, or did not think too highly of it. The story remained untouched and forgotten until 1967. 287 numbered pages.

187. *I Am a Barbarian* (New York: Ace Books, Inc., September 1975)
The first paperback edition of *I Am a Barbarian* has front cover art by Boris Vallejo. There are two variants; one with 15 ERB titles, a second with 17 ERB titles listed. Stock No. 35804, price $1.50. 287 numbered pages.

The Illustrated Tarzan Book No. 1

---FIRST EDITION---

188. *The Illustrated Tarzan Book No. 1, Picturized from the Novel Tarzan of the Apes by Edgar Rice Burroughs* (New York: Grosset & Dunlap, 1929)
This is an abridged yet accurate pictorial retelling of the original Tarzan book, *Tarzan of the Apes*. The black-and-white drawings were done by the soon-to-be famous comic strip artist, Hal Foster, who did Tarzan in the Sunday comic pages, and ultimately quit to concentrate on his own hero, Prince Valiant. The book has hard paper covers with a green cloth spine. It has a dust jacket which has the same color illustration repeated on the front cover. The back of the Grosset & Dunlap dust jacket has a rectangular photograph of Burroughs, and a listing of 25 of Burroughs's books, ending with *The Mucker*. Inside the fly leaf on the back is a photograph of ERB mounted upon his horse, Brigadier Rex, and a very brief biography. There is a separate copyright page missing in the second edition. The distinguishing mark between the two states of the first edition is the last page of the book, which is a list of books by Burroughs. The last page on the first state of the first edition has a list of 25 titles (none of them are underlined). The last title on the list is *The Chessmen of Mars*. The list found on the last page of the *second state* (described in more detail below) has 28 titles ending with *The Mucker*, each underlined. Otherwise, the two variants are identical. The first and second printings of the book originally sold for 50¢. 79 numbered pages.

189. *The Illustrated Tarzan Book No. 1, Picturized from the Novel Tarzan of the Apes by Edgar Rice Burroughs* (New York: Grosset & Dunlap, 1929)
The second state of the first edition is identical to the one above, with the exception of the very last page of the book. A list of books written by Burroughs is a common feature on the last page of G&D books, and the last title on the first printing of the first edition (described above) is *The Chessmen of Mars*. However, the list found on the last page of this, the second state, has been reset; there are three additional titles making 28 titles on the list, and each one is underlined. The last title is now *The Mucker*. The three additional titles are *Tarzan, Lord of the Jungle* (1928), *The War Chief* (1928), and *The Master Mind of Mars*

BY EDGAR RICE BURROUGHS

(1929). We might surmise that someone at Grosset & Dunlap noticed that the list included at the back of the book was out of date, and made it more current by adding their three most recent titles. Otherwise, the two variants are identical. 79 numbered pages.

I. BIBLIOGRAPHY OF BOOKS

Original G&D dust jacket for *The Illustrated Tarzan Book No. 1* (1929)

190. *The Illustrated Tarzan Book No. 1, Picturized from the Novel Tarzan of the Apes by Edgar Rice Burroughs* (New York: Grosset & Dunlap, 1934)
   This 1934 reprinting has no dust jacket, but has the same Foster cover illustration on both the front and back boards. The cardboard binding is not quite

as thick as the first edition. The cloth reinforced spine was replaced with a green *paper* spine, and a reduced price of 25¢ is found in a red circle with a black border on the lower right hand corner of the front cover. The book consists of 78 pages with four of the illustrations omitted—one each from the original pages 76 through 79 of the first printing. There is no page 79 in this edition. Although the cover blurb claims 300 pictures, it contains only 296. 78 numbered pages.

191. *THE BURROUGHS BIBLIOPHILE #2: THE ILLUSTRATED TARZAN BOOK No. 1, Picturized from the Novel TARZAN OF THE APES by Edgar Rice Burroughs* (Kansas City, MO: House of Greystoke, 1967)
This is a reprint of the original 1929 Grosset & Dunlap edition, described above. It was done by Vern Coriell's House of Greystoke. There are two different colors for the paper wraps. The regular edition is in yellow (gold) wraps. There was another variant with blue wraps, which Coriell sent to special friends. It is 8½" × 11" in size.

John Carter of Mars

192. "John Carter and the Giant of Mars" (AMAZING STORIES, January 1941)
This very controversial magazine story has been a problem for Burroughs fans and bibliographers ever since it first appeared. Those who knew ERB's writing style instantly felt that the story was not written by the same person who had written all the other tales of Barsoom. In addition to the stylistic differences and errors, we know that Burroughs left no notation in his notebook of having written it (rather conclusive evidence that ERB did not write it, because he was fastidious about recording the time he spent on his writing). Burroughs' son, the artist John Coleman Burroughs, had written a Big Little Book in 1940 with the same plot, and it seemed likely that this story was the work of John Coleman Burroughs. The issue has been settled: Clarence B. Hyde, president of the Burroughs Bibliophiles, visited John Coleman Burroughs in Tarzana in 1963, and asked him about the authorship of this story, and ERB's son admitted that he wrote it, not his father. When Burroughs scholar Bill Ross visited John Coleman Burroughs in 1976, he too was told that J.C. Burroughs was the actual author of the story. It has a striking front cover painting and two interior black-and-white illustrations by J. Allen St. John. The issue sold for 20¢. It was later published in hardback 14 years after ERB's death as Part One of *John Carter of Mars*.

193. "John Carter and the Giant of Mars" (AMAZING STORIES QUARTERLY, Volume 1, no. 4, fall 1941)

I. BIBLIOGRAPHY OF BOOKS

Ray Palmer took returned copies of AMAZING STORIES and rebound them in groups of three, calling it AMAZING STORIES QUARTERLY. The cover art is by Julian S. Krupa.

194. "Skeleton Men of Jupiter" (AMAZING STORIES, February 1943)
This is recorded in Burroughs' notebook, and is written by the master. Clearly, it is the beginning of a longer story, for John Carter does not finish this story with "the incomparable Dejah Thoris" safely in his arms. The complications were obviously to be dealt with in subsequent stories which were never written. This magazine story has front cover art and two interior black-and-white illustrations by J. Allen St. John. This story was collected in the Canaveral volume listed below, where it is "Part Two" of the 1964 hardback edition.

195. "Skeleton Men of Jupiter" (AMAZING STORIES QUARTERLY, Volume 3, no. 4, fall 1943)
Returned copies of AMAZING STORIES were rebound in groups of three, and called AMAZING STORIES QUARTERLY. This issue has a cover by Malcolm Smith and Julian S. Krupa.

196. "John Carter and the Giant of Mars" (AMAZING STORIES, April 1961)
This is a reprint of the 1941 story in smaller format, with two interior black-and-white illustrations by J. Allen St. John from the 1941 AMAZING.

197. "Skeleton Men of Jupiter" (AMAZING STORIES, January 1964)
This is a reprint of the 1943 story in smaller format with two interior black-and-white illustrations by J. Allen St. John from the 1943 AMAZING.

──────────────── FIRST EDITION ────────────────

198. *John Carter of Mars* (New York: Canaveral Press, Inc., July 24, 1964)
This Canaveral first edition is the sixty-fourth Burroughs hardback, posthumously published in 1964. It is also the last of the Mars books. It is bound in dark blue cloth (and other colors) with black lettering on the front cover and spine. The true first can be determined by the fact that there is an error on the front cover and spine—the title is incorrect. The binder was apparently under the misapprehension that the title was *John Carter and the Giant of Mars*. The title is correct on the dust jacket. Reed Crandall did the dust jacket illustration, the illustrated endpapers and eight interior black-and-white illustrations. There is an introduction by Richard A. Lupoff. The two stories are continuously paginated. Price: $3.50. 208 numbered pages.

199. *John Carter of Mars* (New York: Canaveral Press, Inc., 1964)
The second state, actually a corrected reprinting, has the erroneous title corrected on the spine and front cover. We now find *John Carter of Mars* instead of

John Carter and the Giant of Mars. This edition is bound in light blue cloth (and other colors) with gold lettering on the front cover and spine. 208 numbered pages.

200. *John Carter of Mars* (New York: Ballantine Books, April 1965)
The first Ballantine paperback printing has a cover painting by Robert Abbett. The book has the introduction by Richard A. Lupoff. Stock No. U2041, price 50¢. 157 numbered pages.

201. *John Carter of Mars* (New York: Ballantine Books, October 1973)
The third Ballantine paperback printing has a new cover painting by Gino D'Achille. The book has the introduction by Richard A. Lupoff. Stock No. 23588, price $1.25. 157 numbered pages.

202. *Llana of Gathol* and *John Carter of Mars* (New York: Doubleday, April 1977)
The Science-Fiction Book Club edition is bound in blue-gray boards with white lettering on the spine. The dust jacket art and five interior black-and-white illustrations are by idiosyncratic s-f artist, Richard Corben. The Richard Lupoff introduction is not reprinted. The two stories are consecutively paginated. 314 numbered pages.

203. *John Carter of Mars* (New York: Ballantine–Del Rey, April 1979)
The ninth Ballantine paperback printing has a new cover painting by Michael Whelan. The book omits the introduction by Richard A. Lupoff. Stock No. 27844, price $1.95. 167 numbered pages.

Jungle Girl

204. "**The Land of Hidden Men**" (THE BLUE BOOK MAGAZINE, May–September 1931)
On October 2, 1929, five months after he finished *A Fighting Man of Mars*, ERB turned his hand to writing a tale set in the jungles of Cambodia. The result was this five-part serial which had the working title "**The Dancing Girl of the Leper King.**" The front cover art on the first installment is by Laurence Herndon. In addition, there are seven interior illustrations for each issue by Frank Hoban (some with blue, green or orange color backgrounds). Each issue was 25¢. His next novel was *Tarzan the Invincible.*

205. *Jungle Girl* (Tarzana: Edgar Rice Burroughs, Inc., printed prior to April 15, 1932)

I. BIBLIOGRAPHY OF BOOKS

For several titles, we know that ERB, Inc. produced something called a "printer's dummy," as did A.C. McClurg. On the outside these books look like the first edition. However, on the inside of this book we find only blank pages. It has the coated pages for illustrations in the book, but they too are blank. There is a dust jacket, but the only printing is on the front cover and spine—the back cover and end flaps are blank. These "dummies" may have been printed by ERB, Inc. to help visualize the final product, or they may have been produced to help one or more salesmen sell the book by demonstrating what the finished product was going to look like before the book was finally printed and bound. The exact number of pages is unclear because the pages are unnumbered and unmarked.

──────────── FIRST EDITION ────────────

206. *Jungle Girl* (Tarzana: Edgar Rice Burroughs, Inc., April 15, 1932)

This first edition of Burroughs's thirty-seventh hardback book is bound in the typical blue cloth with red lettering on the front cover and spine. This was the second book which Burroughs published with his own publishing company, and does *not* have the "First Edition" imprint on the copyright page. The dust jacket and six interior black-and-white plates are by Studley Burroughs (ERB's nephew). Price: $2.00. 318 numbered pages.

207. *Jungle Girl* (New York: Grosset & Dunlap, 1933)

The first reprint is bound in standard G&D red cloth with black lettering on the front cover and spine. The dust jacket and *four* (not the original six) interior black-and-white plates are by Studley Burroughs. The tops of the pages are dyed green. Price: 75¢. 318 numbered pages.

208. *Jungle Girl* (New York: Grosset & Dunlap, 1940)

The second reprint is bound in standard G&D red cloth with black lettering on the front cover and spine. The tops of the pages are green, and the dust jacket is the same as the first reprinting, but it can be distinguished by the absence of any interior black-and-white plates. Price: 75¢. 318 numbered pages.

209. *The Land of Hidden Men* (New York: Ace Books, Inc., October 1963)

The first American paperback edition has cover art and a title page drawing by Roy G. Krenkel, Jr. Stock No. F-232, price 40¢. 191 numbered pages.

210. *The Land of Hidden Men* (New York: Ace Books, Inc., November 1969)

The second paperback edition has the same cover art and a title page drawing by Roy G. Krenkel, Jr. Stock No. 47011, price 60¢. 217 numbered pages.

BY EDGAR RICE BURROUGHS

211. *The Land of Hidden Men* (New York: Ace Books, Inc., January 1973)
The third paperback edition has new cover art by Frank Frazetta. Stock No. 47012, price 75¢. 191 numbered pages.

212. *The Land of Hidden Men* (New York: Ballantine–Del Rey, November 1992)
This paperback edition has changed the cover art; the new cover art is by Michael Herring. Stock No. 37837, price $3.99. 200 numbered pages.

Jungle Tales of Tarzan

213. "The New Stories of Tarzan" (THE BLUE BOOK MAGAZINE, September 1916-August 1917)
On March 17, 1916, two days after he finished "The Return of the Mucker" (published as the second half of *The Mucker*), ERB began work on his sixth Tarzan novel, which started out as 12 short stories describing the childhood adventures of the young Tarzan. It was first published as a 12-part serial with one black-and-white illustration for each installment, by Herbert Morton Stoops. Each issue sold for 15¢.

———————————— FIRST EDITION ————————————
214. *Jungle Tales of Tarzan* (Chicago: A.C. McClurg & Co., March 29, 1919)
The first edition of this, Burroughs's eighth hardback to be published, is bound in an unusual bright orange cloth with black lettering on the front cover and spine. "W.F. Hall Printing Company, Chicago" is imprinted on the copyright page. The dust jacket, five sepia plates and 12 interior illustrations are by J. Allen St. John. It sold for $1.40. 319 numbered pages. (Note that McClurg did an unusual *four* printings of this title, described below, printing 63,000 copies in all. It was the second largest printing for any McClurg title.)

215. *Jungle Tales of Tarzan* (Chicago: A.C. McClurg & Co., 1920)
The second printing by McClurg is distinguished by the dark green cloth binding with black lettering on the front cover and spine. The title page is dated *1919*. "W.F. Hall" appears on the copyright page. The dust jacket and 17 black-and-white illustrations are by J. Allen St. John. Price: $1.40. 319 numbered pages.

216. *Jungle Tales of Tarzan* (Chicago: A.C. McClurg & Co., 1920)
The third printing by McClurg is also bound in dark green cloth with black lettering on the front cover and spine, but can be distinguished from the second

printing by the absence of the "W.F. Hall" imprint on the copyright page. Again, the title page is dated *1919*. The dust jacket and 17 black-and-white illustrations are by J. Allen St. John. Price: $1.40. 319 numbered pages.

217. *Jungle Tales of Tarzan* (Chicago: A.C. McClurg & Co., 1921)
The fourth printing by McClurg is bound in dark green cloth, dated *1919*, but has only the frontispiece; the coated page interior illustrations have been eliminated, and so there is no page listing illustrations following the Contents page. Price: $1.40. 319 numbered pages.

218. *Jungle Tales of Tarzan* (New York: Grosset & Dunlap, 1921)
The earliest G&D reprints are bound in a dark red-brown, or the standard dark red cloth boards with black lettering on the front cover and spine. The first reprint is distinguished by an elegant "R" on the spine in the word G<u>R</u>OSSET with a fancy lower curl. The "R" on the subsequent reprintings by G&D is a plain letter without the curl. There are no ERB books listed among the advertised novels at the end of the book. The dust jacket and *thirteen* interior black-and-white illustrations are by J. Allen St. John. On the back of the earliest jacket is ERB's photo in an oval frame. Later jackets have the ERB photograph in a rectangular design. This reprint sold for $1.00. 319 numbered pages.

219. *Jungle Tales of Tarzan* (New York: Grosset & Dunlap, 1922)
This second G&D reprinting is bound in a lighter red cloth with black lettering on the front cover and spine. The dust jacket and thirteen interior black-and-white illustrations are by J. Allen St. John. This reprint has the plain "R" on the spine in "GROSSET." The advertisement pages in the back of the book do not list any ERB books. The book sold for 75¢. 319 numbered pages.

220. *Jungle Tales of Tarzan* (New York: Grosset & Dunlap, 1924)
A later G&D reprinting is bound in a lighter red cloth with black lettering on the front cover and spine. The dust jacket and 13 interior black-and-white illustrations by J. Allen St. John. This reprint has the plain "R" on the spine in "GROSSET." It can be distinguished from the previous reprintings by examining the advertisements at the back of the book. There are 11 ERB books listed in the advertisement section. Later reprintings can be identified by the number of ERB titles listed in the ads at the back: 23 titles (1927), 28 titles (1930), 33 titles (1934) and 37 titles (1936). The book sold for 75¢. 319 numbered pages.

221. *Jungle Tales of Tarzan* (New York: Grosset & Dunlap, 1940)
The 1940 reprint is bound in red cloth with black lettering on the front cover and spine. Like the other reprints from the early 1940s, this can be distinguished from the 1922 reprint by the lack of a frontispiece. The dust jacket is by

J. Allen St. John. This has the plain "R" on the spine in the word "GROSSET." Price: 75¢. 319 numbered pages.

222. *Jungle Tales of Tarzan* (New York: Grosset & Dunlap, 1943)
This is the World War II edition bound in maroon with black lettering on the front cover and spine. The book is thin, having been printed with thinner paper which turns brown and brittle with age. The dust jacket is like the previous reprints; however, there are only ten interior black-and-white drawings by J. Allen St. John (the illustrations for Chapter I and Chapter XII are missing). The title page has a drawing of "Tarzan and the Golden Lion" as a logo on the top of the page. Price: 50¢; reduced to 49¢ after 1945.

223. *Jungle Tales of Tarzan* (New York: Grosset & Dunlap, January 1950)
Like the other 1950s reprints, this originally sold for $1.00 and is bound in a rust-colored brownish-orange *cloth* with pictorial boards and brown lettering on the spine. The end-paper map and board and title page decorations are by Rafael Palacios. The unsigned dust jacket design is by C. E. Monroe, Jr. The decorated title page is by an unidentified artist; it has 12 interior black-and-white drawings by J. Allen St. John. This title was reissued several times over the years, first with the map by Palacios (first $1.00, raised to $1.25 in 1955) and later in a 1958 edition marked $1.50 (without the map of Africa) on the flap of the dust jacket. All of the later reissues had paperbound boards in tan with brown decorations and lettering. 319 numbered pages.

224. *Jungle Tales of Tarzan* (New York: Ace Books, Inc., June 1963)
The first paperback edition is this Ace paperback with front cover art and a title page drawing by Frank Frazetta. Stock No. F-206, price 40¢. 220 numbered pages.

225. *Jungle Tales of Tarzan* (New York: Ballantine Books, July 1963)
The first Ballantine paperback edition has a front cover illustration by Richard Powers. Stock No. F 750, price 50¢. 191 numbered pages.

226. "Tarzan, Jungle Detective" (ELLERY QUEEN'S MYSTERY MAGAZINE, May 1964)
The magazine reprints chapter ten from *Jungle Tales of Tarzan*, "The Battle for Teeka," on pages 67–81. There is a two-page introduction by the editor. There are no illustrations. Price 50¢.

227. *Jungle Tales of Tarzan* (New York: Grosset & Dunlap, 1967)
This hardback reprinting is bound in pictorial boards with a cover design taken from the C.E. Monroe, Jr., dust jacket used in the previous printings. The

title page is decorated by an unidentified artist. Like the previous reprints, this has the same 12 black-and-white drawings by J. Allen St. John. 319 numbered pages.

228. *Jungle Tales of Tarzan* (New York: Ballantine Books, April 1969)
   The third Ballantine paperback edition has a front cover illustration by Robert Abbett. Stock No. 01596, price 50¢. 191 numbered pages.

229. "Tarzan, Jungle Detective" (ELLERY QUEEN'S 1970 ANTHOLOGY, volume 18, 1969)
   This anthology reprints chapter ten from *Jungle Tales of Tarzan*, "The Battle for Teeka," on pages 251–266, and includes the same two-page introduction by the editor. There are no illustrations. Price $1.50.

230. *Jungle Tales of Tarzan* (New York: Ballantine Books, April 1975)
   The sixth Ballantine paperback edition has new front cover art by Neal Adams. Stock No. 24164, price $1.25. 191 numbered pages.

231. "Tarzan's First Love" in *Love Stories* edited by Martin Levin (New York: Quadrangle-New York Times Book Co., 1975)
   This single chapter is anthologized in a collection of 28 short stories around the theme of love. This appeared in Book Club form. 464 numbered pages.

232. *Jungle Tales of Tarzan* (New York: Ballantine Books—A Del Rey Book, June 1991)
   The eighteenth Ballantine paperback edition has new front cover art by Barclay Shaw. Stock No. 34413, price $1.25. 212 numbered pages.

The Lad and the Lion

233. "The Lad and the Lion" (ALL-STORY WEEKLY, June 30; July 7, 14, 1917)
   Burroughs began working on this story in February of 1914, three days after *The Beasts of Tarzan* was finished. It is a 40,000 word novelette with the working title "**Men and Beasts.**" It was serialized in three parts with a front cover illustration on the June 30th issue by Modest Stein which portrays a movie audience watching a projected image of a lad with his arm around a lion, and on the bottom of the page is: "On the screen/Selig Polyscope Co." There are no interior illustrations. Each issue: 10¢.

234. *The Lad and the Lion* (Tarzana: Edgar Rice Burroughs, Inc., April 23, 1940)

For at least three titles, we know that ERB, Inc. produced something called a "printer's dummy." These are sample printings so that the publisher and author get to see samples of the binding, the typeface, the illustrations, and the paper. The ERB, Inc. printer's dummies have the standard front cover and spine (blue pebbled cloth and red lettering in this case), but the back cover is only 3½" wide. This has eight bound sheets: a sample title page and copyright page, list of illustrations, and several sample pages from the final text. There is no dust jacket on this printer's dummy. The exact number of pages is unclear because the pages are unnumbered and unmarked. We know that another ERB, Inc. printer's dummy exists for *Jungle Girl* and *The Deputy Sheriff of Comanche County*.

─────────── FIRST EDITION ───────────

235. *The Lad and the Lion* (Tarzana: Edgar Rice Burroughs, Inc., February 15, 1938)

In ten days in August, 1937, Burroughs rewrote and added another 20,000 words to the original 1914 story, and it became his fiftieth published hardback book. The first edition is bound in the typical ERB, Inc. blue cloth with red lettering on the front cover and spine. The copyright page says "First Edition." The dust jacket appears in two versions: one laminated and one unlaminated. The dust jacket illustration and five interior black-and-white plates are by John Coleman Burroughs, ERB's son. Price: $2.00. 317 numbered pages.

236. *The Lad and the Lion* (New York: Grosset & Dunlap, 1939)

This, the first reprint, is bound in red cloth with black lettering on the front cover and spine, and the tops of the pages are dyed green. The dust jacket by John Coleman Burroughs has two variants. Even though there are no interior illustrations in this edition, some of the G&D dust jackets have the word "Illustrated" on the spine (just like the first edition). Price: 75¢. 317 numbered pages.

237. *The Lad and the Lion* (New York: Canaveral Press, Inc., April 28, 1964)

The second time *The Lad and the Lion* was reprinted, it was bound in tan cloth with black lettering on the front cover and spine. The dust jacket has a photograph of the original John Coleman Burroughs illustration, and announces "ERB'S RAREST BOOK." There are several other titles which might qualify equally well for this sobriquet. This reprint includes the five interior black-and-white illustrations by John Coleman Burroughs. 317 numbered pages.

238. *The Lad and the Lion* (New York: Ballantine Books, September 1964)

I. BIBLIOGRAPHY OF BOOKS

First edition jacket for *The Lad and the Lion* (1938)

I. BIBLIOGRAPHY OF BOOKS

First edition jacket for *The Lad and the Lion* (1938)

BY EDGAR RICE BURROUGHS

First paperback edition with front cover art by R. Bartram. Stock No. U2048, price 50¢. 192 numbered pages.

239. *The Lad and the Lion* (New York: Ace Books, Inc., April 1974)
This Ace paperback printing is the second paperback edition. It has a front cover by Enrich. Stock No. 46870, price 95¢. 189 numbered pages.

Land of Terror

——————— FIRST EDITION ———————
240. *Land of Terror* (Tarzana: Edgar Rice Burroughs, Inc., May 1, 1944)
Burroughs's fifty-sixth hardback book is also the fifth novel set in the inner world of Pellucidar. Although this story, begun in October of 1938, was written directly after *Synthetic Men of Mars*, it was never published in magazine form. This first edition is bound in the usual ERB, Inc. blue cloth with red lettering on the front cover and spine. The colorful dust wrapper art is by John Coleman Burroughs (Burroughs's youngest son). There are no interior illustrations. According to Robert R. Barrett, John Coleman Burroughs also executed a frontispiece and numerous small illustrations intended to be used as chapter headings in the first edition. For some reason, they were not used. However, they were all reprinted by Vernell Coriell in *THE BURROUGHS BIBLIOPHILE #3: DAVID INNES OF PELLUCIDAR* (Kansas City, MO: House of Greystoke, 1968). Price: $2.00. 319 numbered pages.

241. *Land of Terror* (New York: Canaveral Press, Inc., November 15, 1963)
The first and only reprint hardback edition is bound in green cloth with black lettering on the front cover and spine. The dust jacket art and seven interior black-and-white illustrations are by Roy G. Krenkel. Price: $3.50. 319 numbered pages.

242. *Land of Terror* (New York: Ace Books, Inc., January 1964)
This Ace printing is the first paperback edition. It has front cover art and a title page drawing by Frank Frazetta. Stock No. F-256, price 40¢. 175 numbered pages.

243. *Land of Terror* (New York: Ace Books, Inc.)
The second Ace printing has the same front cover art and a title page drawing by Frank Frazetta. Stock No. G-738, price 50¢. 175 numbered pages.

244. *Land of Terror* (New York: Ace Books, Inc.)
The third Ace printing has the same front cover art and a title page drawing by Frank Frazetta. Stock No. 46996, price 60¢. 175 numbered pages.

245. *Land of Terror* (New York: Ace Books, Inc., January 1973)
The fourth Ace printing has new front cover art by Frank Frazetta. Stock No. 46997, price 75¢. 176 numbered pages.

246. *Land of Terror* (New York: Ballantine Books–Del Rey, May 1990)
The first Ballantine paperback has front cover art by David B. Mattingly. Stock No. 36672, price $3.95. 186 numbered pages.

The Land That Time Forgot

247. "The Land That Time Forgot" (THE BLUE BOOK MAGAZINE, August 1918)
In September of 1917, a few months after completing "The Oakdale Affair," Burroughs began work on a highly imaginative short story whose original working title was "**The Lost U-Boat.**" This, and the other two segments, delineate the classic theme of a hitherto undiscovered island filled with prehistoric beasts and men, with an interesting twist on Darwinian evolution as a part of the subplot. This issue sold for 15¢.

248. "The People That Time Forgot" (THE BLUE BOOK MAGAZINE, October 1918)
The same day he finished "**The Lost U-Boat,**" ERB began writing the next installment, whose original working title was "**Cor Sva Jo.**" This issue sold for 20¢.

249. "Out of Time's Abyss" (THE BLUE BOOK MAGAZINE, December 1918)
In May of 1918, three months after completing "**The People That Time Forgot,**" Burroughs began work on the third and concluding installment of the prehistoric island saga. There is one black-and-white illustration for each issue by Quin Hall. Price: 20¢.

──────────────── FIRST EDITION ────────────────

250. *The Land That Time Forgot* (Chicago: A.C. McClurg & Co., June 14, 1924)

The nineteenth hardback in the Burroughs canon, this first edition is bound in light olive green cloth with black lettering on the front cover and spine. The dust jacket of this very popular story is one of the more spectacular from the brush of J. Allen St. John, and the four interior sepia plates are also by St. John. The price marked on the back of the jacket is $2.00. A.C. McClurg printed a respectable 10,000 copies of this first edition. This is one of the biggest of ERB's books, with 422 numbered pages.

251. *The Land That Time Forgot* (New York: Grosset & Dunlap, 1925)
The first reprint is bound in the usual G&D red cloth with black lettering on the front cover and spine. The dust jacket and three interior black-and-white plates by J. Allen St. John are present. The illustrations are facing pages 74, 138, and 170, which disagrees with the page numbers listed in the front matter of the book (a 1930 variant has illustrations facing pages 66, 146, and 178). The earliest G&D printing has no ERB titles listed in the ads at the back of the book. That was soon corrected, with the next printing listing 11 ERB titles at the back, and then 15 titles, and 23 titles. The earliest dust jacket has a list of 12 ERB titles on the back, with a subsequent jacket listing 16, and then 18 ERB titles. There is a 1931 or 1932 printing which has the tops of the pages dyed yellow. Price: 75¢. 422 numbered pages.

252. "The Land That Time Forgot" (AMAZING STORIES, February-April 1927)
It was very unusual for a Burroughs story to be serialized again *after* it had already appeared in hardback (Burroughs sold "second serial rights"), but this is one of those exceptions (among the others were "**Tarzan of the Apes**," "**Tarzan and the Jewels of Opar**," "**The Moon Maid**," "**A Princess of Mars**" and "**At the Earth's Core**"). It is a serial in three parts (the 1927 AMAZING STORIES was an extra large science-fiction magazine) with a cover illustration on the February issue (the first installment) and a black-and-white illustration, each installment, by Frank R. Paul. Price was 25¢ each issue.

253. *The Land That Time Forgot* (New York: Grosset & Dunlap, 1940)
The 1940 G&D reprint is bound in the usual red cloth with black lettering on the front cover and spine. The tops of the pages are dyed green, and there are 33 ERB titles listed in the ads at the back of the book. The dust jacket is by St. John, but the interior black-and-white plates by St. John are gone (the 1940s G&D reprints are identified by their lack of interior illustrations). Price: 75¢. 422 numbered pages.

254. *The Land That Time Forgot* (New York: Canaveral Press, Inc., October 17, 1962)
This Canaveral hardback reprinting is bound in light blue cloth with black

lettering on the front cover and spine. The dust jacket and seven black-and-white interior illustrations are by Mahlon Blaine. Price: $2.75, raised to $2.95 in 1963. 318 numbered pages.

255. *The Land That Time Forgot* and *The Moon Maid* (New York: Dover Publications, Inc., April 1963)

This large Dover paperback edition is the first paperback reprinting. It has the dust jacket art printed on the front cover. It is the same St. John dust jacket design and four interior black-and-white illustrations found on the previous reprints. The stories are consecutively paginated. Price: $2.00. 552 numbered pages.

256. *The Land That Time Forgot* and *The Moon Maid* (New York: Dover Publications, Inc., May 1963)

This hardback Dover edition is bound in brown cloth with gold lettering on the spine. The dust jacket design and four interior black-and-white illustrations by J. Allen St. John are all present. It is consecutively paginated; the price was $3.75. 552 numbered pages.

257. *The Land That Time Forgot* (New York: Ace Books, Inc., July 1963)

First Ace paperback edition of the first installment of the story has cover art and title page drawing by Roy G. Krenkel. Stock No. F-213, price 40¢. 126 numbered pages.

258. *The People That Time Forgot* (New York: Ace Books, Inc., August 1963)

First Ace paperback of the second installment has cover art and title page drawing by Roy G. Krenkel. Stock No. F-220, price 40¢. 124 numbered pages.

259. *Out of Time's Abyss* (New York: Ace Books, Inc., September 1963)

First Ace paperback of the concluding installment has front cover art and title page drawing by Roy G. Krenkel. Stock No. F-233, price 40¢. 125 numbered pages.

260. *The Land That Time Forgot* (New York: Doubleday, June 1975)

The Science-Fiction Book Club edition is tied in with the ERB movie which was released in the same year. It is bound in yellow boards with black lettering on the spine. The dust jacket illustration, by an unnamed artist, was taken from promotional stills from the movie, and six more interior black-and-white film stills. 249 numbered pages.

261. *The Land That Time Forgot* (New York: Ace Books, Inc.)

This is the second Ace paperback edition of the first installment of the story and it utilized the same cover art and title page drawing by Roy G. Krenkel. Stock No. 47020, price 60¢. 126 numbered pages.

262. *The People That Time Forgot* (New York: Ace Books, Inc.)
This Ace paperback printing has the same cover art and title page drawing by Roy G. Krenkel. Stock No. 65941, price 60¢. 124 numbered pages.

263. *Out of Time's Abyss* (New York: Ace Books, Inc.)
Second Ace paperback of the concluding installment has the same front cover art and title page drawing by Roy G. Krenkel. Stock No. 64481, price 60¢. 125 numbered pages.

264. *The Land That Time Forgot* (New York: Ace Books, Inc.)
The third Ace paperback edition of the first installment of the story has new cover art by Frank Frazetta. Stock No. 47021, price 75¢. 153 numbered pages.

265. *The People That Time Forgot* (New York: Ace Books, Inc., January 1973)
Third Ace paperback printing has new cover art by Frank Frazetta. Stock No. 65942, price 75¢. 125 numbered pages.

266. *Out of Time's Abyss* (New York: Ace Books, Inc., March 1973)
Third Ace paperback printing of the concluding installment has a new front cover by Frank Frazetta, which was originally used on the smaller Ace edition of *Land of Terror*. Stock No. 64482, price 75¢. 142 numbered pages.

267. *The Land That Time Forgot* (New York: Ace Books, Inc., January 1979)
The next Ace paperback edition of the first installment of the story has new cover art by Segrelles. Stock No. 47025, price $1.95. 153 numbered pages.

268. *The People That Time Forgot* (New York: Ace Books, Inc.,)
The next Ace paperback printing is a movie "tie-in" which uses the movie poster for a cover. It includes 16 black-and-white photographs from the film. Stock No. 65946, price $1.75. 153 numbered pages.

269. *Out of Time's Abyss* (New York: Ace Books, Inc., 1979)
The next Ace paperback printing of the concluding installment has a cover illustration by Segrelles. Stock No. 64485, price $1.95. 139 numbered pages.

270. *The Land That Time Forgot* (New York: Ballantine Books–Del Rey, February 1992)

The Ballantine paperback edition of the first installment of the story has new cover art by Michael Herring. Stock No. 37407, price $3.99. 138 numbered pages.

271. *The People That Time Forgot* (New York: Ballantine Books–Del Rey, February 1992)
This Ballantine paperback printing has cover art by Michael Herring. Stock No. 37403, price $3.99. 134 numbered pages.

272. *Out of Time's Abyss* (New York: Ballantine–Del Rey, February 1992)
The Ballantine paperback printing of the concluding installment has a cover illustration by Michael Herring. Stock No. 37404, price $3.99. 138 numbered pages.

Llana of Gathol

273. "The City of Mummies" (AMAZING STORIES, March 1941)
In July of 1940, shortly after he finished "**Captured on Venus**" (later retitled "**Slaves of the Fishmen**" from *Escape on Venus*), Burroughs began work on a brand new story of Barsoom. He originally entitled this installment "**The Frozen Men of Mars**," and then "**John Carter and the Pits of Horz**." The front cover illustrations and two black-and-white drawings are by J. Allen St. John. Price: 20¢.

274. "Black Pirates of Barsoom" (AMAZING STORIES, June 1941)
Two weeks after he finished "**The City of Mummies**," Burroughs began work on the second installment of the new tale of Barsoom. The front cover illustrations and two black-and-white drawings are by J. Allen St. John. Price: 20¢.

275. "Yellow Men of Mars" (AMAZING STORIES, August 1941)
Three weeks after completing "**Black Pirates of Barsoom**," ERB started this installment which he entitled "**Escape on Mars**." The front cover illustrations and two black-and-white drawings are by J. Allen St. John. Price: 20¢.

276. "Invisible Men of Mars" (AMAZING STORIES, October 1941)
This tale concluded the new Mars adventures and the four were later published in hardback as *Llana of Gathol*. The front cover illustrations and two black-and-white drawings (each installment) are by J. Allen St. John. Price: 20¢.

BY EDGAR RICE BURROUGHS

277. "The City of Mummies" (AMAZING STORIES QUARTERLY, volume 1, no. 4, fall 1941)
Returned copies of AMAZING STORIES were rebound in groups of three, and called AMAZING STORIES QUARTERLY. Cover by Frank Durban and Julian S. Krupa.

278. "Black Pirates of Barsoom" (AMAZING STORIES QUARTERLY, volume 2, no. 1, winter 1941)
Returned copies of AMAZING STORIES were rebound in groups of three, and called AMAZING STORIES QUARTERLY. Cover by Frank Durban and Julian S. Krupa.

279. "Yellow Men of Mars" and "Invisible Men of Mars" (AMAZING STORIES QUARTERLY, volume 2, no. 2, spring 1942)
Returned copies of AMAZING STORIES were rebound in groups of three, and called AMAZING STORIES QUARTERLY. This issue has a cover by Frank Durban and Julian S. Krupa.

―――――――――― FIRST EDITION ――――――――――
280. *Llana of Gathol* (Tarzana: Edgar Rice Burroughs, Inc., March 26, 1948)
The first edition of the tenth novel of Barsoom, and Burroughs's fifty-ninth hardback publication, is bound in the standard ERB, Inc. blue cloth with red lettering on the front cover and spine. The illustration on the white dust jacket and five interior black-and-white plates are by John Coleman Burroughs (ERB's son). It says "First Edition" on the copyright page. *Llana of Gathol* is dedicated to John Philip Bird (a lieutenant with whom Burroughs became friends in Honolulu in 1942). Price: $2.00. 317 numbered pages.

281. *Llana of Gathol* (New York: Ballantine Books, August 1963)
This, the first paperback edition, has front cover art by Robert Abbett. Stock No. F 762, price 50¢. 191 numbered pages.

282. *Llana of Gathol* and *John Carter of Mars* (New York: Doubleday, 1977)
The Doubleday Science Fiction Book Club issued this green volume with illustrations by the idiosyncratic science-fiction artist, Rich Corben. 314 pages.

283. *Llana of Gathol* (New York: Ballantine Books, October 1973)
This, the fifth paperback printing, has front cover art by Gino D'Achille. Stock No. 23587, price $1.25. 191 numbered pages.

284. *Llana of Gathol* (New York: Ballantine–Del Rey, April 1979)
The eleventh paperback edition has new front cover art by Michael Whelan. Stock No. 27843, price $1.95. 191 numbered pages.

Lost on Venus

285. "Lost on Venus" (ARGOSY WEEKLY, March 4, 11, 18, 25; April 1, 8, 15, 1933)

In August of 1932, three months after "**Pirate Blood**," Burroughs began work on the second of the five Venus novels. It was first printed as a seven-part serial with one cover illustration (the March 4th first installment) by Paul Stahr. One black-and-white illustration for each installment is by Samuel Cahan. Each issue was 10¢.

──────────── FIRST EDITION ────────────

286. *Lost on Venus* (Tarzana: Edgar Rice Burroughs, Inc., February 15, 1935)

The first edition (it is imprinted "First Edition" on the copyright page) of the forty-third hardback by Burroughs is bound in typical ERB, Inc. blue cloth with red lettering on the front cover and spine. The endpapers are illustrated with a map of Venus (Amtor) done by Burroughs himself. The dust jacket and five interior black-and-white plates are by J. Allen St. John. Price: $2.00. 318 numbered pages.

287. *Lost on Venus* (New York: Grosset & Dunlap, 1936)

This, the first hardback reprint, is bound in the usual G&D red cloth with black lettering on the front cover and spine. The tops of the pages are dyed green. The dust jacket and *four* interior black-and-white plates are by J. Allen St. John; ERB's map of Amtor serves as decorated endpapers. Price: 75¢. 318 numbered pages.

288. *Lost on Venus* (Tarzana: Edgar Rice Burroughs, Inc., 1940)

This ERB, Inc. reprint is one of the seven titles bound in red cloth with blue lettering on the front cover and spine (it is easily mistaken for the G&D red cloth). The dust jacket is identical with the first edition jacket, with cover by J. Allen St. John. There is a black-and-white frontispiece, also by St. John. There is no map on the endpapers. Price: 75¢. 318 numbered pages.

289. *Lost on Venus* (New York: Grosset & Dunlap, 1940)

This reprint is bound in the usual G&D red cloth with black lettering on the front cover and spine, without any interior illustrations. The dust jacket is by J. Allen St. John; ERB's map of Amtor serves as decorated endpapers. Price: 75¢. 318 numbered pages.

290. *Lost on Venus* (Tarzana: Edgar Rice Burroughs, Inc., March 26, 1948)

The thinner 1948 ERB reprints are all bound in tan cloth with dark red lettering on the front cover and spine. The dust jacket and black-and-white frontispiece by J. Allen St. John are the same as in the 1940 reprint. Price: $1.00. 318 numbered pages.

291. *Lost on Venus* (New York: Ace Books, Inc., August 1963)
The first Ace paperback edition has cover art and a title page drawing by Frank Frazetta. Stock No. F-221, price 40¢. 192 numbered pages.

292. *The Pirates of Venus and Lost on Venus: Two Venus Novels by Edgar Rice Burroughs* (New York: Dover Publications, Inc., November 1963)
This volume has cover art and 25 interior illustrations by the meticulous Italian artist Fortunino Matania (done originally for the 1934 British weekly magazine THE PASSING SHOW). $1.75. 340 pages.

293. *Lost on Venus* (New York: Canaveral Press, Inc., November 15, 1963)
The Canaveral hardback reprint is bound in tan-green cloth with green lettering on the front cover and spine. The dust jacket and five interior black-and-white illustrations are the regular ones by J. Allen St. John. Canaveral has used Burroughs's own map of Amtor as green decorated endpapers. Price: $3.50. 318 numbered pages.

294. *Lost on Venus* (New York: Ace Books, Inc.)
The second Ace paperback edition has the same cover art and a title page drawing by Frank Frazetta. Stock No. 49500, price 50¢. 192 numbered pages.

295. *Lost on Venus* (New York: Ace Books, Inc.)
The third Ace paperback edition has cover art and a title page drawing by Frank Frazetta. Stock No. 49501, price 60¢. 192 numbered pages.

296. *Lost on Venus* (New York: Ace Books, Inc., March 1973)
The fourth Ace paperback edition has a new larger size with the same cover art by Frank Frazetta, but the title page drawing is missing. Stock No. 49502, price 75¢. 224 numbered pages.

297. *Lost on Venus* (New York: Ace Books, Inc., June 1979)
This Ace paperback edition has a cover by Esteban Maroto. Stock No. 49506, price $1.95. 224 numbered pages.

298. *Lost on Venus* (New York: Ballantine Books, July 1991)
The first Ballantine paperback edition has cover art by Richard Hescox. Stock No. 37009, price $3.95. 200 numbered pages.

I. BIBLIOGRAPHY OF BOOKS

"The Mad King" March 21, 1914

BY EDGAR RICE BURROUGHS

The Mad King

299. "The Mad King" (ALL-STORY WEEKLY, March 21, 1914)
Towards the end of October, 1913, two weeks after he finished the first part of *The Mucker*, Burroughs tried his hand at a short story of royal romance set in the Balkan states of Europe (perhaps inspired by the 1894 Anthony Hope novel, *Prisoner of Zenda*, or by the popular series of novels by George Barr McCutcheon, which began with the 1901 best-seller, *Graustark*). For his story, ERB used the working title **"The Mad King of Lutha."** He finished it in November of 1913; it was the eleventh story Burroughs wrote. It became part one of *The Mad King*. The front cover illustration is by Fred W. Small, and there is one black-and-white headpiece by Modest Stein. Each issue sold for 10¢.

300. "Barney Custer of Beatrice" (ALL-STORY WEEKLY, August 7, 14, 21, 1915)
This story was begun two weeks after he finished the last half of *The Eternal Lover* (**"Sweetheart Primeval"**). It was begun in September of 1914, and was Burroughs' twenty-first story. It is in three parts, and is a sequel to **"The Mad King."** The cover illustration on the August 7th issue (the first installment of the three) is by W. C. Fairchild. There are no interior illustrations. This became the second half of *The Mad King* (discussed below).

───────────── FIRST EDITION ─────────────

301. *The Mad King* (Chicago: A.C. McClurg & Co., September 18, 1926)
This was the twenty-fifth hardback to be published. The copyright page states "Published August, 1926." The first state of the first edition is like the typical McClurgs of this period. It is bound in a dark blue cloth with orange lettering on the front cover and spine. It can be distinguished from the second state by several typographical errors which were corrected in the next printing. A phrase on page 12 is in the wrong place, and on page 92, line 16 is identical with line 22. Maurice B. Gardner pointed these out to McClurg, and the incorrect pages were removed and replaced (cf. Henry Heins, *A Golden Anniversary Bibliography*, page 168). The dust jacket and frontispiece (same picture) are by J. Allen St. John. A.C. McClurg records indicate that the combined printing for the first state and the second corrected state (see below) was only 5,000 copies. Price: $2.00. 365 numbered pages.

302. *The Mad King* (Chicago: A.C. McClurg & Co., 1926)
The second state of the first edition is identical to the first state except the typographical errors on pages 12 and 92 noted above have been repaired by tipping in a new corrected page. It seems to have been bound in a slightly lighter

I. BIBLIOGRAPHY OF BOOKS

"Barney Custer of Beatrice" (part two of *The Mad King*) August 7, 1915

blue cloth with orange lettering on the front cover and spine. The dust jacket and frontispiece are both by J. Allen St. John, just like #301. The existence of a corrected McClurg printing was not noted in Heins' *Bibliography*. Price: $2.00. 365 numbered pages.

303. *The Mad King* (New York: Grosset & Dunlap, 1927)
The G&D reprint is bound in the traditional red cloth with black lettering on the front cover and spine. The earliest printing lists 23 ERB titles in the advertising pages at the back of the book. The dust jacket and frontispiece, by J. Allen St. John, are the same as the first edition. On the back of the earliest dust jacket is a list of 24 ERB books. Price: 75¢. 365 numbered pages.

304. *The Mad King* (New York: Grosset & Dunlap, 1940)
The 1940 G&D reprint is like the 1927 described above (bound in red cloth with black lettering) except there is *no* frontispiece (the 1940s G&D reprints are identified by their lack of interior illustrations). The dust jacket by J. Allen St. John has the same cover as the 1927 reprint described above. Price: 75¢. 365 numbered pages.

305. *The Mad King* (New York: Ace Books, Inc., April 1964)
The first paperback printing has front cover art and a title page drawing by Frank Frazetta. Stock No. F-270, price 40¢. 255 numbered pages.

306. *The Mad King* (New York: Ace Books, Inc.)
The second Ace printing has front cover art and a title page drawing by Frank Frazetta. Stock No. 51401, price 60¢. 255 numbered pages.

307. *The Mad King* (New York: Ace Books, Inc.)
The third Ace printing has a new larger size, with the same front cover art by Frank Frazetta. It also has the Frazetta title page drawing. Stock No. 51402, price 75¢. 252 numbered pages.

308. *The Mad King* (New York: Ace Books, Inc.)
This Ace printing has a front cover by Boris Vallejo. It also has the Frazetta title page drawing. Stock No. 51403, price $1.50. 252 numbered pages.

The Man-Eater

309. "The Man-Eater" (THE NEW YORK EVENING WORLD newspaper, November 15, 16, 17, 18, 19, 20, 1915).

I. BIBLIOGRAPHY OF BOOKS

The first appearance of this story in print was neither in a magazine nor a book. Written in May of 1915, it was first published in a newspaper, THE NEW YORK EVENING WORLD, November 15–20, 1915. The title which Burroughs assigned it was "**Ben, King of Beasts.**" After completing this, he began to work on "**Beyond Thirty.**"

──────────────── FIRST EDITION ────────────────

310. *The Man-Eater* (Lloyd Arthur Eshbach, 1955)
This short story was first published by ERB fan Lloyd Arthur Eshbach, the founder of Fantasy Press, in a 50-page typed offset edition, 8½" × 11", in blue paper covers. According to the publisher, 300 were printed. There are no illustrations. Some collectors consider this the *true* first edition.

311. *Beyond Thirty* and *The Man-Eater* (New York: Science-Fiction & Fantasy Publications, 1957)
Written directly after *The Son of Tarzan* in 1915, originally as a synopsis for a film, *The Man-Eater* was later turned into a short story but was never published in magazine or hardback form during Burroughs' life. Its only printing during Burroughs' lifetime was in the NEW YORK EVENING WORLD newspaper between November 15–20, 1915. This hardback edition is the only hardback edition. The book contains *Beyond Thirty* (previously published in magazine form in 1916 but never in hardback) as well as *The Man-Eater*. The book is bound in red cloth with gold lettering on spine, and clearly states "First Edition" on the copyright page. The white dust jacket has a black-and-white drawing by Gilbert Kane of a futuristic-looking soldier (Jefferson Turck, hero of *Beyond Thirty*) superimposed upon the face of a (saber-toothed?) lioness. There is a three-page prologue, entitled "Edgar Rice Burroughs: A Bit of His Life," by Bradford M. Day, the book's publisher. The two unrelated stories are consecutively paginated. 229 numbered pages.

312. *THE MAN EATER* [sic] (North Hollywood, CA: Fantasy House —Fantasy Reader 5, 1974)
This small 8¼" × 4" paperback book, which omits the hyphen between "Man" and "Eater," has front and back cover designs by Robert Kline. The title page is decorated. It is shaped more like a thick pamphlet than a standard paperback book. The book is subtitled: "**Ben, King of Beasts**" (Burroughs' original working title). It has a brief preface with the story's background and acknowledgment to Danton Burroughs. 93 numbered pages.

BY EDGAR RICE BURROUGHS

Marcia of the Doorstep

NOTE: The 1994 announcement of the imminent publication of Burroughs' longest manuscript, *Marcia of the Doorstep*, heralded an exciting new development in the publication of Burroughs books. Fans have known about the existence of this 1924 manuscript for many decades (Henry Hardy Heins did a thorough analysis of the ms. in 1966, and published a lengthy summary and review in ERB-DOM, #67, February 1973), but the unwillingness of ERB, Inc. to actively promote the creations of ERB, or even to allow publication of anything unless a sizeable amount of money was paid to the corporation, had made it virtually impossible for smaller presses to obtain rights to print any of the remaining unpublished manuscripts. Now there seems to be a new attitude at ERB, Inc. for which those who enjoy reading the books by Burroughs are grateful. Burroughs had finished *Tarzan and the Ant Men* four months before he began work on *Marcia*. It seems clear that this was another unsuccessful bid on the part of ERB to be treated as a "serious" author, and as such this story is much closer to ERB's other "realistic" novel, *The Girl from Hollywood* (written two years earlier). It obviously follows in the same vein, with the action moving between Broadway and Hollywood, conniving lawyers, high society and poverty, mutinies, shipwrecks and desert islands, and true love. Burroughs submitted it to many publishers in the 1924-25 period, and it was rejected by all of them. Discouraged, ERB decided to return to the "highly imaginative fiction" at which he excelled, and started on "The Red Hawk," the third part of *The Moon Maid*.

——————————— FIRST EDITION ———————————

313. *Marcia of the Doorstep* (Hampton Falls, NH: Donald M. Grant, Publishers, 1997)

The imminent publication of this book was announced in 1994, but it was not scheduled to appear until the end of 1997. The book will be published in two versions: a limited deluxe edition ($60) and a regular trade edition ($30). This is the *only* printing of this story. It never appeared in any form previously. Interior illustrations by Ned Dameron.

The Master Mind of Mars

314. "The Master Mind of Mars" (AMAZING STORIES ANNUAL, vol. no. 1, July 15, 1927)

I. BIBLIOGRAPHY OF BOOKS

After finishing *Marcia of the Doorstep* and then "**The Red Hawk**," ERB began to write his fifth story of Mars, which was published complete in this one issue. It has cover art and ten interior black-and-white illustrations by AMAZING STORIES artist Frank R. Paul. Burroughs toyed with several working titles, including "**A Weird Adventure on Mars**" and "**Vad Varo of Barsoom**." The final title is probably that of Hugo Gernsback, the editor. This much larger annual sold for 50¢, and this was the only annual published. A year later, Gernsback began publishing AMAZING STORIES quarterlies.

──────────── FIRST EDITION ────────────

315. *The Master Mind of Mars* (Chicago: A.C. McClurg & Co., March 10, 1928)

Burroughs's twenty-ninth published hardback book has the first edition bound in orange cloth with black lettering on the front cover and spine. The beautiful dust jacket is by J. Allen St. John, as are five interior illustrations, unusual in that they have been printed on coated stock with a yellow background. The black-and-white drawing on title page is also by St. John. A.C. McClurg records indicate that only 5,000 copies of the first edition were printed, and Burroughs stories were not selling as well as they had in the past. This was the last Mars book published by McClurg. Convinced that he could make a larger profit if he were the publisher, Burroughs began to explore the possibility of publishing his own books. Two years later, in 1931, the newly formed ERB, Inc. published its first effort, *Tarzan the Invincible*. The first edition of *The Master Mind of Mars* sold for $2.00 and has 312 numbered pages.

316. *The Master Mind of Mars* (New York: Grosset & Dunlap, 1929)

This, the first reprinting just one year after the first edition, is bound in the usual G&D red cloth with black lettering on the front cover and spine. The earliest printing has 25 ERB titles listed in the advertising pages at the back of the book; subsequent reprintings have 28 titles in the back. The dust jacket and five interior black-and-white illustrations (without a yellow background) are by J. Allen St. John. As with the first edition described above, the title page drawing is by J. Allen St. John. On the back of the earliest G&D jacket is a rectangular photo of ERB and a list of 27 ERB titles. Price: 75¢. 312 numbered pages.

317. *The Master Mind of Mars* (Tarzana: Edgar Rice Burroughs, Inc., March 26, 1948)

The 1948 ERB, Inc. reprints are bound in tan-gray cloth with dark red lettering on the front cover and spine. The dust jacket and title page illustration are present, but no other interior illustrations. The series of 1948 reprintings all sold for $1.00. 312 numbered pages.

318. *Three Martian Novels: Thuvia, Maid of Mars / The Chessmen of Mars / The Master Mind of Mars* (New York: Dover Publications, Inc., April 1962, October 1963, and again at least seven different times)

This compilation volume was one of the very first Burroughs books available in the early 1960s, and presaged the Burroughs revival dominated by the Ace paperbacks and the Canaveral hardbacks. It is a thick paperback with cover and sixteen interior black-and-white illustrations by J. Allen St. John. The stories are continuously paginated. Stock No. T39. Original price $1.75, raised to $1.85 for the October 1963 reprinting. There are 499 numbered pages.

319. *Three Martian Novels: Thuvia, Maid of Mars / The Chessmen of Mars / The Master Mind of Mars* (New York: Peter Smith, 1963).

This is the Dover volume (listed above) bound in a red cloth hardback (with black lettering on the spine only) for the use of libraries. It has 16 St. John illustrations. The book sold for $3.75. 499 numbered pages.

320. *The Mastermind* [sic] *of Mars* (New York: Ace Books, Inc., February 1963)

The first Ace paperback edition has run the two words "Master" and "Mind" together to make "Mastermind." It has a cover illustration and a title page drawing by Roy G. Krenkel, and reproductions of two interior black-and-white drawings by J. Allen St. John. Stock No. F 181, price 40¢. 159 numbered pages.

321. *The Master Mind of Mars* (New York: Ballantine Books, December 1963)

The first paperback printing by Ballantine has cover art by Robert Abbett. Stock No. U2036, price 50¢. 160 numbered pages.

322. *The Master Mind of Mars* (New York: Ballantine Books, February 1969)

The second Ballantine printing of 1969 is identical to the first printing except for the Stock No. 01526. The price remained 50¢.

323. *The Master Mind of Mars* (Kansas City, MO: House of Greystoke, 1971)

This is a large 8½" × 11" publication by Vernell Coriell. It was intended to be part of the BURROUGHS BIBLIOPHILES #5, but the printer misprinted it as the BURROUGHS BULLETIN #5. This reprints the AMAZING STORIES ANNUAL cover (in a two-color version) with 55 numbered pages of text. The illustrations by J. Allen St. John from the first edition are reproduced in black-and-white and the dust jacket illustration is also reprinted. Coriell also included ten of the interior illustrations by the artist "Paul" (Frank R. Paul).

I. BIBLIOGRAPHY OF BOOKS

324. *The Master Mind of Mars* (New York: Ballantine Books, October 1973)
The third paperback printing by Ballantine has new cover art by Gino D'Achille. Stock No. 23583, price $1.25. 160 numbered pages.

325. *The Mastermind* [sic] *of Mars* and *A Fighting Man of Mars* (New York: Doubleday, 1973 [January 1974])
Although this Science-Fiction Book Club edition is dated 1973, H. Heins' research established the actual date of publication as January 1974. It is bound in dark blue cloth with gold lettering on the spine. The dust jacket and six black-and-white illustrations are by Frank Frazetta. Consecutively paginated, 348 numbered pages.

326. *The Master Mind of Mars* (Wytheville, VA: House of Greystoke, 1977)
This is a reprint of the large 8½" × 11" publication by Vernell Coriell described above. It was printed as a triple issue of the BURROUGHS BULLETIN #66/67/68. This reprints the AMAZING STORIES ANNUAL version with illustrations by J. Allen St. John and ten of the pulp interior illustrations by Frank Paul.

327. *The Master Mind of Mars* (New York: Ballantine–Del Rey, May 1979)
The ninth paperback printing by Ballantine has new cover art by Michael Whelan. Stock No. 23783, price $1.95. 160 numbered pages.

The Monster Men

328. "A Man Without a Soul" (THE ALL-STORY, November 1913)
A few weeks after completing **"The Cave Girl"** in March of 1913, ERB began to write his eighth story, whose original working title was **"Number Thirteen."** It is complete in one issue of THE ALL-STORY which sold for 15¢. The cover art is by P. J. Monahan and there is a black-and-white headpiece by Fred W. Small. The title of this story is similar to *The Man Without a Soul*, the name which the British publisher Methuen gave to a completely different story, **"The Return of the Mucker."** The two stories are unrelated. For more information on *The Man Without a Soul*, see #361, 363, 364, 365.

——————————— FIRST EDITION ———————————

329. *The Monster Men* (Chicago: A.C. McClurg & Co., March 15, 1929)
This was the thirty-first hardback by ERB, and this first edition is bound in a pebbled tan cloth with dark green lettering on the front cover and spine. The

BY EDGAR RICE BURROUGHS

"A Man Without a Soul" (*The Monster Men*) November 1913

dust jacket art and title page drawing are by J. Allen St. John. There are no other interior illustrations. The book sold for $2.00; 304 numbered pages. McClurg records indicated that only 5,000 copies of this title were published. This was the last of the non-series titles by Burroughs printed by McClurg.

330. *The Monster Men* (New York: Grosset & Dunlap, 1930)
The earliest G&D reprinting of this title is bound in the usual G&D red cloth with black lettering on front cover and spine, and lists 28 ERB books in the advertising pages at the back of the book. A later reprinting of this title has the tops of the pages dyed yellow. As with the first, the dust jacket painting and title page drawing are by J. Allen St. John. Apparently G&D did not publish very many copies of this title. Price: 75¢. 304 numbered pages.

331. *The Monster Men* (New York: Canaveral Press, Inc., May 17, 1962)
This, the next reprinting of *The Monster Men*, is bound in red cloth with black lettering on the front cover and spine. The dust jacket design and seven interior black-and-white illustrations are by Mahlon Blaine. In 1962, the book sold for $2.75; the price was raised to $2.95 in 1963. 188 numbered pages.

332. *The Monster Men* (New York: Ace Books, Inc., February 1963)
The first paperback printing has a front cover and title page drawing by Frank Frazetta. Stock No. F-182, price 40¢. 159 numbered pages.

333. *The Monster Men* (New York: Ace Books, Inc.)
The second Ace paperback printing has the same front cover and title page drawing by Frank Frazetta. Stock No. 53587, price 60¢.

334. *The Monster Men* (New York: Ace Books, Inc.)
The third Ace paperback printing has new front cover by Enrich. Stock No. 53588, price 75¢. 155 numbered pages.

335. *The Monster Men* (New York: Ace Books, Inc.)
The fifth Ace paperback printing has new front cover by Boris Vallejo. Stock No. 53590. $1.50. 185 numbered pages.

336. *The Monster Men* (New York: Ballantine-Del Rey, September 1992)
The first Ballantine paperback printing has front cover by Michael Herring. Stock No. 37832. $3.99. 198 numbered pages.

BY EDGAR RICE BURROUGHS

The Moon Maid

337. "The Moon Maid" (ARGOSY ALL-STORY WEEKLY, May 5, 12, 19, 26; June 2, 1923)

In June of 1922, about three weeks after finishing *Tarzan and the Golden Lion*, Edgar Rice Burroughs began work on this five-part serial, which became part one of the hardback book, *The Moon Maid*. However, note that although it was printed before "The Moon Men," it was written *after* "The Moon Men," the story which comprises part two of the hardback book. This ARGOSY ALL-STORY WEEKLY serial has a front cover illustration (the May 5th issue) by P. J. Monahan. In addition, there is one interior black-and-white illustration in each issue by an artist identified only as "Stout." Each issue sold for 10¢.

338. "The Moon Men" (ARGOSY ALL-STORY WEEKLY, February 21, 28; March 7, 14, 1925)

While he was working on *Tarzan the Untamed*, between April and May of 1919, Burroughs wrote this story under the working title "**Under the Red Flag,**" a cautionary tale about the dangers of Russian communism. Three years later Burroughs wrote a prequel, "**The Moon Maid,**" describing events leading up to the happenings in this tale. It is a four-part serial. The front cover art for the February 21st issue is by Stockton Mulford. As with "**The Moon Maid,**" there is one interior black-and-white illustration, each installment, but these are by Roger B. Morrison. Each issue 10¢.

339. "The Red Hawk" (ARGSOY ALL-STORY WEEKLY, September 5, 12, 19, 1925)

After finishing *Tarzan and the Ant Men* and then *Marcia of the Doorstep*, Burroughs wrote a sequel to "The Moon Men," thus completing his lengthy story about the future of life on earth. "**The Red Hawk**" was sold by Burroughs as a three-part serial. Modest Stein did the front cover illustration for the September 5th issue, and there is one interior black-and-white illustration, each installment, by Roger B. Morrison. Each issue was 10¢.

―――――――――― FIRST EDITION ――――――――――

340. *The Moon Maid* (Chicago: A.C. McClurg & Co., February 6, 1926)

The first edition of the twenty-fourth hardback by Burroughs is bound in the usual McClurg blue cloth with black lettering on the front cover and spine. The dust jacket art is by J. Allen St. John with the same illustration serving as a sepia frontispiece. This book is unusual because it is almost 25 percent *shorter* than the original magazine stories described above. It is not known whether ERB shortened the book for publication, or whether the McClurg editor did the trimming. The major changes occurred in "**The Moon Men**" middle section. The Ace paperback reprintings, described below, were drawn from the original magazine editions and thus are more complete than the hardback editions. A. C. McClurg records indicate that only 5,000 copies of this title were published. Price: $2.00. 412 numbered pages.

341. *The Moon Maid* (New York: Grosset & Dunlap, 1927)

The first reprint is bound in the usual G&D red cloth with black lettering on the front cover and spine and lists 15 ERB titles in the advertising pages at the back of the book. The dust jacket art is the same as the first edition (by J. Allen St. John), with the same illustration serving as a black-and-white frontispiece. The earliest dust jacket has an oval photo of ERB on the back and lists 16 ERB books in blue letters. On the back of subsequent jackets the ERB photo is enclosed in a rectangular pattern. This hardback printing follows the McClurg edition, and so it too is about 25 percent shorter than the original magazine appearances. Price: 75¢. 412 numbered pages.

342. "Conquest of the Moon" (MODERN MECHANICS AND INVENTIONS, November, December 1928; January, February 1929)

Burroughs sold the "second serial rights" to the three stories that make up *The Moon Maid* to MODERN MECHANICS AND INVENTIONS, so the story was printed in magazine form *after* the hardback was printed. The four parts were published as an abridged serial, with black, white and tinted interior illustrations, each installment, by C. Saunders. The magazine also reprinted "**At the Earth's Core**" and "**A Princess of Mars.**" Each issue sold for 25¢.

343. *The Moon Maid* (New York: Grosset & Dunlap, 1940)

This is identical with the 1927 G&D reprinting except there is *no* frontispiece. Price: 75¢. 412 numbered pages.

344. *The Moon Men* (New York: Canaveral Press, Inc., May 17, 1962)

This reprint, although titled *The Moon Men*, is the book originally published as *The Moon Maid*. It is bound in orange cloth with black lettering on the front cover and spine. The dust jacket art and seven interior black-and-white illustrations are by Mahlon Blaine. Price: $2.75, raised to $2.95 in 1963. 375 numbered pages.

345. *The Moon Maid* (New York: Ace Books, Inc., September 1962)

This is the first paperback printing (of the first half of *The Moon Maid*), and the first Ace paperback edition, with front cover art and title page drawing by Roy G. Krenkel. It contains the original material in the first magazine appearance, not the shorter version in the hardback printing. Stock No. F-157, price 40¢. 176 numbered pages.

346. *The Moon Men* (New York: Ace Books, Inc., October 1962)
The paperback edition (drawn from the original magazine publication) contains "**The Moon Men**" and "**The Red Hawk**," part two and part three sequels to "**The Moon Maid**" with front cover art by Ed Emsh, and title page drawing by Roy G. Krenkel. Stock No. F 159, price 40¢. 222 numbered pages.

347. *The Land That Time Forgot* and *The Moon Maid* (New York: Dover Publications, Inc., April 1963).
This is a large red Dover paperback (T 358) with the original St. John illustrations done for each book. Price: $2.00. 552 pages.

348. *The Land That Time Forgot* and *The Moon Maid* (New York: Dover Publications, Inc., May 1963).
This is a hardback library binding over the Dover paperback with the original St. John interior illustrations. The dust jacket is red with a yellow moon behind St. John's illustration for "**The Moon Maid**." Price: $3.75. 552 pages.

349. *The Moon Maid* (New York: Ace Books, Inc.)
This is the second paperback printing of the first half of *The Moon Maid* with front cover art and title page drawing by Roy G. Krenkel. Stock No. G 745, price 50¢. 176 numbered pages.

350. *The Moon Men* (New York: Ace Books, Inc.)
The paperback edition has the part two and three sequels to *The Moon Maid* with front cover art by Ed Emsh, and title page drawing by Roy G. Krenkel. Stock No. G-748, price 50¢. 222 numbered pages.

351. *The Moon Maid* (New York: Ace Books, Inc.)
The third paperback printing of the first half of *The Moon Maid* has the same front cover art and title page drawing by Roy G. Krenkel. Stock No. 53701, price 60¢. 176 numbered pages.

352. *The Moon Men* (New York: Ace Books, Inc.)
The third paperback edition of part two and three of *The Moon Maid* has the same front cover art by Ed Emsh, and title page drawing by Roy G. Krenkel. Stock No. 53751, price 60¢. 222 numbered pages.

353. *The Moon Maid* (New York: Ace Books, Inc.)
The fourth paperback printing of the first half of *The Moon Maid* has new front cover art by Frank Frazetta. Stock No. 53702, price 95¢. 187 numbered pages.

354. *The Moon Men* (New York: Ace Books, Inc.)
The fourth paperback edition of *The Moon Men* does not include "**The Red Hawk**" as the previous versions did. New front cover art by Frank Frazetta and the title page drawing by Roy G. Krenkel. The Krenkel illustration is omitted from the title page in subsequent Ace printings. Stock No. 53752, price 95¢. 222 numbered pages.

355. *The Moon Maid* (New York: Ballantine–Del Rey, May 1992)
The first Ballantine edition of this title has a cover by Lawrence Schwinger. Stock No. 37405, price $3.99. 202 numbered pages.

356. *The Moon Men* (New York: Ballantine–Del Rey, June 1992)
The first Ballantine edition of *The Moon Men* also includes the third part of this trilogy, "**The Red Hawk.**" Cover art is by Lawrence Schwinger. Stock No. 37406. Price $3.99. 227 numbered pages.

The Mucker

357. "**The Mucker**" (All-Story Cavalier Weekly, October 24, 31; November 7, 14, 1914)
Burroughs began work on his tenth story between August and October, 1913. It was written directly after *The Warlord of Mars* and *The Girl from Farris's*, and was printed as a four-part serial with a front cover illustration (the October 24th issue) by P. J. Monahan. There are no interior illustrations. Each issue was 10¢.

358. "**The Return of the Mucker**" (All-Story Weekly, June 17, 24; July 1, 8, 15, 1916)
On January 24, 1916, a month after he finished "**H.R.H. the Rider,**" Burroughs began working on a sequel to "**The Mucker.**" This was published at 10¢ per issue as a five-part serial with front cover art (June 17th issue) by P. J. Monahan; no interior illustrations. Its working title was "**Out There Somewhere,**" the title of a poem by H. H. Knibbs which Burroughs liked very much. Eleven of the fourteen stanzas of Knibbs' poem are quoted in the story. Two days after finishing this, he began to write *Jungle Tales of Tarzan*.

——————————— FIRST EDITION ———————————

359. *The Mucker* (Chicago: A.C. McClurg & Co., October 31, 1921)
The thirteenth hardback by Burroughs was published in first edition by A.C. McClurg. It is bound in pale green cloth with red lettering on the front cover

BY EDGAR RICE BURROUGHS

and spine. The book is unusual for several reasons. First, it is almost a quarter-inch taller than all the other McClurg first editions. Secondly, this was the only Burroughs book published in England *before* it was published in the United States. The English publisher, Methuen, published part I of *The Mucker* on October 6, 1921, 25 days before this McClurg American first edition. Lastly, this was one of Burroughs' personal favorites, and ERB is quoted as having said that he thought it one of his best novels. The dust jacket art and five interior illustrations are by J. Allen St. John. This was a fairly popular title for McClurg, and their records indicate that 17,000 copies of the first and one reprinting were printed. Original price: $1.90. 414 numbered pages.

360. *The Mucker* (Chicago: A.C. McClurg & Co., 1922)
This McClurg reprinting of *The Mucker* is clearly labeled 1922 on the title page. In other respects it is like the first printing described above. Price: $1.90. 414 numbered pages.

361. *The Man Without a Soul* (London: Methuen, January 26, 1922)
Although this bibliography has excluded foreign editions, this unusual British hardback (and its variants) is included because it has been a source of confusion for collectors for many years; its title is very similar to that of the title used for the 1913 first magazine appearance of *The Monster Men* ("A Man Without a Soul"). However, this is the British first edition of the second half of *The Mucker* ("The Return of the Mucker"). It is bound in red cloth with a rectangular floral decoration encircling the black lettering on the front cover and on the spine. Frank Westwood, honorary secretary of the *Edgar Rice Burroughs Society* shared with me the original jacket with an illustration attributed to Frank Leist; there are no interior illustrations. It was reprinted at least three more times (see below). Price: 6s. 209 numbered pages.

362. *The Mucker* (New York: Grosset & Dunlap, 1922)
The first G&D reprint is bound in red cloth with black lettering on the front cover and spine. The dust jacket art and four black-and-white plates are, like the first edition, by J. Allen St. John. Price: 75¢. 414 numbered pages.

363. *The Man Without a Soul* (London: Methuen, March 1927)
This, the second Methuen edition, is bound in red or blue cloth. According to Frank Westwood, the book is foolscap octavo, "cheap form." The jacket is like the first edition, with an illustration by Frank Leist; there are no interior illustrations. Price: 2s. 209 numbered pages.

364. *The Man Without a Soul* (London: Methuen, December 1928)
This, the third Methuen edition, is bound in red or blue cloth and was printed in December 1928. The book is foolscap octavo, "cheap form." The jacket

I. BIBLIOGRAPHY OF BOOKS

is like the first edition, with an illustration by Frank Leist; there are no interior illustrations. 209 numbered pages.

365. *The Man Without a Soul* (London: Methuen, August 1939)
The fourth edition of this unusual British hardback has a cloth binding with a tan cloth color. It too has the same dust jacket as the previous editions, with an illustration by Frank Leist; there are no interior illustrations. The fourth edition is slightly smaller in size, crown octavo, "cheap form." Price: 3s6d. 209 numbered pages.

366. *The Mucker* (New York: Grosset & Dunlap, 1940)
The second G&D reprint is distinguished from the 1922 reprinting by the absence of illustrations. It is bound in red cloth with black lettering on the front cover and spine. The dust jacket art is by J. Allen St. John. Price: 75¢. 414 numbered pages.

367. *The Mucker* (New York: Canaveral Press, Inc., November 14, 1963)
The book is bound in pale green cloth with black lettering on the front cover and spine. There is a sticker on the copyright page with the names of the original magazine serials. The artwork is the St. John dust jacket design and the same five interior black-and-white illustrations found in previous reprints. Price: $3.50. 414 numbered pages.

368. *The Mucker* (New York: Ballantine Books, January 1966)
The first paperback printing has a front cover illustration by Robert Abbett. Stock No. U6039, price 75¢. 320 numbered pages.

369. *The Mucker* (New York: Ace Books, Inc., June 1974)
The first Ace paperback reprint is just *part one* of the hardback versions of *The Mucker*. It has front cover art by Frank Frazetta. Stock No. 54460, price 95¢, 190 numbered pages.

370. *Return of The Mucker* (New York: Ace Books, Inc., June 1974)
The first Ace paperback is the *part two* sequel to *The Mucker* and it too has cover art by Frank Frazetta. Stock No. 71815, price 95¢. 212 numbered pages.

The Oakdale Affair

371. "The Oakdale Affair" (THE BLUE BOOK MAGAZINE, March 1918)
Written between two of the stories which comprise *Jungle Tales of Tarzan*, this short novel was completed in June of 1917, and was published in one issue

complete for 15¢. Burroughs' working title was "**Bridge and the Oskaloosa Kid.**" There are two interior black-and-white illustrations by Dom J. Lavin. Robert Barrett points out that the same Dom J. Lavin executed a caricature of Burroughs for the famous "The White Paper Club of Chicago" menu celebrating ERB's departure from Chicago in 1919. J. Allen St. John supplied a drawing of a flying pig for the same menu. Several months after finishing this, Burroughs began work on *The Land That Time Forgot* as his next book.

372. "H.R.H. the Rider" (ALL-STORY WEEKLY, December 14, December 21, and December 28, 1918)
   The December 14th cover is illustrated by George Brehm, but the remaining two installments are unillustrated. Note that this story is *unrelated* to "**The Oakdale Affair.**" Each issue was 10¢.

─────────── FIRST EDITION ───────────

373. *The Oakdale Affair* and *The Rider* (Tarzana: Edgar Rice Burroughs, Inc., February 15, 1937)
   The forty-eighth hardback published, this first edition is bound in the usual ERB, Inc. blue cloth with red lettering on the front cover and spine. John Coleman Burroughs, ERB's younger son, painted the wrap-around dust jacket art (using his sister, Joan Burroughs, as one of the models, and her husband, James H. Pierce, as the other) and two interior black-and-white plates (this was the first book he illustrated for his father). The stories are separately paginated. Note that the hardback printings of "**The Oakdale Affair**" published by ERB, Inc. are missing the last 174 lines which conclude the magazine version. In addition, the magazine version of "**The Rider**" had chapter titles; the book does not. Price: $2.00. 172 and 144 numbered pages.

374. *The Oakdale Affair* and *The Rider* (A "Mixed Edition": Grosset & Dunlap, 1937)
   This mixed edition is a remaindered ERB, Inc. first edition, with a Grosset & Dunlap title page and cover. The tops of the pages are stained red and the vertical edges are untrimmed. There were not very many copies of this book with a Grosset & Dunlap title page. 172 and 144 numbered pages.

375. *The Oakdale Affair* and *The Rider* (Grosset & Dunlap, 1938)
   This text has two interior illustrations. The cloth is a smooth blue material, unlike the original first edition which is pebbled. It has "Grosset & Dunlap" in red ink on the spine and cover, but the red lettering is flat on the surface, not indented as on the first edition. The tops of the pages are dyed red. Price: 75¢. 172 and 144 numbered pages.

I. Bibliography of Books

376. *The Oakdale Affair* and *The Rider* (Grosset & Dunlap, 1940)
This G&D reprint, like the others from 1940, has no interior illustrations. Price: 75¢. 172 and 144 numbered pages.

377. *The Oakdale Affair* (New York: Ace Books, Inc., July 1974)
The first paperback edition has cover art by Frank Frazetta. Stock No. 60563, price $1.25. 152 numbered pages.

378. *The Oakdale Affair* (New York: Buccaneer Books, 1977)
This hardcover reprint is bound in black cloth with the title and author's name in yellow letters on the spine. In addition, the publisher's name and colophon is in red ink on the spine. This version contains the original ending from the magazine story, unlike the ERB, Inc. first edition. It was issued without a dust jacket and without illustrations. Price: perhaps $14.50. 152 numbered pages.

379. *The Oakdale Affair* (New York: Charter, August 1979)
This paperback edition has the same cover art by Frank Frazetta used on the prior Ace paperbacks, but smaller with a red border. There are no interior illustrations. This has the original magazine ending with the 174 lines omitted from the hardback first edition. Stock No. 60565. $1.95. 152 numbered pages.

The Outlaw of Torn

380. "The Outlaw of Torn" (NEW STORY MAGAZINE, January, February, March, April, May 1914)
This is the second story Burroughs wrote ("**Under the Moons of Mars**" was the first if we do not count a few amateurish pieces written for family members long before), and it was published as a five-part serial with the same black-and-white headpiece for each installment. The editor of ALL-STORY MAGAZINE had suggested the theme ("along the lines of *Ivanhoe*"), but rejected this story of 13th century England and France when ERB submitted it. His feelings hurt but undaunted, Burroughs then submitted it to NEW STORY MAGAZINE which bought it because of the popularity of his Mars tale. The next story he wrote after this was "**Tarzan of the Apes.**" Each issue of NEW STORY sold for 15¢.

——————————— FIRST EDITION ———————————

381. *The Outlaw of Torn* (Chicago: A.C. McClurg & Co., February 19, 1927)
Although this was the second story Burroughs wrote, he could not get it published in hardback until 13 years later, at which point his name alone could

guarantee good sales. Burroughs added some additional material in the first chapter that was not in the magazine version. The twenty-sixth hardback by ERB, this first edition is bound in red cloth with gold lettering on the front cover and spine. The dust wrapper front illustration is by J. Allen St. John. There are no interior illustrations. It is dedicated "To my friend Joseph E. Bray." Bray was an editor at McClurg, and later became the President and Chairman. A.C. McClurg records indicated that the combined print run was 6,000 copies for both the first edition and the one subsequent reprinting. Price: $2.00. 298 numbered pages.

382. *The Outlaw of Torn* (Chicago: A.C. McClurg & Co., March 1927)
This is labeled the "First Reprinting: March 1927." Like the first edition, this too is bound in red cloth with gold lettering on the front cover and spine. The dust wrapper front illustration is by J. Allen St. John. There are no interior illustrations. Price: $2.00. 298 numbered pages.

383. *The Outlaw of Torn* (New York: Grosset & Dunlap, 1928)
The second reprinting (first by G&D) is bound in red cloth with black lettering on the front cover and spine. The copyright page repeats the McClurg inscription, "First reprinting: March, 1927" even though G&D actually reprinted the title in 1928. In the earliest printing there are 23 ERB books listed in the advertising pages at the back of the book; the next printing lists 25 ERB titles. The dust jacket is by J. Allen St. John; there are no interior illustrations. Price: 75¢. 298 numbered pages.

384. *The Outlaw of Torn* (New York: Ace Books, Inc., November 1968)
The first paperback edition has cover art and a title page illustration by Roy G. Krenkel. Stock No. A-25, price 75¢. 255 numbered pages.

385. *The Outlaw of Torn* (New York: Ace Books, Inc., January 1973)
The second paperback edition has cover art by Frank Frazetta. Stock No. 64510, price 75¢. 255 numbered pages.

386. *The Outlaw of Torn* (New York: Ace Books, Inc.)
The third paperback edition has cover art by Frank Frazetta. Stock No. 64511, price 95¢. 255 numbered pages.

Pellucidar

387. "Pellucidar" (ALL-STORY CAVALIER WEEKLY, May 1, 8; ALL-STORY WEEKLY, May 15, 22, 29, 1915)

I. BIBLIOGRAPHY OF BOOKS

"Pellucidar" May 1, 1915

BY EDGAR RICE BURROUGHS

Begun in November of 1914, this sequel to *At the Earth's Core* (thus the second in the Pellucidar series) was Burroughs's twentieth story. It was initially published as a five-part serial with front cover illustration (the May 1st issue) by Modest Stein. The Stein cover is remarkably similar to the previous cover he did for "At the Earth's Core" (it appears to be a subtly different close-up). Burroughs' own map of the "Empire of Pellucidar" is repeated in each installment except the second; there are no other interior illustrations. In the middle of this serial, ALL-STORY CAVALIER WEEKLY changed its name with the May 15th installment to ALL-STORY WEEKLY. Each issue sold for 10¢. When he finished *Pellucidar*, Burroughs began writing *The Son of Tarzan*.

―――――――――― FIRST EDITION ――――――――――

388. *Pellucidar* (Chicago: A.C. McClurg & Co., September 5, 1923)

This was the seventeenth hardback published by Burroughs. The first edition is bound in red cloth with black lettering on the front cover and spine. The dust jacket and four interior sepia plates are by J. Allen St. John. The map drawn by Burroughs is included. A. C. McClurg records indicate that 10,000 copies of the first edition were printed. Price: $1.75. 322 numbered pages.

389. *Pellucidar* (New York: Grosset & Dunlap, 1924)

The first reprint is bound in the standard G&D red cloth boards with black lettering on the front cover and spine. The dust jacket and four interior black-and-white plates by J. Allen St. John are the same as the first edition. The ERB map of Pellucidar is present. The illustrations on the first printing face page 20, 100, and 232, and there are 11 ERB titles listed in the advertisements in the back of the book. The next reprinting has illustrations facing pages 16, 96, and 232, and has 11 ERB titles in the back. Another printing has illustrations facing pages 16, 102, and 232. A 1927 printing has 15 ERB titles at the back. On the back of the earliest G&D dust jacket is a photo of ERB in an oval device, and 8 ERB titles. 322 numbered pages.

390. *Pellucidar* (New York: Grosset & Dunlap, 1928 and after)

There is a printing in or after 1928 which has a dark red cloth cover and 25 ERB titles listed in the advertisements at the end of the book. Illustrations are facing pages 16, 96, and 232. The dust jacket and four interior black-and-white plates by J. Allen St. John are the same as the earlier editions. The ERB map of Pellucidar is present. 322 numbered pages.

391. *Pellucidar* (New York: Grosset & Dunlap, 1940)

This reprint is bound in the standard G&D red cloth boards with black lettering on the front cover and spine. The difference is that the four interior black-and-white plates by J. Allen St. John are omitted. The ERB map of Pellucidar is present. Price: 75¢. 322 numbered pages.

392. *Pellucidar* (New York: Ace Books, Inc., October 1962)
This is the first American paperback printing. It has a cover and title page art by Roy G. Krenkel, plus Burroughs' map of Pellucidar. Stock No. F-158, price 40¢. 160 numbered pages.

393. *Pellucidar* (New York: Canaveral Press, Inc., October 25, 1962)
This Canaveral hardback is bound in yellow cloth with black lettering on the front cover and spine. Mahlon Blaine did the dust jacket illustration, the illustrated endpapers, a map of Pellucidar and four interior black-and-white illustrations. Price: $2.75, raised to $2.95 in 1963. 180 numbered pages.

394. *At the Earth's Core / Pellucidar / Tanar of Pellucidar: Three Science Fiction Novels by Edgar Rice Burroughs* (New York: Dover Publications, Inc., December 1963)
This Dover paperback collection has dark blue covers with yellow lettering on the front cover and spine. An illustration by J. Allen St. John provides the cover art and 12 black-and-white illustrations; in addition there is one illustration by Paul F. Berdanier. The three stories are consecutively paginated. Price: $2.00. 433 numbered pages.

395. *At the Earth's Core / Pellucidar / Tanar of Pellucidar: Three Science Fiction Novels by Edgar Rice Burroughs* (New York: Peter Smith, 1963)
This is a hardback library cover over the Dover inside pages. It uses the J. Allen St. John twelve black-and-white illustrations. In addition, there is one black-and-white illustration by Paul F. Berdanier for *Tanar of Pellucidar*. The three stories are consecutively paginated. Price: $3.50. 433 numbered pages.

396. *Science Fiction Classics* (Secaucus, NJ: Castle, 1982)
Pellucidar is included in this anthology of five ERB stories. It is bound in orange cloth with black lettering on spine. The dust jacket design and 25 black-and-white illustrations are by J. Allen St. John; one black-and-white illustration is by Paul F. Berdanier, and there is one black-and-white map of Pellucidar. Consecutively paginated with 451 numbered pages. There are variants. More details can be found under the last entry for *The Chessmen of Mars*, #104, 105, 106.

397. *Pellucidar* (New York: Ace Books, Inc.)
This is the second American paperback printing. It has the same cover and title page art by Roy G. Krenkel, plus Burroughs' map of Pellucidar. Stock No. G-734, price 50¢. 160 numbered pages.

BY EDGAR RICE BURROUGHS

398. *Pellucidar* (New York: Ace Books, Inc.)
This is the third American paperback printing. It has cover and title page art by Roy G. Krenkel, plus Burroughs' map of Pellucidar. Stock No. 65851, price 60¢. 160 numbered pages.

399. *Pellucidar* (New York: Ace Books, Inc., September 1972)
This is the fourth Ace paperback printing. It has new cover art by Frank Frazetta but includes Burroughs' map of Pellucidar. Stock No. 65852, price 75¢. 191 pages.

400. *Pellucidar* (New York: Ballantine–Del Rey, May 1990)
This is the first Ballantine paperback printing. It has cover art by David B. Mattingly and ERB's own map of Pellucidar. Stock No. 36669, price $3.95. 182 pages.

Pirate Blood

NOTE: The 34,000 word novelette *Pirate Blood* was written after *Tarzan and the City of Gold* (in the first half of 1932) under the penname John Tyler McCulloch, and submitted to various magazine publishers, all of whom rejected it. Burroughs seems to have put it away and begun work on his next novel, *Lost on Venus*. *Pirate Blood* was never published in any form during ERB's life. It was found in Burroughs' safe long after his death in 1950, and presently it exists only as a part of the paperback books listed below. Note that this story can also be found under the heading *The Wizard of Venus*, #839.

──────────── FIRST EDITION ────────────
401. *The Wizard of Venus* (New York: Ace Books, Inc., August 1970)
This paperback printing is the true first edition of *Pirate Blood*, the sixty-ninth story to be published (but never in hardback). The front cover art is by Roy G. Krenkel. The book advertises a title page drawing by Krenkel, but, in a letter to Robert R. Barrett, Donald A. Wolheim (the DAW editor) said the omission occurred because he had gone on vacation and did not leave instructions for his temporary replacement (the title page drawing first appeared in another Ace paperback, Anthony Boucher's *The Complete Werewolf*). Beneath the cover title we find: "Including the first publication anywhere of *Pirate Blood* Burroughs' last great adventure novel." Stock No. 90190, price 60¢. Consecutively paginated; 158 numbered pages.

402. *The Wizard of Venus* (New York: Ace Books, Inc., January 1973)
This second paperback printing also contains *Pirate Blood*. The front cover illustration and a title page drawing are by Roy G. Krenkel (the title page drawing error has been corrected in the second edition). Stock No. 90191, price 75¢. 158 pages.

403. *The Wizard of Venus and Pirate Blood* (New York: Ace Books, Inc., June 1979)
Although the copyright page states that this is the third printing (which is Stock No. 90192), actually this is the *fourth* Ace reprinting. The front cover art is by Esteban Maroto. Stock No. 90193, price $1.95. Contains *Pirate Blood*. 248 pages.

404. *The Wizard of Venus and Pirate Blood* (New York: Ballantine–Del Rey, July 1991)
The first authorized Ballantine–Del Rey printing has been given the new descriptive title, *The Wizard of Venus and Pirate Blood*, with cover illustration by Richard Hescox. Stock No. 37012, price $3.95. 186 pages.

Pirates of Venus

405. "Pirates of Venus" (ARGOSY WEEKLY, September 17, 24; October 1, 8, 15, 22, 1932)
In September of 1931 Burroughs completed *Tarzan and the Leopard Men*, and a month later he began work on a new series set on Venus, with a new hero, Carson Napier (named after a friend ERB had made while he was in the cavalry in Arizona more than thirty years earlier). It was published as a six-part serial, 10¢ each issue, with a front cover illustration on the September 17th issue by Paul Stahr. In addition, there is one interior black-and-white illustration, each installment, by Samuel Cahan. Finishing this, he immediately began working on *Tarzan and the City of Gold*.

——————————— FIRST EDITION ———————————

406. *Pirates of Venus* (Tarzana: Edgar Rice Burroughs, Inc., February 15, 1934)
The first edition of the forty-first hardback by ERB is bound in the typical blue cloth with red lettering on the front cover and spine. The copyright page says "First Edition." The dust jacket cover and five interior black-and-white illustrations are by J. Allen St. John. The map of Venus (Amtor) drawn by Burroughs himself serves as decorated endpages. Price: $2.00. 314 numbered pages.

407. *Pirates of Venus* (Tarzana: Edgar Rice Burroughs, Inc., after February 1934)

The second printing by ERB, Inc. is bound in the typical blue cloth with orange lettering on the front cover and spine. On this one, the copyright imprint "First Edition" is *omitted*. The dust jacket cover and five interior black-and-white illustrations are by J. Allen St. John. The map of Venus serves as decorated endpages. Price: $2.00. 314 numbered pages.

408. *Pirates of Venus* (New York: Grosset & Dunlap, 1935)

The first G&D reprint is bound in red cloth with black lettering on the front cover and spine. The tops of the pages are dyed green. J. Allen St. John did the dust jacket and *four* (one omitted) interior black-and-white plates. The endpapers are decorated like the ERB, Inc. printings. ERB's map of Amtor (Venus) is present. The earliest jacket has "Illustrated" on the middle of the spine. Price: 75¢. 314 numbered pages.

409. *Pirates of Venus* (New York: Grosset & Dunlap, 1940)

The third reprint is bound in red cloth with black lettering on the front cover and spine, and the page tops are dyed green. It has the St. John dust jacket but, like all the other 1940s G&D reprints, it lacks all interior black-and-white plates. The map is also omitted. 314 numbered pages.

410. *Pirates of Venus* (Tarzana: Edgar Rice Burroughs, Inc., 1940)

The ERB, Inc. reprint is one of seven reprinted titles bound in red cloth with blue lettering on the front cover and spine. The dust jacket and frontispiece by J. Allen St. John are identical with the first edition jacket. Price: 75¢. 314 numbered pages.

411. *Pirates of Venus* (Tarzana: Edgar Rice Burroughs, Inc., March 26, 1948)

The 1948 ERB reprints are thinner than the others, and bound in tan cloth with dark red lettering on the front cover and spine. This reprint uses the same dust jacket illustration and frontispiece by J. Allen St. John. Price: $1.00. 314 numbered pages.

412. *Pirates of Venus* (New York: Canaveral Press, Inc., November 16, 1962)

This reprint is bound in tan cloth with black lettering on the front cover and spine. The dust jacket design was adapted from the St. John original by Sam Sigaloff. Four interior black-and-white illustrations by J. Allen St. John, plus ERB's map of Amtor. Price: $2.75, raised to $2.95 in 1963. 314 numbered pages.

413. *Pirates of Venus* (New York: Ace Books, Inc., January 1963)
The first Ace paperback edition has a cover illustration and a title page drawing by Roy G. Krenkel. Stock No. F-179, price 40¢. 173 numbered pages.

414. *The Pirates of Venus* and *Lost on Venus: Two Venus Novels by Edgar Rice Burroughs* (New York: Dover Publications, Inc., November 1963)
This volume has cover art and twenty-five interior illustrations by the meticulous Italian artist Fortunino Matania (done originally for the 1934 British weekly magazine THE PASSING SHOW). $1.75. 340 pages.

415. *Pirates of Venus* (New York: Canaveral Press, Inc., 1975)
This second Canaveral reprint is bound in red cloth with black lettering on the front cover and spine. It is clearly labeled "1975." 314 numbered pages.

416. *Pirates of Venus* (New York: Ace Books, Inc.)
The second Ace paperback edition has the same cover illustration and a title page drawing by Roy G. Krenkel. Stock No. 66500, price 50¢. 173 numbered pages.

417. *Pirates of Venus* (New York: Ace Books, Inc.)
The third Ace paperback edition has the same cover illustration and a title page drawing by Roy G. Krenkel. Stock No. 66501, price 60¢. 173 numbered pages.

418. *Pirates of Venus* (New York: Ace Books, Inc., March 1973)
The fourth Ace paperback edition has cover art by Roy G. Krenkel, originally on the small Ace edition of *A Fighting Man of Mars*. Stock No. 66502, price 75¢. 205 numbered pages.

419. *Pirates of Venus* (New York: Ace Books, Inc., June 1979)
This Ace paperback edition has new cover art by Esteban Maroto. Stock No. 66506, price $1.95. 205 numbered pages.

420. *Pirates of Venus* (New York: Ballantine–Del Rey, July 1991)
The first Ballantine paperback edition has cover illustration by Richard Hescox. Stock No. 37008, price $3.95. 183 pages.

A Princess of Mars

421. "Under the Moons of Mars" (THE ALL-STORY, February, March, April, May, June, July, 1912)

BY EDGAR RICE BURROUGHS

This is the first story Edgar Rice Burroughs ever wrote (if we do not count two childish efforts written years before), begun in July 1911 and finally completed and sent to the editor at THE ALL-STORY on September 28, 1911, four weeks after his thirty-sixth birthday. This introduced the world to the interplanetary romance between John Carter, hero extraordinaire of uncertain age, and Dejah Thoris, the proud Martian princess of incomparable beauty. The manuscript was accepted and published as a six-issue serial under the penname "Norman Bean" (uncomfortable about having written such outlandish fantasy, he had wanted to use the penname "Norma*l* Bean"). The original had several working titles, including "**My First Adventure on Mars**" and "**The Green Martians.**" The $400 check which Burroughs received from ALL-STORY was for a story entitled "**Dejah Thoris, Martian Princess,**" but that was changed to "**Under the Moons of Mars**" by the managing editor of ALL-STORY, Thomas Newell Metcalf (who later became editor at ARGOSY). This magazine version does not have the six-page Foreword that was included in the hardback publication. There is no cover illustration, but there is the same black-and-white headpiece by Fred W. Small for each installment. Each issue was sold for 10¢ until July, when the price was raised to 15¢. After selling this, the enthusiastic Burroughs began work on a medieval adventure, *The Outlaw of Torn*, which almost put an end to his writing career.

422. *A Princess of Mars* (Chicago: A.C. McClurg & Co., September 1917)

This is the pre-publication paperback copy of this book. We know that ERB referred to these as "advance sheets" rather than as "review copies." It is assumed that their purpose was to make available early review copies for the benefit of major newspapers, but that is not certain. Not knowing the book's purpose, it is difficult to make an estimate of how many of these were published, but it was not many, perhaps only a dozen or fewer. We do know that a review of *Tarzan of the Apes* was published a week or so before the official publication date of the book, but it is not known whether the reviewer had received a paperback review copy, or just a hardback released prior to the official date of publication. The cover is the McClurg dust wrapper by Frank Schoonover. The interior is *not* identical to the McClurg first edition described above. The book has no illustrations, no page listing illustrations and no Table of Contents, although the chapters all have their proper names. The Prologue which provides the frame for the story is missing; the story begins with page 1. 326 (+1) numbered pages.

──────────────── FIRST EDITION ────────────────

423. *A Princess of Mars* (Chicago: A.C. McClurg & Co., October 10, 1917)

This profoundly seminal work (written in 1911) singlehandedly created the "interplanetary romance" form of science fiction. Although it was the first story written by ERB, it was the fifth hardback which Burroughs published. ERB

First G&D dust jacket for *A Princess of Mars* (1918)

added a six-page Foreword to the hardback book. The first edition is bound in dark brown cloth with red lettering on the front cover and spine. There is a red circle on the cover (representing Mars, the Red Planet). The dust jacket painting of John Carter, sword in hand with Dejah Thoris behind him, and five sepia plates are by Frank E. Schoonover. On the jacket, the phrase "A Princess of Mars" is in a white band across the top, and the author's name appears under the word "Mars." There is a "W. F. Hall" imprint on the copyright page. Dedicated "To my son Jack" (John Coleman Burroughs). McClurg records unearthed by Alan M. Freedman indicate that 10,200 copies of *A Princess of Mars* were printed. Original price: $1.35. 326 (+1) numbered pages.

424. *A Princess of Mars* (New York: Grosset & Dunlap, 1918)

G&D issued numerous reprints almost yearly until 1940. The earliest 1918 printing has a yellow-brown cover with red letters (the interior illustration faces p. 130). Another reprinting has a dark blue cover with red letters (illustration facing p. 130), while a third has olive-green cloth with orange letters (with an illustration facing p. 146). The dark green cover has red letters and illustration facing p. 138 (probably 1922, because six ERB titles are listed in the ads at the back of the book). A later reprinting, bound in pale green with brown letters is probably from 1927. The olive-green binding with red letters (illustration facing p. 146) is probably from 1930. A light green cover, brownish-red letters, and an orange stain on the top of the pages is probably from 1933 or 1934. Like the first edition, these early reprintings used the dust jacket and four interior black-and-white illustrations by Frank E. Schoonover. The G&D dust jacket differed from the McClurg jacket by cutting off the top ½" of the painting, and adding "BY EDGAR RICE BURROUGHS" in small capital letters, and underneath that, "Author of TARZAN OF THE APES." The earliest jackets did *not* have a photo of ERB on the rear and mention only *A Princess of Mars*. Later jackets list more ERB titles. The various years of the reprints can be determined by carefully examining the advertisements for G&D books found at the back of the volume. Each reprint sold for 75¢. 326 (+1) numbered pages.

425. "Carter of the Red Planet" (MODERN MECHANICS AND INVENTIONS, April-July 1929)

Burroughs sold the second serial rights to this classic tale in 1928. This is an abridged four-part serial of "**A Princess of Mars**" with two interior illustrations, each installment, by C. Saunders. The April issue was a double ERB issue, since it also contained the last installment of "**Lost Inside the Earth**" (*At the Earth's Core*). Each issue cost 25¢.

426. *A Princess of Mars* (New York: Grosset & Dunlap, 1940)

This 1940s G&D reprint can be identified by its lack of illustrations. It is bound in light blue with yellow lettering on the front cover and spine, and the pages have a yellow stain on their tops. The dust jacket is by Frank E. Schoonover; the back includes a photo of ERB and lists 28 ERB titles. Price: 75¢. 326 (+1) numbered pages.

427. *A Princess of Mars* (Tarzana: Edgar Rice Burroughs, Inc., March 26, 1948)

As with the other 1948 ERB, Inc. reprints, this is bound in tan-gray boards with dark red lettering and a circle representing the planet Mars on the front cover; dark red lettering on the spine. The dust jacket and frontispiece (same picture) are by Frank E. Schoonover. Price: $1.00. 326 (+1) numbered pages.

428. *A Princess of Mars* (New York: Ballantine Books, January 1963)

The first U.S. paperback edition of *A Princess of Mars* has front cover art by Robert Abbett. Stock No. F 701, price 50¢. 159 numbered pages.

429. *A Princess of Mars* and *A Fighting Man of Mars: Two Martian Novels by Edgar Rice Burroughs* (New York: Dover Publications, Inc., May 1964)

This is a large paperback edition with cover design taken from the hardback first edition illustrations of Frank E. Schoonover. Four black-and-white interior illustrations by Schoonover and one by Hugh Hutton. Consecutively paginated, 356 numbered pages. Stock No. T1140. $1.75. 356 pages.

430. *A Princess of Mars* and *A Fighting Man of Mars: Two Martian Novels by Edgar Rice Burroughs* (New York: Dover Publications, Inc.)

This Dover paperback has the original interior illustrations but a two-color cover illustration from Frank E. Schoonover. This printing uses Stock No. 21140-1 and sold for $3.00. The title was reprinted several times. 356 pages.

431. *A Princess of Mars* (New York: Doubleday, 1970)

The Science-Fiction Book Club edition is bound in tan cloth with green lettering on the spine. The inspiring dust jacket painting of John Carter and Dejah Thoris, and four excellent interior black-and-white line drawings are by Frank Frazetta. 179 numbered pages.

432. *A Princess of Mars* (New York: Ballantine Books, October 1973)

The fifth Ballantine paperback edition has new front cover art by Gino D'Achille. Stock No. 23578, price $1.25. 159 numbered pages.

433. *A Princess of Mars* (New York: Ballantine–Del Rey, May 1979)

The thirteenth Ballantine paperback printing has new front cover art by Michael Whelan. Stock No. 27834, price $1.95. 159 numbered pages.

434. *A Princess of Mars* (New York: Carroll & Graff Publishers, Inc., 1989)
This paperback uses front cover art by Kiko. $2.95. 159 numbered pages.

435. *A Princess of Mars* and *At the Earth's Core* (Norwalk, CT: The Easton Press, 1996)
This is a quality leather bound edition with an introduction by L. Sprague de Camp and illustrations by Ron Miller, is available by subscribing to the "Masterpieces of Science Fiction" series. Price $38.50. 318 (+xvi) pages.

The Resurrection of Jimber-Jaw

436. "The Resurrection of Jimber-Jaw" (ARGOSY WEEKLY, February 20, 1937)
Several months after he finished "**Tarzan and the Magic Men**" (the first half of *Tarzan the Magnificent*), ERB wrote this short story (whose original working title was "**Elmer**") in three days in March 1936. It has a front cover illustration by Emmett Watson and one interior black-and-white illustration by Samuel Cahan.

─────────── FIRST EDITION ───────────

437. *Tales of Three Planets* (New York: Canaveral Press, Inc., April 27, 1964)
The hardback first edition of Burroughs's sixty-second hardback book is bound in blue cloth with black lettering on the front cover and spine. It says "First Edition" on the copyright page. The book contains "**Beyond the Farthest Star**" (Part II is also referred to as "**Tangor Returns**"), "**The Resurrection of Jimber-Jaw**" and "**The Wizard of Venus**." Roy G. Krenkel did the dust jacket ink illustrations and ten interior black-and-white illustrations. Arlene Williamson did the illustrated endpaper interior maps of Poloda. The stories are consecutively paginated. 282 numbered pages.

438. "**The Resurrection of Jimber-Jaw**" in *Masterpieces of Science Fiction*, edited by Sam Moskowitz (Cleveland and New York: The World Publishing Company, 1966)
This anthology includes ERB's story on pages 377–399. There are no interior illustrations. Price $6.50. 552 pages.

439. "**The Resurrection of Jimber-Jaw**" in *The Pulps* (New York: Chelsea House, 1970)
This edition appears in two forms. The first was published by Chelsea House, edited by Tony Goodstone. It is bound in yellow decorated cloth with

I. Bibliography of Books

black lettering on the front cover and spine. The illustrated dust jacket is a montage of many different pulp magazine covers. There is an inexpensive reprinting of the book distributed by Bonanza Books, a division of Crown Publishers. The story includes one black-and-white interior illustration by Samuel Cahan for the original ARGOSY WEEKLY magazine appearance in 1937. 239 numbered pages.

440. "The Resurrection of Jimber-Jaw" in *Masterpieces of Science Fiction*, edited by Sam Moskowitz (Westport, CT: Hyperion Press, Inc., 1974)
This is a reprint of the earlier World Publishing Company anthology which includes ERB's story on pages 377–399. There are no interior illustrations. The light blue cloth bound book sold for $12.95; the paperback was $4.95. 552 pages.

441. "The Resurrection of Jimber-Jaw" in *The Fantastic Pulps*, edited by Peter Haining (New York: St. Martin's Press, 1976)
This hardback anthology is bound in red cloth with gold lettering on the spine. The ERB story appears on pages 42–61. The dust jacket illustration is by Frank R. Paul. There are no interior illustrations for the ERB story, but there is a portfolio of pulp illustrations. The book sold for $10.00. 418 numbered pages.

442. "The Resurrection of Jimber-Jaw" in *The Fantastic Pulps*, edited by Peter Haining (New York: Vintage Books, October 1976)
This is a paperback version of the St. Martin's Press edition described above. The ERB story is between pages 42–61. There are no interior illustrations for the ERB story. Price $2.95. Stock No. V-109. 418 pages.

The Return of Tarzan

443. "The Return of Tarzan" (NEW STORY MAGAZINE, June, July, August, September, October, November, December 1913)
This was the fifth story written by Edgar Rice Burroughs, completed in January of 1913 immediately after *The Gods of Mars*. The ALL-STORY WEEKLY magazine readers were clamoring for a resolution to the romance between Tarzan and Jane, left unresolved at the end of *Tarzan of the Apes*. In the first part of this book Tarzan spends some time in the drawing rooms and salons of Paris, so its first working title was "**Monsieur Tarzan**," and then "**The Ape-Man.**" When ERB submitted it to Thomas Metcalf, the editor at ALL-STORY, it was rejected. Burroughs revised it according to Metcalf's suggestions, and again it was rejected. He felt betrayed. Rather than revising or rewriting it again, he turned around and submitted it to the editor at NEW STORY MAGAZINE, who promptly purchased it for $1,000, considerably more than ALL-STORY would have paid. The

BY EDGAR RICE BURROUGHS

N.C. Wyeth dust jacket illustration for *The Return of Tarzan* (1915)

first printing was as a seven-part serial with front cover art in the June issue (Tarzan dressed as a European astride a horse) and in the August issue (Tarzan in the tree tops) by famed illustrator, N.C. Wyeth. There is one black-and-white headpiece for each installment by an unidentified artist. Each issue cost 15¢.

444. *The Return of Tarzan* (Chicago: A.C. McClurg & Co., prior to March 1915)

Thanks to the perspicacity of Brian Kirby, at one time a mint condition "printer's dummy" of this book passed through my hands. On the outside it looked just like a mint copy of the first edition of *The Return of Tarzan*. However, on the inside, it had only about the first 30 pages of text and the rest was completely blank pages. This was done by McClurg so that the publisher and the author could see what the finished product was going to look like before the book was finally printed. The book I saw did not have a dust jacket. It probably had 356 pages, but most of them were unnumbered and unmarked. We know that other McClurg printer's "dummies" exist for *The Beasts of Tarzan*, *The Son of Tarzan*, *The Cave Girl*, and *The Eternal Lover*. The printer's dummy for *The Beasts of Tarzan* is stamped "unique salesman's copy," and so it seems that McClurg referred to these as "unique salesman's copies." ERB, Inc. also produced at least three printer's dummies, including *Jungle Girl*, *The Lad and the Lion*, and *The Deputy Sheriff of Comanche County*.

445. *The Return of Tarzan* (Chicago: A.C. McClurg & Co., prior to March 10, 1915)

A paperbound copy of this book was printed before the hardback was published. ERB referred to these as "advance sheets," perhaps reflecting their original purpose. The cover for *The Return of Tarzan* is a plain brown stiff paper wrapper with a McClurg postcard advertisement affixed to it. Unlike the other "pre-publication" copies, this one does not have the dust jacket illustration on its cover. The interior is identical with the first edition described below. 365 numbered pages.

―――――――― FIRST EDITION ――――――――

446. *The Return of Tarzan* (Chicago: A.C. McClurg & Co., March 10, 1915)

The first edition of the second hardbound book in the Burroughs Tarzan saga is bound in dark green cloth with shiny gold lettering on the front cover and spine. The dust jacket is the N.C. Wyeth illustration used on the August (third) magazine installment cover. There are twenty-six interior black-and-white headpieces by J. Allen St. John (the first time St. John illustrated a Burroughs book). There is also a "W. F. Hall" imprint on the copyright page. The first edition dust jacket has a price of "*$1.30*" on the spine. A.C. McClurg printed a total of 15,000 copies of the first and six reprintings. 365 numbered pages.

447. *The Return of Tarzan* (Chicago: A.C. McClurg & Co., after March 10, 1915)

McClurg issued at least *six* additional reprintings of this, but all are dated 1915 on the title page. However, they bear a title page imprint which identifies the book as the "Second Edition," "Third Edition," or "Sixth Edition," etc. All other points are the same as the McClurg first edition described as #446 above. The dust-jacket has the price imprinted on the spine. 365 numbered pages.

448. *The Return of Tarzan* (New York: A.L. Burt Company, Publishers, 1916)

The first A.L. Burt reprint is bound in dark green cloth with white lettering on the front cover and spine. The book uses the same first edition dust jacket painting by N.C. Wyeth and 26 interior black-and-white headpieces by J. Allen St. John. Price: 50¢. 365 numbered pages.

449. *The Return of Tarzan* (New York: A.L. Burt Company, Publishers, 1916-1929)

Burt reprinted *The Return of Tarzan* almost yearly until 1929. These come with different cloth covers (primarily shades of green and blue-gray), but can be identified as later Burt reprints by the black lettering on the front cover and spine. The dust jacket is the same one by N.C. Wyeth. It also uses the 26 interior black-and-white headpieces by J. Allen St. John. 365 numbered pages. An approximation of the actual date of the reprint can be ascertained by carefully examining the announcement of Burt books found at the end of the volume; if an ERB book from 1927 is advertised there, obviously the reprint cannot be any earlier than 1927! The price of the 1917 printing was 60¢, the 1919 printing, 75¢.

450. *The Return of Tarzan* (New York: Grosset & Dunlap, 1927)

The first of the G&D reprints is bound in red cloth with black lettering on the front cover and spine, and we find a list of 15 ERB titles in the advertising pages at the back. G&D used the same N.C. Wyeth jacket illustration, and on the back of the earliest jacket we find a photo of ERB and a list of 24 ERB books in blue ink inside a blue border (and only 18 ERB titles listed on the reverse of the jacket). This G&D reprint has the 26 interior black-and-white headpieces by J. Allen St. John. Price: 75¢. 365 numbered pages.

451. *The Return of Tarzan* (New York: Grosset & Dunlap, 1935)

Grosset & Dunlap seems to have reprinted this book many times. They are all bound in red cloth with black lettering on the front cover and spine and use the same N.C. Wyeth jacket illustration and the 26 interior black-and-white headpiece decorations by J. Allen St. John. The date is determined by the number of Burroughs books found listed in the advertising at the back of the book. There are 23 titles (1928), 25 titles, 28 titles, 29 titles, and 33 titles (1935). 365 numbered pages.

I. Bibliography of Books

452. *The Return of Tarzan* (Racine, WI: Whitman Publishing, 1936).
This is one of the small papercovered Big Little Books published for children. This series of books measures 3½" wide by 4⅜" high, and averages about 1¼" in width. The cover is by Hugh Hutton, and there are 209 interior illustrations by Rex Maxon, abridged from the 1929 daily newspaper comic strip. Stock No. 1102. 432 pages. For more information on these, see #932–968.

453. *The Return of Tarzan* ("Armed Services Edition #O-22" published by arrangement with the Edgar Rice [sic] Publishing Co., Tarzana: California. No date [1943])
This is a rare pocket-sized paperback edition (6½" × 4½") issued in 1943 by The Armed Services, Inc., a non-profit organization established by the Council on Books in Wartime. It bears the A.C. McClurg & Co. copyright date of 1915 on the title page. Despite the small size, the paperback is complete and unabridged. The number "O-22" comes from Burroughs' Tarzana telephone number during this time: Owensmouth 220. There is a decorated front cover with a picture of the British Methuen edition dust jacket but no interior illustrations. 287 numbered pages.

454. *The Return of Tarzan* (New York: Grosset & Dunlap, 1943)
This "Madison Square" inexpensive reprint is bound in maroon cloth with black lettering on the front cover and spine. It has the same dust jacket by N.C. Wyeth. The title page has a decoration by J. Allen St. John; no interior illustrations. This is the thin cheap "Wartime Edition" with Madison Square imprint on dust jacket. The price was 50¢ until 1945, when it was changed to 49¢. 314 numbered pages.

455. *The Return of Tarzan* (New York: Grosset & Dunlap, April 1948)
The first of this series of 1948 G&D reprints sold for $1.00. It is bound in orange *cloth* pictorial covers with a black drawing on front cover and black lettering on spine. The dust jacket art is by C. Edmund Monroe, Jr. The end paper map and board and title page drawings are by Rafael Palacios. In 1955, it was reissued with tan *paper* pictorial boards (dark red lettering) at $1.25 and again, in 1958, without the decorated endpapers, for $1.50. 314 numbered pages.

456. *The Return of Tarzan* (New York: Ballantine Books, July 1963)
The first Ballantine paperback edition has front cover art by Richard Powers. Stock No. F 746, price 50¢. 221 numbered pages.

457. *The Return of Tarzan* (New York: Grosset & Dunlap, 1967)
This G&D reprint has a full color illustrated cloth cover, art by C. Edmund Monroe, Jr. There was no dust jacket on this series of G&D reprints. The series is called "Books for Boys and Girls." Stock No. 2631. $1.95. 314 numbered pages.

BY EDGAR RICE BURROUGHS

458. *The Return of Tarzan* (Racine, WI: Whitman Publishing, 1967)
This abridged version is bound in a pictorial binding. The cover art is by Al Anderson. The illustrated end-papers and twelve interior illustrations are by Al Anderson and Sparky Moore. There is no dust jacket. 214 pages.

459. *The Return of Tarzan* (New York: Ballantine Books, February 1967)
The third Ballantine paperback edition has a new front cover, with Ron Ely (who played Tarzan on the television series during this period) paddling a canoe. A red banner on the front cover says "See the NBC Network Program TARZAN on Friday Nights." Stock No. U2002, price 50¢. 221 numbered pages.

460. *The Return of Tarzan* (New York: Ballantine Books, April 1969)
The fifth Ballantine paperback edition has new front cover art by Robert Abbett. Stock No. 01592, price 50¢. 221 numbered pages.

461. *The Return of Tarzan* (New York: Ballantine Books, April 1975)
The eighth Ballantine paperback edition has new front cover art by Neal Adams. Stock No. 24160, price $1.25. 221 numbered pages.

I. BIBLIOGRAPHY OF BOOKS

The Rider

462. "H.R.H. the Rider" (ALL-STORY WEEKLY, December 14, 21, 28, 1918)
One week after completing *Tarzan and the Jewels of Opar*, ERB began writing this short story in October 1915. It was sold for 10¢ an issue as a three-part serial with a rather whimsical cover illustration on the first installment by George Brehm. There are no interior illustrations. This has chapter titles which were omitted in the hardback publication. The "H.R.H" in the title is a British acronym which stands for "His Royal Highness."

———————— FIRST EDITION ————————
463. *The Oakdale Affair* and *The Rider* (Tarzana: Edgar Rice Burroughs, Inc., February 15, 1937)
This first edition is the forty-eighth hardback by ERB to be published, and the twelfth published by ERB, Inc. As with the other ERB, Inc. firsts, it is bound in blue cloth with red-orange lettering on the front cover and spine. It has the "First Edition" imprint on the copyright page. The full wrap-around dust jacket illustration by John Coleman Burroughs is the first one that Burroughs' son ever did (his sister, Joan Burroughs, and her husband, Jim Pierce, were the models). In addition, there are two interior black-and-white illustrations also by John Coleman Burroughs. The two stories are separately paginated. Note that the hardback printings of *The Oakdale Affair* are missing the last two pages of the magazine version. Price: $2.00. 172 and 144 numbered pages. (This book is also listed under the heading of *The Oakdale Affair*, #373.)

464. *The Oakdale Affair* and *The Rider* (A "Mixed Edition": Grosset & Dunlap, 1937)
It is unclear whether a "mixed edition" of this title actually exists. If it did, we should find the ERB, Inc. first edition distributed with a Grosset & Dunlap title page and dust jacket.

465. *The Oakdale Affair* and *The Rider* (Grosset & Dunlap, 1938)
This red cloth hardback reprint has two interior illustrations. Price: 75¢. 172 and 144 numbered pages.

466. *The Rider* (New York: Ace Books, Inc., October 1974)
The first paperback edition has a front cover painting by Frank Frazetta. Stock No. 72280, price $1.25. There are at least two variants with different advertisements; priority not established. 154 numbered pages.

BY EDGAR RICE BURROUGHS

Savage Pellucidar

467. "The Return to Pellucidar" (AMAZING STORIES, February 1942)
After working on *Llana of Gathol*, Burroughs began this, the first of a series of four short novelettes linked together to form his last Pellucidar novel. He spent a week in September 1940 writing this story, whose original working title was "Hodon and O-aa." There are two interior black-and-white illustrations by J. Allen St. John. The issue cost 25¢.

468. "Men of the Bronze Age" (AMAZING STORIES, March 1942)
It took Burroughs a week in October 1940, to produce the second of four short stories which would later be published in hardback as a novel entitled *Savage Pellucidar*. J. Allen St. John provided two interior black-and-white illustrations. 25¢.

469. "Tiger Girl" (AMAZING STORIES, April 1942)
The third part of *Savage Pellucidar* took four days of November 1940 to write. As with the previous installments, J. Allen St. John did two interior black-and-white illustrations. The issue cost 25¢.

470. "The Return to Pellucidar," "Men of the Bronze Age," "Tiger Girl" (AMAZING STORIES QUARTERLY, fall 1942).
These three stories were reprinted with the original interior art in a 752-page quarterly in the fall of 1942. The front cover is by Julian S. Krupa and the back cover by McCall. Original price: 35¢.

471. "Savage Pellucidar" (AMAZING STORIES, November 1963)
This novelette remained unpublished during the author's lifetime even though it was written in October of 1944, six years before the death of Burroughs. This installment completes the tale. There are two black-and-white interior illustrations by Larry Ivie. The issue cost 50¢.

──────────── FIRST EDITION ────────────

472. *Savage Pellucidar* (New York: Canaveral Press, Inc., November 25, 1963)
The title Burroughs had in mind for this book was "**Girl of Pellucidar.**" This Canaveral printing is the first edition. The first edition has a tipped-in copyright page (the original copyright information was erroneous). It is bound in blue cloth with blue lettering on the front cover and spine. On the dust jacket appears the announcement: "First NEW Burroughs in fifteen years." Following tradition, the dust jacket and six interior black-and-white illustrations are by

J. Allen St. John (the same illustrations used in the magazines). There is a map of Pellucidar used as illustrated endpapers. Price: $3.50. 274 numbered pages.

473. *Savage Pellucidar* (New York: Ace Books, Inc., May 1964)
The first paperback edition has cover art and title page drawing by Frank Frazetta (which was later used on the Ace and Tempo printings of *Cave Girl*). Stock No. F-280, price 40¢. 221 numbered pages.

474. *Savage Pellucidar* (New York: Ace Books, Inc.)
The second paperback edition has the same cover art and title page drawing by Frank Frazetta. Stock No. G-739, price 50¢. 221 numbered pages.

475. *Savage Pellucidar* (New York: Ace Books, Inc.)
The third paperback edition has the same cover art and title page drawing by Frank Frazetta. Stock No. 75131, price 60¢. 221 numbered pages.

476. *Savage Pellucidar* (New York: Ace Books, Inc., January 1973)
The fourth paperback edition has new cover art by Frank Frazetta. Stock No. 75132, price 75¢. 255 numbered pages.

477. *Savage Pellucidar* (New York: Ballantine–Del Rey, May 1990)
The first Ballantine edition has cover art by David B. Mattingly. Stock No. 36673, price $3.95. 231 pages.

The Scientists Revolt

NOTE: The only commercial publication of this story, written in 1922, was in the 1939 magazine appearance described below. The only reprints are in several Burroughs fanzines in the 1970s. Because of this, I am inclined to say that there really isn't a genuine first edition. However, the three 1971 ERB-DOM issues (#2 below) were the first fanzine printing, and the 1974 BURROUGHS BULLETIN version is the only appearance of Burroughs's original words. Thus some collectors would consider these both to be highly desirable, and perhaps call them the first editions.

478. "The Scientists Revolt" (FANTASTIC ADVENTURES, July 1939)
This cautionary short story was written in three weeks in November, 1922, immediately after "The Moon Maid," under the working title "Beware!"

Burroughs submitted it under the pseudonym "John Tyler McCulloch" to see if it would sell without his famous name on it. It was not one of his better stories, and he was not able to sell it until 17 years later, when finally he submitted it under his own name. It was published in this large oversized magazine with four interior black-and-white illustrations by Julian S. Krupa, but it was significantly rewritten by Ray Palmer, the editor of FANTASTIC ADVENTURES.

479. "The Scientists Revolt" (ERB-DOM, January, February, March 1971)
This is a reduced photographic reproduction of the Fantastic Adventures version, with the Ray Palmer changes. It appeared in 1971 in three issues: #42, #43 and #44 of the excellent Burroughs fanzine, ERB-DOM, published by Camille "Caz" Cazedessus. Issue 43 also offers an excellent Neal MacDonald, Jr., double page illustration. These issues are rather small in size, approximately 5½" x 8½".

480. "Beware!" by John Tyler McCulloch (BURROUGHS BULLETIN, #39, July 1974)
This is the first publication of "The Scientists Revolt" as originally written and titled by ERB in 1922 under the McCulloch pseudonym. This does not have the Ray Palmer changes, and the story is very different. The cover art and two interior illustrations of the Vern Coriell fanzine publication are by Richard Corben.

481. "The Scientists Revolt" by Edgar Rice Burroughs (BURROUGHS BULLETIN #40, August 1974)
This is another photographic reprint of the FANTASTIC ADVENTURES story of 1939 with the Julian S. Krupa illustrations and the Ray Palmer editing. It is printed in the larger 8½" x 11" size, closer to the original oversized magazine publication. Vern Coriell, the publisher, commissioned new cover art by Herb Arnold.

The Son of Tarzan

482. "The Son of Tarzan" (ALL-STORY WEEKLY, December 4, 11, 18, 25, 1915; January 1, 8, 1916)
This very popular Tarzan novel was written between January 21 and May 11, 1915, directly after *Pellucidar*. It was published as a six-part serial with front cover illustration (the December 4th installment) by P. J. Monahan. Each issue cost 10¢. There were no interior illustrations. There were chapter titles in the serial which were not used in the hardback publication. Completing this, Burroughs next wrote "Ben, King of Beasts" (published as *The Man-Eater*) and then "Beyond Thirty."

I. BIBLIOGRAPHY OF BOOKS

"The Son of Tarzan" December 4, 1915

483. *The Son of Tarzan* (Chicago: A.C. McClurg & Co., prior to March 1917)

McClurg issued an early paperback version of this title prior to hardback publication, just as it did with the first three Tarzan titles and with *A Princess of Mars*. ERB referred to these as "advance sheets." The cover is the St. John dust jacket illustration, and the interior is the same as the first edition above. 394 numbered pages.

484. *The Son of Tarzan* (Chicago: A.C. McClurg & Co., prior to March 1917)

For several early titles, we know that McClurg produced something called a "printer's dummy." On the outside these books look like the first edition. However, on the inside of the book we find only some pages of text and illustrations and the rest is completely blank. These "dummies" were probably printed by McClurg to help the publisher visualize the binding and typeface, and it could be used by salesmen to sell the book by demonstrating what the finished product was going to look like before the book was finally printed and bound. The exact number of pages is unclear because most pages were unnumbered and unmarked. We know that other McClurg "printer's dummies" exist for *The Return of Tarzan, The Beasts of Tarzan, Cave Girl* and *The Eternal Lover*, and it is very possible that there were dummies produced for other McClurg ERB titles as well. A printer's dummy for the Volland edition of *The Tarzan Twins* exists. ERB, Inc. also produced some (*Jungle Girl, The Lad and the Lion* and *The Deputy Sheriff of Comanche County* are known).

─────────── FIRST EDITION ───────────

485. *The Son of Tarzan* (Chicago: A.C. McClurg & Co., March 10, 1917)

The first edition of Burroughs's fourth published hardback book is bound in green cloth with gold lettering on the front cover and spine. The copyright page has a W.F. Hall printer's imprint. The full wrap-around dust jacket and numerous extraordinary interior black-and-white pen drawings are by J. Allen St. John. The dedication page to Hulbert Burroughs was accidentally omitted by McClurg. After Burroughs complained, it was inserted (see below). Thus, the first state of the first edition is without a dedication page. This was a fairly popular McClurg Tarzan title; McClurg printed a total of 32,000 copies of the first and three later reprintings. Price: $1.30. 394 numbered pages.

486. *The Son of Tarzan* (Chicago: A.C. McClurg & Co., 1917)

The second state of the first edition is identical to #2 above, except that it has a dedication page to Hulbert Burroughs (ERB's eldest son, who died of a heart attack on August 8, 1991, two days before his 82nd birthday). Price: $1.30. 394 numbered pages.

I. BIBLIOGRAPHY OF BOOKS

487. *The Son of Tarzan* (Chicago: A.C. McClurg & Co., 1918)
The 1918 reprint is identical to the second state except that it has 1918 on the title page. The dedication page to Hulbert Burroughs is present on this one, and all subsequent editions. Price: $1.30.

488. *The Son of Tarzan* (Chicago: A.C. McClurg & Co., 1918)
This 1918 reprint is like #5 above, except that on the copyright page there is no W.F. Hall printer's imprint. Price: $1.30.

489. *The Son of Tarzan* (New York: A.L. Burt Company, Publishers, 1918)
Burt reprinted this title numerous times until 1928. It is bound in pale green cloth with black lettering on the front cover and spine. George McWhorter notes the existence of variants bound in gray cloth and dark green. "1917" appears on the title page. The dust jacket has been changed; the McClurg first edition jacket is a full wrap-around jacket, but all reprint jackets have used only the front part of the illustration. The illustrated spine and back cover of the jacket have been eliminated. The frontispiece, decorated title page and fabulous interior black-and-white illustrations by J. Allen St. John are the same as in the first edition. The dedication page to Hulbert Burroughs (omitted in the first state of the first edition) is present in this reprint and all subsequent reprints. The 1918 printing sold for 50¢; the 1919 reprinting cost 75¢. 394 numbered pages.

490. *The Son of Tarzan* (New York: Grosset & Dunlap, 1927)
This, the first G&D reprint, is bound in the usual red cloth with black lettering on the front cover and spine. The dust jacket, frontispiece, title page and numerous interior black-and-white illustrations are the same as in the first edition (by J. Allen St. John). On the back of the earliest G&D dust jacket there is a photograph of ERB and a list of 24 ERB titles in blue ink inside a fancy blue border, and on the reverse of the jacket we find only 18 ERB titles listed. A later book variation has the tops of the pages dyed green. Dust jackets from the 1930s have a yellow background with a sketch of ERB on the back panel. The dedication page is present. Price: 75¢. 394 numbered pages.

491. *The Son of Tarzan* (Racine, WI: Whitman, 1939)
This small illustrated children's book is one of the Big Little Book series. It has paper boards. This series of books measures 3½" wide by 4⅜" high, and averages about 1¼" in width. There is a cover illustration by Henry Vallely, and the interior illustrations are abridged from the Rex Maxon 1929-1930 daily newspaper comic strips. Number 1477. 432 pages. For more on these, see #932–968.

492. *The Son of Tarzan* (New York: Grosset & Dunlap, 1940)
This is bound in red cloth with black lettering on the front cover and spine, and the tops of the pages are dyed green. The dust jacket and numerous interior

black-and-white illustrations by St. John are present. Like the other 1940s G&D reprints, this can be distinguished from the earlier 1927 reprint by the absence of a frontispiece and the omission of St. John's name from the title page, but the other decorations on the title page are present, as is the dedication page to Hulbert Burroughs. Price: 75¢. 394 numbered pages.

493. *The Son of Tarzan* (New York: Grosset & Dunlap, 1943)
The thin wartime edition is bound in maroon cloth with black lettering on the front cover and spine. The same J. Allen St. John dust jacket, with "Madison Square" logo readily visible. Bill Ross notes that there are at least three different dust jacket variations on this book, ranging from full color, two color, and black-and-white. As with the other World War II wartime printings, the top the title page presents J. Allen St. John's most famous drawing, Tarzan and his golden lion. To save money, all interior illustrations were omitted. The book sold for 50¢ until 1945, when the price was changed to 49¢. 312 numbered pages.

494. *The Son of Tarzan* (New York: Ace Books, Inc., April 1963)
The first paperback, and the only Ace paperback edition, has a cover painting and a title page drawing by Frank Frazetta. Stock No. F-193, price 40¢. 255 numbered pages.

495. *The Son of Tarzan* (New York: Ballantine Books, July 1963)
The first Ballantine paperback edition has a front cover illustration by Richard Powers. Stock No. F-748, price 50¢. 222 numbered pages.

496. *The Son of Tarzan* (New York: Ballantine Books, November 1963)
The second Ballantine paperback edition is unchanged. Stock No. U2004, price 50¢. 222 numbered pages.

497. *The Son of Tarzan* (New York: Ballantine Books, April 1969)
The third Ballantine paperback edition has new cover art by Robert Abbett. Stock No. 01594, price 50¢. 222 numbered pages.

498. *The Son of Tarzan* (New York: Ballantine Books, April 1975)
The sixth Ballantine paperback edition has new cover art by Neal Adams. Stock No. 24162, price $1.25. 222 numbered pages.

499. *Tarzan of the Apes* (New York: Avenel, 1988)
This anthology volume is bound in maroon cloth with gold lettering on the spine. There is a very attractive J. Allen St. John dust jacket (which appeared originally for *Tarzan at the Earth's Core*). The anthology contains a reprinting of the original magazine version of *Tarzan of the Apes*, and *The Son of Tarzan*,

Tarzan at the Earth's Core and *Tarzan Triumphant*. The interior black-and-white illustrations are by several artists: reprints of J. Allen St. John; reprints of Studley Burroughs; and original drawings by Esteban Maroto. The four stories are consecutively paginated with 848 numbered pages.

Swords of Mars

500. "Swords of Mars" (THE BLUE BOOK MAGAZINE, November, December 1934; January, February, March, April 1935)
 The eighth Burroughs Mars story was written directly after *Tarzan and the Lion Man*, and right before *Tarzan's Quest*. Burroughs worked on it for six weeks at the end of 1933. It was first published as a six-part serial with cover illustrations on two issues. Joseph Chenoweth did the cover on the December 1934 issue; Ondrek Zaula (aka Henry Soulen) did the January 1935 issue. In addition, each issue contains six interior black-and-white illustrations by Robert Fink, and sold for 15¢.

———————————— FIRST EDITION ————————————

501. *Swords of Mars* (Tarzana: Edgar Rice Burroughs, Inc., February 15, 1936)
 Swords of Mars was Burroughs's forty-fifth published hardback. The first edition is bound in a rather porous blue cloth with orange lettering on the front cover and spine. The copyright page says "First Edition." J. Allen St. John did the wrap-around dust jacket painting and five interior black-and-white plates. There are two states of the dust jacket: one laminated; one unlaminated. This book is unusual inasmuch it was written between November 6, 1933, and December 15, 1933, as Burroughs' marriage to his first wife, Emma, was coming apart. After Burroughs and Florence Gilbert were married in 1935, Burroughs arranged it so that the first words in the Preface and the twenty-four separate chapters form an acrostic: "To Florence with all My Love Ed." Price: $2.00. 315 numbered pages.

502. *Swords of Mars* (New York: Grosset & Dunlap, 1937)
 The first hardback reprint is bound in red cloth with black lettering on the front cover and spine. It has all five interior plates. The dust jacket is the same J. Allen St. John wrap-around illustration. Price: 75¢. 315 numbered pages.

503. *Swords of Mars* (New York: Grosset & Dunlap, 1938?)
 This reprint is bound in red cloth with black lettering on the front cover and spine. It is identical with the G&D edition above but it has only two mono-

chrome interior illustrations. The dust jacket is the same J. Allen St. John wraparound illustration. Price: 75¢. 315 numbered pages.

504. *Swords of Mars* (Tarzana: Edgar Rice Burroughs, Inc., 1940)

This reprint is one of the seven titles ERB, Inc. bound in red cloth with blue lettering. It has the same dust jacket illustration as the first edition, but only one interior illustration (the frontispiece) by J. Allen St. John. There are three different dust jacket variations found on this reprinting. One is laminated and identical to the jacket on the first edition, except the $2 price on the inner front flap has been trimmed off (the book sold for 75¢). A second variant is unlaminated, and has the publisher's name on the spine, BURROUGHS, enclosed in a yellow box. There is a third jacket, unlaminated, which has "A John Carter of Mars Romance" just below the title, and a circle with "The 8th Mars Novel" in the lower right corner. On the rear inner flap, all three jackets have an advertisement for and a photograph of the book *Tarzan and the Leopard Men*.

505. *Swords of Mars* (Tarzana: Edgar Rice Burroughs, Inc., March 26, 1948)

As with the other 1948 ERB, Inc. reprints, this thinner reprinting is bound in tan boards with dark brown lettering on the front cover and spine. This jacket is slightly different from the three variants noted above. The 1948 jacket has a yellow rectangular box on the bottom of the spine with BURROUGHS inside the box but does *not* say "8th Mars Novel" or "John Carter of Mars Romance" on the front. In addition, the back inner flap has a list of 22 ERB titles which were available in the 1948 tan binding (the earlier jacket has a photograph of the book *Tarzan and the Leopard Men* on the inner flap). Price: $1.00. 315 numbered pages.

506. *Swords of Mars* (New York: Ballantine Books, May 1963)

The first paperback edition has cover art by Bob Abbett. Stock No. F 728, price 50¢. 191 numbered pages.

507. *Swords of Mars* (New York: Ballantine Books, October 1973)

The fifth paperback edition has cover art by Gino D'Achille. Stock No. 23585, price $1.25. 191 numbered pages.

508. *Swords of Mars* and *Synthetic Men of Mars* (New York: Doubleday, January 1975)

The Science-Fiction Book Club edition is bound in red cloth with white lettering on the spine. As with the earlier volumes in this series, the dust jacket art and six interior black-and-white illustrations are beautifully done by Frank Frazetta. The two stories are continuously paginated with 345 numbered pages.

509. *Swords of Mars* (New York: Ballantine–Del Rey, April 1979)
The eleventh paperback edition has new cover art by Michael Whelan. Stock No. 27841, price $1.95. 191 numbered pages.

Synthetic Men of Mars

510. "The Synthetic Men of Mars" (ARGOSY WEEKLY, January 7, 14, 21, 28; February 4, 11, 1939)
This imaginative six-part serial was begun in March of 1938, a year after Burroughs had finished writing *Tarzan and the Forbidden City*. It has a front cover illustration (the January 7th first installment) by Rudolph Belarski. In addition, each issue has one black-and-white illustration by Samuel Cahan, and sold for 10¢ apiece.

──────────── FIRST EDITION ────────────

511. *Synthetic Men of Mars* (Tarzana: Edgar Rice Burroughs, Inc., March 15, 1940)
The first edition of Burroughs' fifty-fourth published book is bound in the usual pebbled blue cloth with orange lettering on the front cover and spine. The book's copyright page is imprinted "First Edition." John Coleman Burroughs did the dust jacket art, five interior black-and-white plates, and a line-drawing on the spine of the book. Like other ERB books of this period, the dust jacket is in two states: one laminated; one unlaminated. Price: $2.00. 315 numbered pages.

512. *Synthetic Men of Mars* (Tarzana: Edgar Rice Burroughs, Inc., March 26, 1948)
The first hardback reprint is bound in the standard 1948 reprinting's tan cloth with dark brown lettering on the front cover and spine, with the same line drawing also on the spine. The same jacket art and frontispiece by John Coleman Burroughs. Price: $1.00. 315 numbered pages.

513. *Synthetic Men of Mars* (New York: Ballantine Books, June 1963)
This, the first paperback reprint, has a front cover by Robert Abbett. Stock No. F 739, price 50¢. 160 numbered pages.

514. *Synthetic Men of Mars* (New York: Ballantine Books, October 1973)
The fifth paperback reprinting has new front cover art by Gino D'Achille. Stock No. 23586, price $1.25. 160 numbered pages.

515. *Swords of Mars* and *Synthetic Men of Mars* (New York: Doubleday, January 1975)
The Science-Fiction Book Club edition is bound in red cloth with white lettering on the spine. As with the earlier volumes in this series, the dust jacket art and six interior black-and-white illustrations are beautifully done by Frank Frazetta. The two stories are continuously paginated with 345 numbered pages.

516. *Synthetic Men of Mars* (New York: Ballantine–Del Rey, October 1979)
The eleventh paperback reprinting has new front cover art by Michael Whelan. Stock No. 27842, price $1.95. 160 numbered pages.

Tales of Three Planets

--- FIRST EDITION ---

517. *Tales of Three Planets* (New York: Canaveral Press, Inc., April 27, 1964)
Tales of Three Planets is the sixty-second hardback by Burroughs, and an anthology volume which compiles four short and unrelated Burroughs stories ranging from 1936 ("The Resurrection of Jimber-Jaw") to 1941 ("The Wizard of Venus"), none of which had been previously published in hardbound. This volume has two different colors for the cloth binding: one is bound in blue, one in tan, both with black lettering on the front cover and spine. The copyright page says "First Edition." Roy G. Krenkel did the dust jacket and 13 interior black-and-white illustrations. The volume contains "**Beyond the Farthest Star**," "**Tangor Returns**," "**The Resurrection of Jimber-Jaw**" and "**The Wizard of Venus**." Artist Arlene Williamson did the endpaper maps of Poloda and other interior maps based on sketches by Burroughs. Introduction by Richard A. Lupoff, the editor. Consecutively paginated, 282 numbered pages.

518. *Tales of Three Planets* (New York: Canaveral Press, Inc., 1975)
This reprinting of *Tales of Three Planets* is clearly labeled "1975" on the title page. Otherwise, the interior is identical with the first edition described above.

NOTE: See also the separate entries for *The Wizard of Venus* (#839– 845) and *The Resurrection of Jimber-Jaw* (#436, 437) in this book.

I. BIBLIOGRAPHY OF BOOKS

Tanar of Pellucidar

519. "Tanar of Pellucidar" (THE BLUE BOOK MAGAZINE, March-August 1929)
This six-part serial was written between September and November 1928, four months after *Tarzan and the Lost Empire*, and right before *Tarzan at the Earth's Core*. It has a front cover illustration on each of the first five installments by Frank Hoban. Hoban also did a great many interior black-and-white illustrations. There is a map by ERB included in the first three installments. Each issue sold for 25¢.

---FIRST EDITION---

520. *Tanar of Pellucidar* (New York: Metropolitan, May 29, 1930)
The thirty-third hardback by Burroughs first appeared in hardback in this first edition bound in dark blue cloth with black lettering on the front cover and spine. There is a wrap-around dust jacket and a black-and-white frontispiece by Paul F. Berdanier. The book is dedicated to Joan Burroughs Pierce II (ERB's granddaughter). Price: $2.00. 312 numbered pages.

521. *Tanar of Pellucidar* (New York: Grosset & Dunlap, 1931)
The first reprint is this early G&D bound in red cloth with black lettering on the front cover and spine, and with the tops of the pages dyed green. The earliest printing has 30 ERB titles listed in the advertisements at the back of the book. The dust jacket art and frontispiece are the same as the Metropolitan first edition by Paul F. Berdanier. Price: 75¢. 312 numbered pages.

522. *Tanar of Pellucidar* (New York: Grosset & Dunlap, 1940)
The second reprint is bound in red cloth with black lettering on the front cover and spine. The dust jacket is the same as the Metropolitan first edition by Paul F. Berdanier, but the book can be distinguished from the 1931 reprinting by the absence of a frontispiece. Price: 75¢. 312 numbered pages.

523. *Tanar of Pellucidar* (New York: Canaveral Press, Inc., October 19, 1962)
The Canaveral reprint is bound in tan cloth with dark brown lettering on the front cover and spine. The new dust jacket design and seven interior black-and-white illustrations are by Mahlon Blaine. Price: $2.75, raised to $2.95 in 1963. 245 numbered pages.

524. *Tanar of Pellucidar* (New York: Ace Books, Inc., December 1962)
The first paperback edition has Roy G. Krenkel's cover illustration and title page drawing. Stock No. F-171, price 40¢. 224 numbered pages.

BY EDGAR RICE BURROUGHS

525. *At the Earth's Core / Pellucidar / Tanar of Pellucidar: Three Science Fiction Novels by Edgar Rice Burroughs* (New York: Dover Publications, Inc., December 1963)
   This Dover paperback collection has dark blue covers with yellow lettering on the front cover and spine. An illustration by J. Allen St. John provides the cover art and 12 black-and-white illustrations; in addition there is one illustration by Paul F. Berdanier. The three stories are consecutively paginated. Price: $2.00. 433 numbered pages.

526. *At the Earth's Core / Pellucidar / Tanar of Pellucidar: Three Science Fiction Novels by Edgar Rice Burroughs* (New York: Peter Smith, 1963)
   This is a hardbound library binding whose inside is identical with the Dover paperback collection. Although this is a hardback, it did not have a dust jacket. The three stories are consecutively paginated. Price: $3.50. 433 numbered pages.

527. *Tanar of Pellucidar* (New York: Ace Books, Inc.)
   The second paperback edition has the same Roy G. Krenkel cover illustration and title page drawing. Stock No. G-735, price 50¢. 224 numbered pages.

528. *Tanar of Pellucidar* (New York: Ace Books, Inc.)
   The third paperback edition has the same Roy G. Krenkel cover illustration and title page drawing. Stock No. 70791, price 60¢. 224 numbered pages.

529. *Tanar of Pellucidar* (New York: Ace Books, Inc., January 1973)
   The fourth paperback edition has new Frank Frazetta cover art. Stock No. 79792, price 75¢. 250 numbered pages.

530. *Tanar of Pellucidar* (New York: Ballantine-Del Rey, May 1990)
   The first Ballantine paperback edition has a cover illustration by David B. Mattingly. Stock No. 36670, price $3.95. 229 numbered pages.

Tarzan and the Ant Men

531. "Tarzan and the Ant Men" (ARGOSY ALL-STORY WEEKLY, February 2, 9, 16, 23; March 1, 8, 15, 1924)
   This is the tenth Tarzan story, and was shorter in the magazine version than in the hardback book. It first appeared as a seven-part serial with a first-installment front cover illustration by Stockton Mulford. In addition, Roger B. Morrison supplied one interior black-and-white illustration for each issue. The cost

was 10¢ apiece. Burroughs had completed *The Bandit of Hell's Bend* a month before starting this story on June 20, 1923.

―――――――――――― FIRST EDITION ――――――――――

532. *Tarzan and the Ant Men* (Chicago: A.C. McClurg & Co., September 30, 1924)

This was the twentieth hardback ERB published, and his tenth in the Tarzan series. The first edition is bound in brown cloth with dark brown lettering on the front cover and spine. There is an exquisite wrap-around dust jacket and a sepia frontispiece which is a reversed mirror-image of the jacket, done by J. Allen St. John. There is a four-page appendix at the back by Robert Hobart Davis entitled "How Burroughs Wrote the Tarzan Tales." Davis was the editor at ALL-STORY when ERB submitted his very first manuscripts in 1911. The hardback edition restored Burroughs' original material on Esteban Miranda and the native girl, and the later elements of the Miranda subplot, and the original wording of the last two chapters. A.C. McClurg records indicate that 10,000 copies of the first edition were printed. Price: $2.00. 346 (+4) pages.

533. *Tarzan and the Ant Men* (A "Mixed Edition": McClurg and Grosset & Dunlap, 1925)

This edition is bound in orange cloth with black lettering on the front cover and spine. The spine says "Grosset & Dunlap" but we find "A.C. McClurg & Co." on the title page. It is not clear whether the frontispiece of the first edition exists on this version. Some collectors report the frontispiece is omitted, and others have copies where the frontispiece is present. The dust jacket is a Grosset & Dunlap dust jacket with the same St. John illustration. This also contains the four-page article at the end by Robert H. Davis. Price: 75¢. 346 (+4) numbered pages.

534. *Tarzan and the Ant Men* (New York: Grosset & Dunlap, 1925)

The G&D is bound in the usual bright red cloth with black lettering on the front cover and spine. There are 11 ERB books listed in the advertising pages at the back of the book. Later printings list 15, 23, 25, or more titles at the back of the book. In the 1930s, there is a variant with the tops of the pages dyed yellow. The dust jacket and frontispiece are the same as the previous reprint above, but the Davis article is omitted. On the reverse side of the very earliest G&D dust jacket we find 13 ERB titles listed. Price: 75¢. 346 numbered pages.

535. *Tarzan and the Ant Men* (New York: Grosset & Dunlap, 1940)

There are two differences between this reprinting and the 1925 reprint above. First, the frontispiece by St. John is omitted (in general, the 1940s series of G&D reprints seem to have been without interior illustrations). In addition, the tops of the pages are dyed green. 346 numbered pages.

BY EDGAR RICE BURROUGHS

Original McClurg first edition dust jacket for *Tarzan and the Ant Men* (1924)

536. *Tarzan and the Ant Men* (New York: Grosset & Dunlap, 1943)
The thin inexpensive World War II wartime edition is bound in dark red or maroon cloth with black lettering on the front cover and spine. It uses the same dust jacket by J. Allen St. John, except the jacket has the "Madison Square" label on the spine. The title page is decorated with the justly famous St. John "Tarzan and the Golden Lion" logo. There is no frontispiece. The book was sold for 50¢ until 1945, when the price was changed to 49¢. 346 numbered pages.

537. *Tarzan and the Ant Men* (Racine, WI: Whitman Publishing Company, 1945)
This is one of the Better Little Books cheaply made and designed for children. This series of books measures 3½" wide by 4⅜" high, and averages about 1¼" in width. The cover is by ERB's son, John Coleman Burroughs, with 171 interior illustrations by Rex Maxon abridged from the 1932 newspaper strip. For more information on these, see #932–968. Book no. 144. 352 pages.

538. *Tarzan and the Ant Men* (New York: Grosset & Dunlap, January 1950)
The first reprinting of the 1950 series is bound in green decorated cloth with black lettering on the spine. The dust jacket painting is by an artist who remains unidentified (Heins mistakenly identifies the artist as E. Monroe, p. 64). The endpages are decorated with a map of Africa, and there is a title page drawing, both by Rafael Palacios. There are no interior illustrations. The 1950 G&D printing sold for $1.00; it was reissued in 1955 with tan paper boards for $1.25, and later printed in 1958 without the end-paper maps for $1.50. 346 numbered pages.

539. *Tarzan and the Ant-Men* (New York: Ballantine Books, July 1963)
This is the first U.S. paperback edition with a front cover illustration by Richard Powers. Stock No. F 754, price 50¢. 188 numbered pages.

540. *Tarzan and the Ant Men* (New York: Grosset & Dunlap, 1967)
This hardback is bound in pictorial boards with front cover art by an artist who remains unidentified. The title page has the Rafael Palacios decorations but there are no interior illustrations. Stock No. 2632. 346 numbered pages.

541. *Tarzan and the Ant-Men* (New York: Ballantine Books, October 1969)
This is the third U.S. paperback edition with a new front cover illustration by Robert Abbett. Stock No. 01752, price 50¢. 188 numbered pages.

542. *Tarzan and the Ant-Men* (New York: Ballantine Books, November 1976)

BY EDGAR RICE BURROUGHS

This is the sixth Ballantine paperback edition with a new front cover illustration by Boris Vallejo. Stock No. 24169, price $1.25. 188 numbered pages.

Tarzan and the Castaways

543. "Tarzan and the Champion" (THE BLUE BOOK MAGAZINE, April 1940)
Written in July of 1939, this Burroughs story appeared complete in one issue of BLUE BOOK for 25¢ with seven tinted and black-and-white illustrations by L. R. Gustavson. This became the second story in the hardback *Tarzan and the Castaways*.

544. "Tarzan and the Jungle Murders" (THRILLING ADVENTURES, June 1940)
This story written by ERB in January, 1939, was originally entitled "Murder in the Jungle." It appeared complete in one issue for 10¢, with front cover illustration by Rudolph Belarski and 12 interior black-and-white illustrations by C. A. Murphy. This became the third story in the trilogy published as *Tarzan and the Castaways*.

545. "The Quest of Tarzan" (ARGOSY WEEKLY, August 23, 30; September 6, 1941)
When Burroughs finished "Beyond the Farthest Star," he began writing this story in November of 1940. The tale was serialized in three parts with a cover illustration (August 23rd) and one interior black-and-white illustration, each installment, by the famous fantasy artist, Virgil Finlay. Each issue cost 10¢. The magazine version is different in many subtle ways from the book, including character name changes, minor alterations in the characteristics of some characters, and the ending has been reworked slightly. It was later published in hardback as the first part of *Tarzan and the Castaways*. It is assumed that the Canaveral book reflects the actual words of ERB, and the ARGOSY version has been modified by an editor.

────────────── FIRST EDITION ──────────────

546. *Tarzan and the Castaways* (New York: Canaveral Press, Inc., 1965)
Clearly marked FIRST EDITION, this is the sixty-fifth hardback (there are 68 hardbacks in all, including *Marcia of the Doorstep* and *You Lucky Girl!*) by ERB. The first state of the first edition is bound in dark green with black lettering, and has erroneously listed a copyright date for the title. It is listed twice on the copyright page, once for 1941 and again, for 1965 instead of 1964. The

great fantasy artist, Frank Frazetta, did the dust jacket art and six interior black-and-white illustrations. The back of the dust jacket has an advertisement for Richard A. Lupoff's *Edgar Rice Burroughs: Master of Adventure*. There is also a "Bibliographic Note" by Richard A. Lupoff. Price: $3.50. 229 numbered pages.

547. *Tarzan and the Castaways* (New York: Canaveral Press, Inc., 1965)
Also marked FIRST EDITION, the second state of the first edition is bound in smooth brown or rose colored cloth with dark brown lettering, front cover and spine. The copyright error has been corrected, and has the title listed only *once* on the copyright page, for 1964. The same Frank Frazetta dust jacket art, and six interior black-and-white illustrations are present. There is also a "Bibliographic Note" by Richard A. Lupoff. 229 numbered pages.

548. *Tarzan and the Castaways* (New York: Ballantine Books, July 1965)
First Ballantine paperback edition with front cover art by Robert Abbett. Stock No. U2024, price 50¢. 191 numbered pages.

549. *Tarzan and the Castaways* (New York: Ballantine Books, March 1974)
Second Ballantine paperback printing with different lettering and a cropped reproduction of the Abbett cover. Price 50¢. 191 numbered pages.

550. *Tarzan and the Castaways* (New York: Canaveral Press, Inc., 1975)
This is a reprint of the 1965 Canaveral first edition. The binding is textured and the lettering is gold. The front of the dust jacket is the same as the first edition; however, the back of the jacket has a photograph of Edgar Rice Burroughs instead of an ad for Lupoff's *Edgar Rice Burroughs: Master of Adventure*.

551. *Tarzan and the Castaways* (New York: Ballantine Books, September 1977)
Fourth Ballantine paperback printing has a new cover by Boris Vallejo. Price $1.75. 191 numbered pages.

552. "**The Quest of Tarzan**" (Michael Conran, A free supplement to issue #34 of the fanzine EDGAR RICE BURROUGHS NEWS DATELINE, May 1989).
This is a quality full-size reprinting of the magazine appearance of "**The Quest of Tarzan.**" It has a full color cover by Mike Cody, and the back cover is a reproduction of the Virgil Finlay art used on the cover of the August 23, 1941, ARGOSY WEEKLY. The editor, Michael Conran, provides an interesting but brief analysis of the changes the ARGOSY editor made to ERB's original manuscript, and a summary of the differences between the first edition and the 1975 reprint.

BY EDGAR RICE BURROUGHS

Tarzan and the City of Gold

553. "Tarzan and the City of Gold" (ARGOSY, March, 12, 19, 26; April 2, 9, 16, 1932)
This Tarzan story, written in November of 1931 directly after *Pirates of Venus*, was initially published as a serial in six parts with the front cover painting by Paul Stahr. In addition, there is one interior black-and-white illustration by Samuel Cahan for each installment. In the March 12th first issue is a brief autobiographical sketch by Burroughs with a photograph. Each issue cost 10¢. Finishing this, Burroughs began work on **"Pirate Blood."**

FIRST EDITION
---

554. *Tarzan and the City of Gold* (Tarzana: Edgar Rice Burroughs, Inc., September 1, 1933)
The first edition of Burroughs' fortieth hardback is bound in the usual pebbled blue cloth with orange lettering on the front cover and spine. This is the first book to come from ERB, Inc. to have the copyright page clearly marked "First Edition," reflecting the author's growing recognition of the value of his books to collectors (the first four titles published by ERB, Inc. did not say "First Edition" but are easily distinguished by their blue covers). There is a dust jacket and five interior black-and-white plates by J. Allen St. John. Price: $2.00. 316 numbered pages.

---

555. *Tarzan and the City of Gold* (Tarzana: Edgar Rice Burroughs, Inc., 1934)
This is identical with the first edition described above, but the copyright page is marked "Second Edition." There is a dust jacket and five interior black-and-white plates by J. Allen St. John. It is probable that there were fewer copies of the second printing than there were in the first; the book seems noticeably rarer than the first edition. Price: $2.00. 316 numbered pages.

556. *Tarzan and the City of Gold* (New York: Grosset & Dunlap, 1935)
The first G&D reprint is bound in red cloth with black lettering on the front cover and spine, and the page tops are dyed green. It uses the same St. John dust jacket and five black-and-white illustrations. The title page is decorated with "Tarzan and the Golden Lion" logo by St. John. The back panel of the earliest dust jacket lists 34 ERB books and has a synopsis of *Tarzan Triumphant* on the back flap. Price: 75¢. 316 numbered pages.

557. *Tarzan and the City of Gold* (New York: Grosset & Dunlap, 1935)
The second G&D reprint is bound in red cloth with black lettering on the front cover and spine. This is distinguished from #556 above by the omission of

all five of the interior St. John plates, but it includes the frontispiece. Price: 75¢. 316 numbered pages.

558. *Tarzan and the City of Gold* (New York: Grosset & Dunlap, 1940)
The 1940 reprint is bound in the usual red cloth with black lettering on the front cover and spine. It also has the St. John dust jacket and decorated title page, but lacks the frontispiece and all other interior illustrations (typical of the 1940s G&D reprints). Price: 75¢. 316 numbered pages.

559. *Tarzan and the City of Gold* (Tarzana: Edgar Rice Burroughs, Inc., March 26, 1948)
This 1948 reprint is bound in the usual tan-gray boards with blue lettering on the front cover and spine. The dust jacket and frontispiece are those by J. Allen St. John. Price: $1.00. 316 numbered pages.

560. *Tarzan and the City of Gold* (Racine, WI: Whitman Publishing Company, October 6, 1952)
This "Authorized Abridged Edition" is bound in rust-colored boards with a blue and yellow cover illustration and lettering. It is clearly marked "No. 2307" which is the Whitman series number. There is a dust jacket illustration (front and back) by Don McLoughlin. In addition, there are illustrated endpapers and 12 interior black-and-white illustrations by Jesse Marsh. 250 numbered pages.

561. *Tarzan and the City of Gold* (Racine, WI: Whitman Publishing Company, 1954)
This book, #1533 in the Whitman series, lacks the dust jacket and instead is bound in pictorial boards (the same dust wrapper art by Don McLoughlin). Illustrated endpapers, title page, and numerous interior illustrations in blue tint by Tony Sgroi. The same abridged edition. 282 numbered pages.

562. *Tarzan and the City of Gold* (New York: Ace Books, Inc., June 1963)
The first paperback appearance has front cover art and a title page drawing by Frank Frazetta. Stock No. F-205, price 40¢. 191 numbered pages.

563. *Tarzan and the City of Gold* (New York: Ballantine Books, March 1964)
The first Ballantine paperback has cover art by Richard Powers. Stock No. U2016, price 50¢. 190 numbered pages.

564. *Tarzan and the City of Gold* (Racine, WI: Whitman Publishing Company, 1966)
This Whitman edition is ⅛" taller than the previous Whitman edition. It

is bound in shiny laminated pictorial boards (using the same dust wrapper art by Don McLoughlin). It uses the same illustrated endpapers, title page, and numerous interior tinted illustrations (some blue, some green, some mauve) by Tony Sgroi. The endpapers are green tint on one side, mauve on the other. The title page illustration is also mauve. The text is the same "authorized abridged" edition. 282 numbered pages.

565. *Tarzan and the City of Gold* (New York: Ballantine Books, April 1970)
The second Ballantine paperback edition has new cover art by Robert Abbett. Stock No. 01910, price 75¢. 190 numbered pages.

566. *Tarzan and the City of Gold* (New York: Ballantine Books, November 1975)
The fourth Ballantine paperback edition has new cover art by Neal Adams. Stock No. 24486, price $1.25. 190 numbered pages.

567. *Tarzan and the City of Gold* (New York: Ballantine–Del Rey, June 1991)
The eleventh Ballantine paperback edition uses the same cover art by Neal Adams. Stock No. 28987, price $3.95. 190 numbered pages.

Tarzan and the Forbidden City

568. "The Red Star of Tarzan" (ARGOSY WEEKLY, March 19, 26; April 2, 9, 16, 23, 1938)
After completing *Carson of Venus*, Burroughs began work on this controversial Tarzan story, written between October and November of 1937. It was published as a six-part serial, 10¢ each issue, with a front cover illustration on the March 19th installment (with Tarzan looking very much like Johnny Weissmuller) by Rudolph Belarski. Each issue also has one interior black-and-white illustration by Samuel Cahan. The book is Burroughs' revised version of Rob Thompson's adaption of an earlier ERB plot, which was then used for the 1934 Tarzan radio serial entitled "Tarzan and the Diamond of Asher." This ARGOSY WEEKLY Tarzan tale is significantly different from the book published by ERB, Inc. in September 1938. Robert R. Barrett reports that Chandler Whipple, editor at ARGOSY turned ERB's manuscript over to Ben Nelson and Burroughs Mitchell, the son of Edward Page Mitchell, to rewrite and expand. In general, Burroughs allowed editors to make changes, but when the hardback book was finally published, it was always ERB's own words. Neither the magazine nor book versions

are considered one of the better Tarzan books. In addition, ERB himself wrote the continuity for the newspaper comic strip of the same title which ran from September 2 to September 30, 1937, before the ARGOSY story was published.

───────── FIRST EDITION ─────────

569. *Tarzan and the Forbidden City* (Tarzana: Edgar Rice Burroughs, Inc., September 15, 1938)

Clearly marked "First Edition," this is the fifty-first hardback published by Burroughs. It is bound in the traditional pebbled blue cloth with red lettering on the front cover and spine. There are many important differences between this hardback story and the version printed as **"The Red Star of Tarzan,"** the first magazine printing described above, including an additional villain added to the hardback. John Coleman Burroughs (ERB's youngest son) did the dust jacket illustration, the color frontispiece, and four interior black-and-white plates. This is the only ERB book which has a *color* frontispiece. As with other books of this period, there is both a laminated and unlaminated jacket. 315 numbered pages. Henry Hardy Heins' *Golden Anniversary Bibliography* tentatively lists a 1940 reprint, but no such book has ever turned up. Heins suggested that perhaps ERB, Inc. remaindered their first edition in Grosset & Dunlap dust jackets in 1940. In this context, Burroughs scholar and collector C.B. Hyde notes that it was not unusual for genuine ERB, Inc. first editions to drop in price from $2.00 to 75¢ (the price of the G&D reprints) when a new ERB title was published. In the absence of any definitive information, a 1940 reprint is not listed separately in this book.

570. *Tarzan in* [sic] *the Forbidden City* (Los Angeles: Bantam Books, 1940)

This reprint is significant because it is the very first ERB book to be published as a paperback. This 4½" × 6" book is a 100 page abridgment, and is marked as "No. 23" in the Bantam series (there were 29 titles in all). The series was sold for 10¢ from vending machines at airports and train stations until about 1943. This title appears with at least three different covers. It is unknown which is first, although the two without cover illustrations are thought to be earliest. They are usually listed as follows:

(1) Green cover border with "Bantam Books" in large white letters, title space and blurb in black letters on a *yellow*-orange block with a rooster trademark logo in red in a yellow-orange circle. The spine is orange with black letters.

(2) Green cover but the title block is *blue* and the trademark logo rooster is purple on a blue circle. The spine is green with black letters.

(3) This one has an *illustrated* laminated cover by an unknown artist ("Gretter"?), with a drawing of Tarzan's upper torso with his face in profile, and a snarling lion crouching behind his right shoulder. "Tarzan" is in bright red letters, and "in the Forbidden City" is in black letters. The Bantam logo is in the lower right of the cover. The spine is green with yellow lettering. Each is 100 numbered pages.

571. *Tarzan and the Forbidden City* (Tarzana: Edgar Rice Burroughs, Inc., March 26, 1948)
The 1948 reprint is bound in the usual tan-gray boards with blue lettering on the front cover and spine. The dust jacket art is the same, but the color frontispiece has been replaced by a monochromatic reproduction of the dust jacket illustration, cropped to eliminate the lettering. Price: $1.00. 315 numbered pages.

572. *Tarzan and the Forbidden City* (Racine, WI: Whitman Publishing Company, October 6, 1952)
This abridgement is bound in pale blue decorated boards with an ape on the front cover and dark brown lettering on the spine. The dust jacket artist is Don McLoughlin. The endpapers are illustrated and there are 17 interior black-and-white illustrations, all by comic book artist Jesse Marsh. This is Whitman series #2306. It was sold for 49¢. 250 numbered pages.

573. *Tarzan and the Forbidden City* (Racine, WI: Whitman Publishing Company, 1954)
The dust jacket illustration on this abridged Whitman edition has been printed on the pictorial boards (no dust jacket). The new endpages, illustrated title page, and interior illustrations are by Tony Sgroi. #1520 on the spine. Price: 49¢. 282 numbered pages.

574. *Tarzan and the Forbidden City* (New York: Ballantine Books, March 1964)
This is the first Ballantine paperback printing. It has front cover art by Richard Powers. Stock No. U2020, price 50¢. 191 numbered pages.

575. *Tarzan and the Forbidden City* (Racine, WI: Whitman Publishing Company, 1966)
This Whitman edition is ⅛" taller than the previous Whitman edition. It is bound in shiny laminated pictorial boards (using the same dust wrapper art by Don McLoughlin). It uses the same illustrated endpapers, title page, and numerous interior tinted illustrations (some blue, some green, some mauve) by Tony Sgroi. The endpapers are green tint on one side, mauve on the other. The title page illustration is also mauve. The text is the same "authorized abridged" edition. Stock No. 1520:49. 282 numbered pages.

576. *The Red Star of Tarzan* (Kansas City, MO: BURROUGHS BULLETIN #41-44, 1974)
This is a photographic reprint of the ARGOSY WEEKLY serial listed above as #568. It has the same front cover illustration by Rudolph Belarski, and all interior black-and-white illustrations found in the original. Vern Coriell did his usual thorough job of providing relevant information in a brief preface. A very

professional fanzine publication in stiff paper covers. The book measures 5½" × 8". 56 unnumbered pages.

577. *Tarzan and the Forbidden City* (New York: Ballantine Books, September 1977)
This is the fourth Ballantine printing. It has a new front cover by Boris Vallejo. Stock No. 25960, price $1.75. 191 numbered pages.

Tarzan and "The Foreign Legion"

———————————FIRST EDITION———————————

578. *Tarzan and "The Foreign Legion"* (Tarzana: Edgar Rice Burroughs, Inc., August 22, 1947)
The last Tarzan story published by ERB, Inc., and the last Tarzan story published during Burroughs' lifetime, this was inspired by ERB's activities as a war correspondent. It was written between June and September 1944, during World War II while he was living in Honolulu. This first edition was the fifty-eighth hardback published, and is bound in the usual ERB, Inc. blue cloth with red lettering on the front cover and spine. The copyright page "First Edition" imprint is present. John Coleman Burroughs provided the dust jacket and five interior black-and-white illustrations. There is a prefatory note by ERB dated Honolulu, 11 September 1944. This is one of the easiest to find of all the ERB, Inc. published first editions. Price: $2.00. 314 numbered pages. Two years after completing this tale, Burroughs started one more Tarzan novel, but only got as far as 83 typewritten pages. The manuscript was completed by Joe R. Lansdale in 1994 and printed in 1995 by Dark Horse as *Tarzan: The Lost Adventure* (see #741–746).

579. *Tarzan and "The Foreign Legion"* (New York: Ballantine Books, March 1964)
The first U.S. paperback edition has Richard Powers cover art. Stock No. U2022, price 50¢. 192 numbered pages.

580. *Tarzan and "The Foreign Legion"* (New York: Ballantine Books, September 1977)
The fourth Ballantine paperback edition has new Boris Vallejo cover art. Stock No. 25962, price $1.75. 192 numbered pages.

BY EDGAR RICE BURROUGHS

Tarzan and the Golden Lion

581. "Tarzan and the Golden Lion" (ARGOSY ALL-STORY WEEKLY, December 9, 16, 23, 30, 1922; January 6, 13, 20, 1923)
This seven-part serial, written between February and May 1922, directly after *The Girl from Hollywood*, had a front cover illustration (December 9th) by P. J. Monahan. In addition, there is one interior black-and-white illustration, each installment, by Stout. Each issue cost 10¢. The ARGOSY editor, Robert Davis, wrote a Foreword to the magazine version which was not included in the book. Finishing this, Burroughs began to write "**The Moon Maid.**"

―――――――――――― FIRST EDITION ――――――――――――
582. *Tarzan and the Golden Lion* (Chicago: A.C. McClurg & Co., March 24, 1923)
The first edition of the ninth Tarzan story, and sixteenth hardback by ERB, is bound in a mustard-yellow cloth (Heins describes it as "olive") with black lettering on the front cover and spine. The dust jacket and eight interior sepia plates are by J. Allen St. John. These illustrations are the source for the classic image of Tarzan walking, spear in hand, alongside his golden lion. There are variations in the thickness of this book: some are rather thick, others are the standard width. This is a fairly easy first edition to find, because McClurg published 25,000 copies of the first edition, compared to a 5,000-15,000 copy average printing for most of the other titles. Price: $1.90. 333 numbered pages.

―――――――――――――――――――――――――――――――

583. *Tarzan and the Golden Lion* (New York: Grosset & Dunlap, 1924)
The first reprinting is bound in red cloth with black lettering on the front cover and spine. The same dust jacket and eight interior black-and-white illustrations by J. Allen St. John. This is distinguished from the second G&D reprinting by the fact that three of the page numbers listed on the Illustrations page are incorrect. They are correct for the original McClurg printing, but G&D put them elsewhere. Price: 75¢. 333 numbered pages.

584. *Tarzan and the Golden Lion* (New York: Grosset & Dunlap, 1924)
The second reprinting is also bound in red cloth with black lettering on the front cover and spine and had the same dust jacket and eight interior black-and-white illustrations by J. Allen St. John. This is distinguished from the first G&D reprinting by the fact that the Illustrations page numbers are corrected for the G&D pages. Price: 75¢. 333 numbered pages.

585. *Tarzan and the Golden Lion* (New York: Grosset & Dunlap, 1927)
This "Photoplay" edition was printed to take advantage of the release of the film by the same name starring Jim Pierce (who later became ERB's son-in-law)

as Tarzan. It is bound in orange cloth with black lettering on the front cover and spine. The dust wrapper is quite different from all previous printings: the colorful dust jacket and four black-and-white illustrations are stills from the movie featuring Jim Pierce. George McWhorter's *Catalog* (page 107) notes that the copyright page mistakenly attributes the copyright to Grosset & Dunlap, 1924. Actually, this was Grosset & Dunlap's error, switching copyright pages on two reprint editions they were apparently putting out at the same time. *The Iron Horse* by Edwin C. Hill (also a photoplay edition) has the full "Copyright Edgar Rice Burroughs 1923" page! Price: 75¢. 333 numbered pages.

586. *Tarzan and the Golden Lion* (New York: Grosset & Dunlap, 1929)
This second printing of the "Photoplay" edition is virtually identical to the 1927 edition described above; however, the G&D advertising section (the last pages of the book) lists advertisements for *Tarzan, Lord of the Jungle* and *The Master Mind of Mars*, which were not reprinted by Grosset & Dunlap until 1929. There are at least four different Photoplay editions with different advertisements for Burroughs titles at the back. Each sold for 75¢. 333 numbered pages.

587. *Tarzan and the Golden Lion* (New York: Grosset & Dunlap, 1930)
This Photoplay reprint is bound in orange cloth with black lettering on the front cover and spine. The dust jacket and eight interior black-and-white plates are by J. Allen St. John. The G&D advertising pages at the back of the book do *not* list *Tarzan and the Lost Empire*. 333 numbered pages.

588. *Tarzan and the Golden Lion* (New York: Grosset & Dunlap, 1931)
Reprinted one year later, this Photoplay copy is bound in typical G&D red cloth with black lettering on the front cover and spine. Dust jacket and eight interior black-and-white plates by J. Allen St. John. In the G&D advertising section at the rear of the book is found an advertisement for *Tarzan and the Lost Empire* (G&D 1931). Price: 75¢. 333 numbered pages.

589. *Tarzan and the Golden Lion* (New York: Grosset & Dunlap, 1940)
Also bound in typical G&D red cloth with black lettering on the front cover and spine. Dust jacket design by J. Allen St. John. This is not a Photoplay edition, and it has *no* interior illustrations (typical of the 1940s G&D reprints). Price: 75¢. 333 numbered pages.

590. *Tarzan and the Golden Lion* (New York: Grosset & Dunlap, 1943)
This is the thin "Madison Square" World War II cheap wartime edition bound in a dark red-maroon cloth with black lettering on the front cover and spine. The dust jacket and title page "Madison Square" logo are by J. Allen St. John. There are no interior illustrations. The "Madison Square" label is on the dust jacket. The book sold for 50¢ until 1945, and then 49¢ thereafter. 332 numbered pages.

BY EDGAR RICE BURROUGHS

©1993, Thomas Yeates

591. *Tarzan and the Golden Lion* (Racine, WI: Whitman Publishing Company, 1943)
This small but thick (3½" by 4⅜") inexpensive children's illustrated Big Little Book has paper boards. The striking cover image is by John Coleman Burroughs, and the 209 interior illustrations are reprintings of the Rex Maxon 1930-1931 daily newspaper strips. Robert R. Barrett notes that the first five illustrations of this title were not from the comic strip but were new to this book. Stock No. 1448. 432 pages.

592. *Tarzan and the Golden Lion* (New York: Grosset & Dunlap, July 1949)
This is bound in tan decorated *cloth* with black lettering on the spine. The dust jacket art is by C. Edmund Monroe. There is a decorated title page and end-paper maps of Africa by Rafael Palacios. There are no interior illustrations. This edition sold for $1.00. 332 numbered pages. There was a subsequent reprinting using tan paper boards instead of cloth, but including the end-paper maps. It sold for $1.25 in 1955. Later, G&D reprinted this title once again in 1958, without the end-paper maps, and sold it for $1.50.

593. *Tarzan and the Golden Lion* (New York: Ballantine Books, July 1963)
The first paperback printing has Richard Powers front cover art. Stock No. F-753, price 50¢. 191 numbered pages.

I. BIBLIOGRAPHY OF BOOKS

594. *Tarzan and the Golden Lion* (New York: Grosset & Dunlap, 1967)
This reprint hardback is bound in pictorial boards with white lettering on the front cover and spine. The front cover art is by C. E. Monroe. There is a decorated title page and no other interior illustrations. Stock No. 2633. 332 pages.

595. *Tarzan and the Golden Lion* (New York: Ballantine Books, October 1969)
The third paperback printing has a new cover by Robert Abbett. Stock No. 01751, price 50¢. 191 numbered pages.

596. *Tarzan and the Golden Lion* (New York: Ballantine Books, November 1976)
The sixth paperback printing has a new cover by Boris Vallejo. Stock No. 24168, price $1.25. 191 numbered pages.

Tarzan and the Jewels of Opar

597. "Tarzan and the Jewels of Opar" (ALL-STORY WEEKLY, November 18, 25; December 2, 9, 16, 1916)
About a month after completing "**Beyond Thirty,**" Burroughs began work on his fifth Tarzan story. He completed it in six weeks and one day, between September and October 1915. Robert Davis, the editor at ALL-STORY WEEKLY, accepted it, edited out approximately 7,000 words, and published it as a five-part serial with a front cover illustration on the November 18th issue by P. J. Monahan. Each issue sold for 10¢. There are no interior illustrations. A week after he finished this classic Tarzan novel, ERB began work on a short story which he called "**H.R.H. the Rider.**"

―――――――――― FIRST EDITION ――――――――――

598. *Tarzan and the Jewels of Opar* (Chicago: A.C. McClurg & Co., April 20, 1918)
This is the fifth Tarzan novel, and the sixth hardback published by Edgar Rice Burroughs. There is additional material about La of Opar to the hardback which did not appear in the magazine serial. The first edition is bound in dark green cloth with gold lettering on the front cover and spine. The dust jacket and eight coated halftone sepia plates are by J. Allen St. John. St. John also did the lettering on the dust jacket and the title page. The frontispiece depicts Tarzan seated in a tree, about to loose an arrow. There is a circle pattern made up of dots running through the title on the front cover. The imprint "W.F. Hall" appears on the copyright page. A price of $1.35 appears on the jacket spine. A.C. McClurg records indicate that a combined total of 50,000 copies of the first and one reprint-

ing were printed. It is interesting to note that approximately 7,300 words are in this book which were *not* in the original magazine appearance. It is believed that they were excised by the editor at ALL-STORY WEEKLY. 350 numbered pages.

599. *Tarzan and the Jewels of Opar* (Chicago: A.C. McClurg & Co., 1919)

This first reprint, from 1919, is bound in a very dark green cloth with gold lettering on the front cover and spine. It differs from the first edition only in that the 1919 date appears on the title page. Price: $1.35. 350 numbered pages.

600. *Tarzan and the Jewels of Opar* (New York: A.L. Burt Company, Publishers, 1919)

The earliest reprint by Burt is bound in dark green or gray with black lettering on the front cover and spine. The typeface and circle of dots pattern on the cover is identical to the McClurg first edition. This version also has a "Cuneo-Henneberry" printer's imprint on the copyright page, and the St. John dust jacket, but only one interior illustration, the frontispiece of Tarzan sitting in a tree, aiming an arrow. Original price was 75¢. 350 numbered pages.

601. *Tarzan and the Jewels of Opar* (New York: A.L. Burt Company, Publishers, 1920)

This title was so popular that there was an immediate Burt reprinting. It is bound in light blue cloth with black lettering on the front cover and spine. As with the first edition and previous A.L. Burt reprint,, the author's name appears on the bottom of the cover in two lines, "Edgar Rice / Burroughs." It has the "Cuneo-Henneberry" printer's imprint on the copyright page. The color of the cloth cover has changed, and the size of the book has changed: this is 4⅞" × 7⁷⁄₁₆" (standard Burt size was 5" × 7½"). In addition, the frontispiece has changed: it uses a different St. John illustration, "Tarzan Crept Forward, Chulk and Taglat Following Behind." The dust jacket and frontispiece are by J. Allen St. John. This book originally sold for 75¢. 350 numbered pages.

602. *Tarzan and the Jewels of Opar* (New York: A.L. Burt Company, Publishers, 1920?)

These later Burt reprintings are bound in light green, medium blue, medium gray, light green, medium green, and olive green cloth covers. Three marks distinguish these reprints from the earlier ones: (1) on the copyright page there is *no* "Cuneo-Henneberry" printer's mark; (2) on the front cover, the author's name has been reset to a slightly different typeface and now appears in one line instead of two, and (3) there is no circular pattern of dots surrounding the book title. The dust jacket and frontispiece are by J. Allen St. John. The year of publication for these later reprints can be approximated by examining the ERB books advertised at the back of the book. Price 75¢. 350 numbered pages.

I. BIBLIOGRAPHY OF BOOKS

"Tarzan and the Jewels of Opar" November 18, 1916

603. "**Tarzan and the Jewels of Opar**" (THE VIRGINIA LEADER, June-December 1920; January and February, 1921; supplementary issue March 1921)
This Tarzan tale was serialized in this small digest sized magazine of about

20 pages, printed for a boy's organization similar to the Boy Scouts called the "Lone Scouts and Junior Naval Reserves." The publisher is identified as J. Welford Barker. There are interior illustrations by artist Frank Parker, identified as "P." The June 1920 and January 1921 issues have a Tarzan cover illustration also by "P" (other issues may also have ERB cover illustrations). The story was not quite finished in the February issue, and so a supplement completing the story was sent to each subscriber in March, 1921. Each issue sold for 5¢.

604. *Tarzan and the Jewels of Opar* (A "Mixed Edition": McClurg and Grosset & Dunlap, 1927)
Some remaining McClurg pages were rebound by Grosset & Dunlap in the usual red cloth with black lettering on the front cover and spine. The St. John dust jacket and all eight interior illustrations (the McClurg pages) are present. Price: 75¢. 350 numbered pages.

605. *Tarzan and the Jewels of Opar* (New York: Grosset & Dunlap, 1927)
The first true G&D reprint is bound in the usual red cloth with black lettering on the front cover and spine, and has 23 ERB titles listed in the advertising pages at the back of the book. The St. John dust jacket and one frontispiece of Tarzan and the two apes following behind, are unchanged. G&D reprinted this title numerous times in the next twelve years; the only thing that changes is the list of book titles which appear at the very end of the book: 25 titles, 28 titles, 30 or 33 titles, etc. In the 1930s, one variation has the tops of the pages dyed yellow, and later still, green. Price: 75¢. 350 numbered pages.

606. *Tarzan and the Jewels of Opar* (Racine, WI: Whitman Publishing Company, 1940)
This Better Little Book is an illustrated retelling of the story intended for children. It was the equivalent of a child's comic book. It is bound in paper boards and measures 3¾" wide by 4½" high. The cover illustration is by Robert Weisman, with 214 interior illustrations by Rex Maxon. The interior is abridged from the 102 daily panels (4 illustrations each day making 408 total) originally printed in the 1930 daily newspaper comic strip (episodes concerning La of Opar are omitted). Stock No. 1495. 432 pages.

607. *Tarzan and the Jewels of Opar* (New York: Grosset & Dunlap, 1940)
This reprint is bound in the standard G&D red cloth with black lettering on the front cover and spine. The tops of the pages are dyed green. It is distinguished from the prior G&D reprintings by the absence of any interior art by J. Allen St. John. 350 numbered pages.

608. *Tarzan and the Jewels of Opar* (New York: Grosset & Dunlap, 1943)
The World War II thin and cheap "Madison Square" wartime edition is bound in maroon cloth with black lettering on the front cover and spine. The

I. BIBLIOGRAPHY OF BOOKS

dust jacket is the same cover illustration as in the previous editions; there is no frontispiece, but there is a small decoration on the title page by J. Allen St. John. Original price was 50¢, and then 49¢ after 1945. 350 numbered pages.

609. *Tarzan and the Jewels of Opar* (New York: Grosset & Dunlap, January 1950)

The first of the post-war reprintings initially sold for $1.00 and are bound in decorated blue-green *cloth* with black lettering on the spine. The dust jacket illustration is by C. Edmund Monroe, Jr. As with the other post-war reprints, this has illustrated endpapers (a map of Africa) and decorated title page by Rafael Palacios. Subsequent reprintings had paperbound boards in tan with brown decorations and lettering. The price was raised to $1.25 in 1955. The last reprinting (1958) omitted the end-paper map, and sold for $1.50. 350 numbered pages.

610. *Tarzan and the Jewels of Opar* (New York: Ace Books, Inc., May 1963)

The first paperback edition has a cover painting and title page drawing by Frank Frazetta. In addition the editor has supplied a subtitle: "The Jungle Secret of / The Lost Atlantis." Stock No. F 204, price 40¢. 192 numbered pages.

611. *Tarzan and the Jewels of Opar* (New York: Ballantine Books, July 1963)

The first Ballantine paperback edition has cover art by Richard Powers. Stock No. F 749, price 50¢. Ballantine printed the first ten Tarzan books simultaneously in July 1963, and they were sold out almost immediately. This title was reprinted again in November 1963. 158 numbered pages.

612. "Tarzan and the Jewels of Opar" plus art portfolio (Kansas City, MO: House of Greystoke, 1964)

This is an interesting paperbound book done by Vern Coriell. The front cover says "The Burroughs Bibliophile / PRESENTS / Tarzan / and the / Jewels of Opar." This edition was designed to accompany a folio of 17 exceptionally fine pen-and-ink line drawings which J. Allen St. John drew especially for the art director of the CHICAGO HERALD, and which were used to illustrate the 1918 newspaper appearance of this story. These illustrations were discovered in 1954 by Burroughs art enthusiast Robert R. Barrett. The text itself is primarily a reproduction of the original ALL-STORY WEEKLY magazine appearance of 1916. However, some segments are from THE VIRGINIA LEADER ("Virginia's Best Boy's Magazine" from 1920) and contain illustrations by Frank Parker. Mr. Coriell has provided a detailed pictorial bibliography at the end of the publication. 124 numbered pages.

613. *Tarzan and the Jewels of Opar* (New York: Grosset & Dunlap, 1967)
This hardback reprint is bound in pictorial boards with the same cover art by C. E. Monroe. The title page is decorated. There are no interior illustrations. Stock No. 2634. 349 (+1) numbered pages.

614. *Tarzan and the Jewels of Opar* (New York: Ballantine Books, April 1969)
This is the third Ballantine paperback printing. It has new cover art by Robert Abbett. Stock No. 01595, price 50¢. 158 numbered pages.

615. *Tarzan and the Jewels of Opar* (New York: Ballantine Books, April 1975)
The sixth Ballantine paperback printing has new cover art by Neal Adams. Stock No. 24163, price 50¢. 158 numbered pages.

616. *Tarzan and the Jewels of Opar* (New York: Ballantine–Del Rey, May 1991)
The nineteenth Ballantine paperback printing has new cover art by Barclay Shaw. Stock No. 32161, price $3.95. 184 numbered pages.

Tarzan and the Leopard Men

617. "Tarzan and the Leopard Men" (THE BLUE BOOK MAGAZINE, August, September, October, November, December 1932; January 1933)
This Tarzan story was written between July and September 1931. About a week later, Burroughs began work on *Pirates of Venus*. This Tarzan tale was printed as a six-part serial with front cover illustrations on the first three issues by Joseph Chenoweth. Frank Hoban provided numerous interior black-and-white illustrations in each installment. This was during the great depression, and the August issue sold for 25¢, but the price per issue dropped to 15¢ in September because magazine sales were falling.

──────────── FIRST EDITION ────────────

618. *Tarzan and the Leopard Men* (Tarzana: Edgar Rice Burroughs, Inc., September 7, 1935)
This first edition was the forty-fourth hardback book published by Edgar Rice Burroughs. It is bound in the usual ERB, Inc. blue cloth with orange lettering on the front cover and spine. It has the usual "First Edition" imprint on the copyright page. It has a J. Allen St. John dust jacket and four interior black-

I. BIBLIOGRAPHY OF BOOKS

Original ERB, Inc. first edition dust jacket for *Tarzan and the Leopard Men* (1935)

and-white plates by St. John. There is a laminated and an unlaminated version of the dust jacket. Price: $2.00. 332 numbered pages.

619. *Tarzan and the Leopard Men* (New York: Grosset & Dunlap, 1937)
The first reprint is bound in red cloth with black lettering on the front cover and spine. The dust jacket and two interior plates are by J. Allen St. John (two plates are omitted). The endpapers are unusual; they have a reproduction of the Grosset & Dunlap dust jacket illustration from *Tarzan of the Apes* cut out, with the following message: "On the trail of reckless adventure, Tarzan encounters new breathtaking dangers! I am sure you will find more exciting thrills than ever before as you follow his spectacular daring through this book." A printed signature by Burroughs follows. The book sold for 75¢. 332 numbered pages.

620. *Tarzan and the Leopard Men* (New York: Grosset & Dunlap, 1938?)
This reprint is just like the 1937 reprint above, except it does not have the unusual endpapers, just the standard plain blank pages. 75¢, 332 numbered pages.

621. *Tarzan and the Leopard Men* (Tarzana: Edgar Rice Burroughs, Inc., 1940)
This reprint is one of the seven ERB, Inc. titles bound in red cloth with blue lettering on the front cover and spine. The first edition St. John dust jacket illustration and the frontispiece are present. Price: 75¢. 332 numbered pages.

622. *Tarzan and the Leopard Men* (Tarzana: Edgar Rice Burroughs, Inc., March 26, 1948)
This reprint is bound in the usual 1948 tan-gray boards with blue lettering on the front cover and spine. It has the same dust jacket wrap-around painting and black-and-white frontispiece by J. Allen St. John. Price: $1.00. 332 numbered pages.

623. *Tarzan and the Leopard Men* (New York: Ballantine Books, March 1964)
The first paperback printing has Richard Powers cover art. Stock No. U2018, price 50¢. 192 numbered pages.

624. *Tarzan and the Leopard Men* (New York: Ballantine Books, April 1970)
The second paperback printing has new Robert Abbett cover art. Stock No. 01912, price 75¢. 192 numbered pages.

625. *Tarzan and the Leopard Men* (New York: Ballantine Books, November 1975)

The fourth paperback printing has a new Neal Adams cover. Stock No. 24488, price $1.25. 192 numbered pages.

Tarzan and the Lion Man

626. "Tarzan and the Lion Man" (LIBERTY, November 11, 18, 25; December 2, 9, 16, 23, 30, 1933; January 6, 1934)

On February 9, 1933, three months after completing *Lost on Venus*, ERB began work on another Tarzan novel. It was accepted by LIBERTY and printed in a nine-part serial with eighteen impressive interior illustrations by Ray Dean, executed in black-and-white wash. Twelve of these have been color tinted. Each issue sold for 5¢. The magazine serial is slightly shorter than the book; it is thought that the LIBERTY editor may have made deletions. Six months after completing this, Burroughs returned to Mars with his next tale, *Swords of Mars*.

─────────────── FIRST EDITION ───────────────

627. *Tarzan and the Lion Man* (Tarzana: Edgar Rice Burroughs, Inc., September 1, 1934)

The first edition of the forty-second hardback by Burroughs is unusual because it is bound in *gray* decorated cloth (not the usual blue) with black lettering and a red "Janus" illustration from the dust jacket on the front cover and spine. The front of the first edition dust jacket has a red, black and gold "Janus" style face, with one facing left and the other facing right. The back has an advertisement for *Pirates of Venus*. There are five interior black-and-white plates by J. Allen St. John. Burroughs is reported to have felt that this was the weakest Tarzan story he had published. 318 numbered pages.

628. *Tarzan and the Lion Man* (Tarzana: Edgar Rice Burroughs, Inc., 1935)

The second ERB, Inc. printing is also bound in *gray* decorated cloth, although the book is about ⅛" thinner than the first. The interior is the same as the first edition with five interior plates. Bill Ross believes this may have been one of the "Mixed editions" with a Grosset & Dunlap dust jacket put over the ERB, Inc. printing and sold as a G&D book. It is unclear whether this sold for the ERB, Inc. price of $2.00, or the G&D price of 75¢. 318 numbered pages.

629. *Tarzan and the Lion Man* (New York: Grosset & Dunlap, 1936)

The first reprint is bound in the usual G&D red cloth with black lettering on the front cover and spine. The reprint dust jacket art (by St. John) is completely different from the first edition jacket illustration (the illustration on page

132 of the first edition was used for the reprint jacket). In addition, there are two (*not* five) interior black-and-white plates by St. John. One variant has the interior illustration facing page 280; another has the interior illustration facing page 282. The earliest dust jacket lists 37 ERB titles on the rear panel and has the price, 75¢, on the upper corner of the front flap. Price: 75¢. 318 numbered pages.

630. *Tarzan and the Lion Man* (New York: Grosset & Dunlap, 1940)
This reprint is distinguished from the earlier 1936 edition by its complete lack of all interior illustrations (typical of the 1940s G&D reprint series). It is bound in the usual G&D red cloth with black lettering on front cover and spine. Price: 75¢. 318 pages.

631. *Tarzan and the Lion Man* (Tarzana: Edgar Rice Burroughs, Inc., 1940)
The third ERB, Inc. printing is one of the seven titles bound in red cloth with blue lettering on the front cover and spine. The dust jacket is the same as the first edition jacket. In addition, there is a J. Allen St. John illustration on the cover and spine. There is only the one frontispiece by St. John. There are two types of red cloth used: one typical, the other a textured material that has a pressed pattern in the cloth to simulate the weave of cloth. Price: 75¢. 318 numbered pages.

632. *Tarzan and the Lion Man* (Tarzana: Edgar Rice Burroughs, Inc., March 26, 1948)
The 1948 reprint in tan-gray boards has a St. John decoration and lettering in blue on the front cover and spine. The dust jacket follows the Grosset & Dunlap reprint pattern, not the first edition jacket illustration by St. John on the front cover. The book uses the St. John frontispiece. Price: $1.00. 318 numbered pages.

633. *Tarzan and the Lion Man* (New York: Ace Books, Inc., July 1963)
The first paperback edition has Frank Frazetta front cover art and title page drawing. Stock No. F-212, price 40¢. 223 numbered pages.

634. *Tarzan and the Lion Man* (New York: Ballantine Books, March 1964)
First Ballantine paperback edition (but second paperback printing) has front cover art by Richard Powers. Stock No. U2017, price 50¢. 192 numbered pages.

635. *Tarzan and the Lion Man* (New York: Ballantine Books, April 1970)
The second Ballantine paperback printing uses new front cover art by Robert Abbett. Stock No. 01911, price 75¢. 192 numbered pages.

636. *Tarzan and the Lion Man* (New York: Ballantine Books, November 1975)
The fourth Ballantine paperback printing uses new front cover art by Neal Adams. Stock No. 24487, price $1.25. 192 numbered pages.

Tarzan and the Lost Empire

637. "Tarzan and the Lost Empire" (BLUE BOOK, October, November, December 1928; January, February, 1929)
This Tarzan story was written between March and May 1928. Burroughs' original title was "**Tarzan and the Lost Tribe**," and he began work on it directly after he finished *Tarzan and the Tarzan Twins with Jad-Bal-Ja, the Golden Lion*. This was published as a five-part serial with four Frank Hoban front cover illustrations in color (October, November, December and January) and 41 interior black-and-white illustrations. There were titles for each chapter. Each issue sold for 25¢. Four months after he finished this, Burroughs returned to the inner world of Pellucidar for "**Tanar of Pellucidar**."

──────────── FIRST EDITION ────────────

638. *Tarzan and the Lost Empire* (New York: Metropolitan Books, Inc., September 28, 1929)
This is ERB's thirty-second published hardback. Burroughs became convinced that he could make more money than A.C. McClurg & Co. was paying him in royalties, so he terminated his 15 year arrangement with McClurg. He took this Tarzan manuscript to Metropolitan Books, and this is the first of four books which Metropolitan published. The first edition is bound in smooth orange cloth with black lettering on the front cover and spine. There is a wrap-around dust jacket design and a black-and-white frontispiece by A. W. Sperry. Chapter titles of the magazine serial were omitted in the hardback. Price: $2.00. 313 numbered pages.

639. *Tarzan and the Lost Empire* ("Mixed Edition," New York: Metropolitan Books, Inc. and Grosset & Dunlap, 1931)
This is another "mixed edition" with Metropolitan pages (and a Metropolitan title page) bound in a Grosset & Dunlap binding and cover. It is bound in red cloth with black lettering on the front cover and spine and the tops of the pages are dyed green. The Grosset & Dunlap dust jacket design and black-and-white frontispiece are by A. W. Sperry. Price: 75¢. 313 numbered pages.

640. *Tarzan and the Lost Empire* (New York: Grosset & Dunlap, 1931)
The earliest reprint is bound in the usual red cloth with black lettering on

BY EDGAR RICE BURROUGHS

Original Metropolitan first edition dust jacket for *Tarzan and the Lost Empire* (1929)

the front cover and spine, and there are no advertisements at the end of the book. The G&D dust jacket and frontispiece are by A. W. Sperry, as with the "mixed edition." A later printing from the early 1930s has the tops of the pages dyed yellow, and a single page of advertisements begins to be included at the end of the book after 1933. Price: 75¢. 313 numbered pages.

641. *Tarzan and the Lost Empire* (New York: Grosset & Dunlap, 1940)
This reprint is bound in the usual red cloth with black lettering on the front cover and spine. It uses the same G&D dust jacket by A. W. Sperry, but there are no interior illustrations. The tops of the pages have been dyed green. Price: 75¢. 313 numbered pages.

642. *Tarzan and the Lost Empire* (Tarzana: Edgar Rice Burroughs, Inc., March 26, 1948)
The first ERB, Inc. reprint is bound in the usual tan-gray boards with blue lettering on the front cover and spine. The dust jacket and frontispiece are the A. W. Sperry art. Price: $1.00. 313 numbered pages.

643. *Tarzan and the Lost Empire* (Racine, WI: Whitman Publishing Company, 1948)
A Better Little Book with cover art that is a copy of a panel by Jesse Marsh from the first Dell Tarzan "one-shot" comic book #134, "Tarzan and the Devil Ogre." The 141 interior illustrations are by Rex Maxon from his 1930 daily comic strip. This is a small yet thick book with cardboard covers, intended for children. This book measures 3½" wide by 4⅜" high. Whitman number 1442. 288 pages. For more information on these, see #932–968.

644. *Tarzan and the Lost Empire* (New York: Dell, August 1951)
This 1951 Dell printing is the first paperback edition. It has front cover art by Robert Stanley and a back cover illustration of a map by Ruth Bellew. Dell Stock No. 536, price 25¢. 192 numbered pages.

645. *Tarzan and the Lost Empire* (New York: Ace Books, Inc., November 1962)
This first Ace paperback edition has cover art and a title page drawing by Frank Frazetta. Stock No. F-169, price 40¢. 192 numbered pages.

646. *Tarzan and the Lost Empire* (New York: Ballantine Books, October 1963)
The first Ballantine paperback edition has a cover illustration by Richard Powers. Stock No. F 777, price 50¢. 159 numbered pages.

647. *Tarzan and the Lost Empire* (New York: Ballantine Books, October 1969)
The second Ballantine paperback printing has a new cover illustration by Robert Abbett. Stock No. 01754, price 50¢. 159 numbered pages.

648. *Tarzan and the Lost Empire* (New York: Ballantine Books, November 1976)
The sixth Ballantine paperback printing has a new cover illustration by Boris Vallejo. Stock No. 24171, price $1.25. 159 numbered pages.

Tarzan and the Madman

―――――――――― FIRST EDITION ――――――――――

649. *Tarzan and the Madman* (New York: Canaveral Press, Inc., June 9, 1964)
The book says "First Edition" on the copyright page. This Tarzan novel was written during January and February, 1940, but never published in magazine form. When it was finally collected and published posthumously in hardback, it became the sixty-third book by ERB. It is bound in several different colors (my copy is light green cloth with black lettering on the front cover and spine). The Reed Crandall dust jacket is accompanied by eight interior black-and-white illustrations. Price: $3.50. 236 numbered pages. When Burroughs finished writing this, he began to work on *Escape on Venus*.

650. *Tarzan and the Madman* (New York: Ballantine Books, February 1965)
The first paperback printing has cover art by Robert Abbett. Stock No. U2023, price 50¢. 160 numbered pages.

651. *Tarzan and the Madman* (New York: Canaveral Press, Inc., 1975)
This printing is identical with the Canaveral first edition described above except for the date "1975" clearly marked on the title page.

652. *Tarzan and the Madman* (New York: Ballantine Books, September 1977)
The fourth Ballantine printing has a new cover illustration by Boris Vallejo. Stock No. 25963, price $1.75. 160 numbered pages.

I. BIBLIOGRAPHY OF BOOKS

Tarzan and the Tarzan Twins

NOTE: There are two separate children's stories under this heading. The first is the beautifully illustrated 1927 Volland book and its reprintings described below. The second is an immediate sequel whose events begin the next day (written in 1928). It appeared as a large (9½" × 7½") "BIG BIG BOOK" printed nine years later (1936) called *Tarzan and the Tarzan Twins with Jad-Bal-Ja, the Golden Lion*. This is more like a large coloring book with stiff cardboard covers and poor-quality paper. Note that in addition to these two, there is a smaller 1934 Whitman Big Little Book, and a Dell Fast Action Book (like a Big Little Book) entitled *Tarzan with the Tarzan Twins in the Jungle* (an adaptation of the 1927 Volland story with different artwork). For more information on these Dell and Whitman books, see #932–968.

653. *The Tarzan Twins* (Joliet–New York–Boston: Volland, before October 1927)
   This is a "printer's dummy" of this book. It appears to have all interior pages blank. The dust jacket art by Douglas Grant is reproduced in shades of gray on the jacket. It probably has 126 numbered pages. Printer's dummies were also produced by A.C. McClurg and by ERB, Inc. for many of their titles.

———————— FIRST EDITION ————————

654. *The Tarzan Twins* (Joliet–New York–Boston: Volland, October 10, 1927)
   The first edition is bound in pictorial boards with yellow lettering on front cover. The spine is just blue cloth with no lettering. The dust jacket art is by Douglas Grant. The front cover art, the illustrated endpapers, and the six color and thirty-six black-and-white illustrations are all by Douglas Grant. The book is clearly marked "First Edition" on the copyright page. Price: $1.50. 126 numbered pages.

655. *The Tarzan Twins* (Joliet–New York–Boston: Volland, 1927)
   Volland printed a "Second edition" in late 1927, but sold it in a beautiful pictorial box instead of a dust jacket. The front cover of the box is the same as the illustration on the front cover of the book. Price: $1.50.

656. *The Tarzan Twins* (Joliet–New York–Boston: Volland, 1927-1932?)

BY EDGAR RICE BURROUGHS

Front cover of *The Tarzan Twins* (Volland, 1927)

Between 1927 and 1932 there were at least seven editions printed by Volland. They are identical to the first edition, except each edition number is clearly printed on the copyright page, as "Fifth Edition" or "Seventh Edition," etc. In 1931, the price was reduced to $1.00, and then to 75¢ in 1932.

I. BIBLIOGRAPHY OF BOOKS

Front cover: *Tarzan and the Tarzan Twins with Jad-Bal-Ja, the Golden Lion* (1936)

———————— FIRST EDITION ————————
657. *Tarzan and the Tarzan Twins with Jad-Bal-Ja, the Golden Lion* (Racine, WI: Whitman Publishing Company, March 9, 1936)

BY EDGAR RICE BURROUGHS

This large (9½" × 7½") book is bound in pictorial boards with front cover art and interior drawings designed as a coloring book by Juanita Bennett (she also illustrated the Whitman Big Little Book of *Tarzan of the Apes* in 1933). It is clearly marked number 4056 in the Whitman series. The book sold for 29¢. 314 numbered pages. On the spine of the copy usually treated as the true first edition is the title and author's name, the Whitman catalog number 4056, and a small circular picture of Tarzan's face in profile.

There is one variant edition (it is unclear whether it was published before or after the copy described above): omitting the printed title and illustration, this has only the Whitman catalog number #4056 visible on the spine. Although Henry Heins' bibliography lists a third variant, subsequent investigation by Robert R. Barrett revealed that the book believed to be a variant was actually identical with the first version described above.

658. *Tarzan and the Tarzan Twins* (New York: Canaveral Press, Inc., November 30, 1963)

This book is not labeled "First Edition" on the copyright page. It is bound in yellow cloth with dark brown lettering on the front cover and spine. The dust jacket art and 19 interior black-and-white illustrations are by Roy G. Krenkel. This volume combines the text of both the 1927 Volland *The Tarzan Twins* and the 1936 Whitman *Tarzan and the Tarzan Twins*. Price: $3.50. 192 numbered pages.

659. *The Tarzan Twins* (Racine, WI: Whitman Publishing Company, 1934)

This is one of the small (3½" wide by 4⅜" high) and cheaply printed Big Little Books designed for children. This cover is by Hal Arbo, and it has 189 interior illustrations by Juanita Bennett telling the same story as in the larger book described above, condensed and slightly rewritten. Stock No. 770. It was reprinted in 1935. 432 pages. For more information on these children's Big Little Books, see #932–968.

660. *The Tarzan Twins* (Racine, WI: Whitman Publishing Company, 1935)

This is a variant of #770 above but it has no number. The cover is a reprint of the illustration on page 409 and the back cover reprints the illustration from page 83; same interior illustrations by Juanita Bennett. The cardboard covers and spine are thinner than the standard Big Little Books. 422 numbered pages.

661. *The Tarzan Twins* (Racine, WI: Whitman Publishing Company, 1935)

This is a third version of this title, with a soft cover by Juanita Bennett and 23 interior illustrations by Bennett reprinted from the Big Little Book, but it is only 48 pages. It was stapled together. This variant was an unusual size, 3½" × 5¾" and was a free give-away booklet.

662. *The Illustrated Tarzan Book No. 23* (Kansas City, MO: House of Greystoke, 1968)

This comes from Vernell Coriell and is a 6¾" × 9½" paperbound (in yellow wraps) edition with a cover illustration taken from one of the interior panels. It reproduces the 1937-1938 newspaper strip "Tarzan Under Fire" (based upon *Tarzan and the Tarzan Twins with Jad-Bal-Ja, the Golden Lion*) with 336 interior pictures by William Juhré.

663. *Tarzan and the Tarzan Twins* (New York: Canaveral Press, Inc., 1974)

A reprinting of the 1963 Canaveral first edition, clearly marked "1974" on the title page.

Tarzan at the Earth's Core

664. "Tarzan at the Earth's Core" (THE BLUE BOOK MAGAZINE, September 1929 through March 1930)

A few weeks after completing *Tanar of Pellucidar*, on December 6, 1928, Burroughs began work on a related Tarzan story, originally titled "**Tarzan and Pellucidar.**" It is a favorite with many fans. It was first published as a seven-part serial with front cover illustrations for each installment by Frank Hoban. In addition, Frank Hoban supplied 53 interior black-and-white illustrations. Each issue sold for 25¢. This story, which mixes the two realms of Tarzan and the inner world, is generally considered one of the better Tarzan novels.

───────── FIRST EDITION ─────────

665. *Tarzan at the Earth's Core* (New York: Metropolitan Books, Inc., November 28, 1930)

The first edition of ERB's thirty-fourth hardback book is bound in light green cloth (a second state is bound in orange) with black lettering on the front cover and spine. A very attractive wrap-around dust jacket illustration and different black-and-white frontispiece are by J. Allen St. John. ERB wrote a Foreword for this book which did not appear in the magazine serial. Price: $2.00. 301 pages.

666. *Tarzan at the Earth's Core* (New York: Metropolitan Books, Inc., and Grosset & Dunlap, 1932)

A "mixed edition" with Metropolitan title page and interior and Grosset & Dunlap binding and dust jacket. It is bound in red cloth with black lettering on

BY *EDGAR RICE BURROUGHS*

Original Metropolitan first edition dust jacket for *Tarzan at the Earth's Core* (1930)

the front cover and spine, and the page tops are green. The dust jacket and frontispiece illustrations by St. John are the same as the first edition. The earliest jacket lists 30 ERB titles on the reverse inside of the jacket. Price: 75¢. 301 numbered pages.

667. *Tarzan at the Earth's Core* (New York: Grosset & Dunlap, 1932)
The first G&D reprint is bound in red cloth with black lettering on the front cover and spine, and the pages have a green top. The dust jacket and frontispiece by St. John are the same as the first edition. The earliest jacket lists 30 ERB titles on the reverse inside of the jacket. Price: 75¢. 301 numbered pages.

668. *Tarzan at the Earth's Core* (New York: Grosset & Dunlap, 1940)
The 1940 G&D reprint is bound in red cloth with black lettering on its front cover and spine, and the tops of the pages are dyed green. It has the St. John dust jacket. It can be distinguished from the 1932 reprint by the fact that there are *no* interior illustrations. Price: 75¢. 301 numbered pages.

669. *Tarzan at the Earth's Core* (Tarzana: Edgar Rice Burroughs, Inc., March 25, 1948)
The first ERB, Inc. reprint is bound in the standard tan-gray boards with blue lettering on the front cover and spine. It uses the same St. John dust jacket and frontispiece. Price: $1.00. 301 numbered pages.

670. *Tarzan at the Earth's Core* (New York: Canaveral Press, Inc., November 28, 1962)
This reprint is bound in beige cloth with black lettering on the front cover and spine. The dust jacket, illustrated endpapers and eight interior black-and-white illustrations are by Frank Frazetta. Price: $2.75, raised to $2.95 in 1963. 301 numbered pages.

671. *Tarzan at the Earth's Core* (New York: Ace Books, Inc., January 1963)
The first U.S. paperback edition has cover art and title page drawing by Frank Frazetta. Stock No. F-180, price 40¢. 223 numbered pages.

672. *Tarzan at the Earth's Core* (New York: Ballantine Books, March 1964)
The first Ballantine paperback edition has cover art by Richard Powers. Stock No. U2013, price 50¢. 191 numbered pages.

673. *Tarzan at the Earth's Core* (New York: Canaveral Press, Inc., 1974)
This reprint is bound in tan cloth, but is otherwise identical with the 1962

printing. The date is clearly marked. Illustrations are by Frank Frazetta. 301 numbered pages.

674. *Tarzan at the Earth's Core* (New York: Ace Books, Inc.)
The second Ace paperback edition has the same cover art and title page drawing by Frank Frazetta. Stock No. G 736, price 50¢. 223 numbered pages.

675. *Tarzan at the Earth's Core* (New York: Ace Books, Inc.)
The third Ace paperback edition has the same cover art and title page drawing by Frank Frazetta. Stock No. 79851, price 60¢. 223 numbered pages.

676. *Tarzan at the Earth's Core* (New York: Ace Books, Inc., March 1973)
The fourth Ace paperback edition has the same cover art by Frank Frazetta. The book is a larger size than previous Ace printings. Stock No. 79852, price 75¢. 256 numbered pages.

677. *Tarzan at the Earth's Core* (New York: Ballantine Books, April 1970)
The third Ballantine paperback printing has a new cover illustration by Robert Abbett. Stock No. 01907, price 75¢. 191 numbered pages.

678. *Tarzan at the Earth's Core* (New York: Ballantine Books, November 1975)
The fifth Ballantine paperback printing has a new cover illustration by Neal Adams. Stock No. 24483, price $1.25. 191 numbered pages.

Tarzan Clans of America

This 32-page booklet, published in 1939, contains the rules of the "Tarzan Clans of America," a somewhat idealistic experiment on the part of Edgar Rice Burroughs himself, to inculcate clean living, health, courage, chivalry and outdoor values for young men. The model was clearly the Boy Scouts of America. Johnny Weissmuller was the "Chief of Chiefs," and ERB's personal secretary and friend, Cyril Rothmund, "Chief Scribe." The Tarzan Clans was an experiment which was not really successful. It is not known how many were printed; there were at least 200 or so copies. We know that 60 copies were supplied to MGM to give out at a screening of the 1939 *Tarzan Finds a Son* film, and ERB, Inc. may have sent out a hundred or more to young members. Additional information can be found in Henry Heins, *A Golden Anniversary Bibliography*, p. 90.

679. **"Tarzan Clans of America"** (Edgar Rice Burroughs, Inc., May 22, 1939)

This "Official Guide" has orange paper covers with a cover illustration by John Coleman Burroughs, inspired by a line drawing by J. Allen St. John (found on page 112 of the McClurg edition of *The Beasts of Tarzan*). The booklet includes a table of contents, rules and instructions for forming a new clan group, duties of procedures at meetings, initiation ritual, a Tarzan Pledge and Tarzan "Clan Grip," lyrics to four songs (but no melodies provided), a section on sports and games, and a 500-word Ape-English Dictionary. Virtually everything in the booklet is the work of Burroughs. Membership in the Tarzan Clans of America cost $1.00, and for that the member received this booklet, a membership card, one new ERB, Inc. hardback first edition (autographed), and one year's worth of dues. 32 pages.

Tarzan Jr.

Burroughs had been dealing with the film industry since 1915, and with the huge success of the 1932 Johnny Weissmuller–Maureen O'Sullivan *Tarzan, the Ape Man* and the succeeding series of films, Edgar Rice Burroughs had many friends and acquaintances in Hollywood. In 1937, movie star Colleen Moore asked ERB to contribute a few lines from a Tarzan novel for the library of her miniature Fairy Castle, a doll house designed and built for her by Hollywood set designers. Burroughs was given a small one-inch-square leather-bound book already stamped "Tarzan" and "Edgar Rice Burroughs" in gold, and Miss Moore expected him to copy a few lines from a Tarzan book and then sign his name to the book. Instead, ERB actually hand-lettered a short, humorous and pun-filled 21-page fairy tale illustrated with hand-colored illustrations on facing pages by Burroughs and his son, John Coleman Burroughs. A rather willful princess wanders into the Forbidden Forest, and is rescued by Tarzan Jr. as a lion is about to eat her. The princess and Tarzan Jr. are married, and lived "happily forever after."

There is only one copy of the book, and it is on a miniature bookshelf in the doll-sized Fairy Castle which presently resides in The Museum of Science and Industry in Chicago. Burroughs collector Michael Conran researched this book, and provides photographs of the book and of each page, in the fanzine of which he is editor, EDGAR RICE BURROUGHS NEWS DATELINE, No. 24, 11/86. I am indebted to Mr. Conran for all the information contained here.

─────────────── FIRST EDITION ───────────────

680. "Tarzan Jr." (July-August 1937)

This work is not listed in the notebook Burroughs used to keep track of his writing (probably because ERB was not paid for it), but when he wrote it, he was probably at work on *Carson of Venus*. We know that in the summer of 1937, ERB received an unusual request from film star Colleen Moore. She asked him to contribute a few lines for a small book to go on the bookshelf in her doll house. Burroughs responded with this 21 page humorous fairy tale. Book size: 1" × 1". There exists only one copy of this miniature book, and it is in the doll house which is in The Museum of Science and Industry in Chicago.

Tarzan, Lord of the Jungle

681. "Tarzan, Lord of the Jungle" (THE BLUE BOOK MAGAZINE, December 1927; January-May 1928)

A few months after he finished writing the Volland version of *The Tarzan Twins* in January 1927, Burroughs began a story which he entitled "**Tarzan the Invincible.**" He worked on it from May to July 1927. It was serialized in six parts with front cover illustrations for the first two issues: December 1927 illustrated by an unidentified artist; January 1928 by J. Allen St. John (this was St. John's first magazine illustrations for an ERB story). Each issue sold for 25¢. There are numerous interior black-and-white illustrations by Frank Hoban.

─────────────── FIRST EDITION ───────────────

682. *Tarzan, Lord of the Jungle* (Chicago: A.C. McClurg & Co., September 15, 1928)

This is the thirtieth hardback book published by ERB, and the last *Tarzan* title published by A.C. McClurg. The first edition is bound in green cloth with black lettering on the front cover and spine. The dust wrapper and five interior sepia plates are by J. Allen St. John. The book includes a map of the Valley of the Sepulcher by Burroughs himself, who often drew maps while writing his novels. There is a title page decoration by St. John. The first edition combined with the four subsequent reprintings totalled only 7,500 copies, according to the research of Alan M. Freedman. Price: $2.00. 377 numbered pages.

683. *Tarzan, Lord of the Jungle* (Chicago: A.C. McClurg & Co., after September 1928)

I. BIBLIOGRAPHY OF BOOKS

Original McClurg first edition dust jacket for *Tarzan, Lord of the Jungle* (1928)

Several McClurg reprint editions are bound in green cloth with black lettering on the front cover and spine. They are labeled "Second Printing," "Third Printing," and "Fourth Printing." All points are identical with the first edition described above. Price: $2.00. 377 numbered pages.

684. *Tarzan, Lord of the Jungle* (New York: Grosset & Dunlap, 1929)
As is typical of the G&D reprints, this is bound in red cloth with black lettering on the front cover and spine. The dust jacket and *four* interior black-and-white plates are by J. Allen St. John (one omitted for the reprint edition). The map by ERB is present. A later variation from the 1930s has the tops of the pages dyed yellow. On the back of the earliest G&D dust jacket is a rectangular photo of Burroughs and a list of 28 ERB book titles, and on the reverse of the jacket there are 25 ERB titles listed. In the 1930s, the back of the jacket was yellow with a sketch of ERB. Price: 75¢. 377 numbered pages.

685. *Tarzan, Lord of the Jungle* (New York: Grosset & Dunlap, 1939)
Bound in red cloth with black lettering on the front cover and spine. The dust jacket and *three* interior black-and-white plates are by J. Allen St. John (two omitted). Price: 75¢. 377 numbered pages.

686. *Tarzan, Lord of the Jungle* (New York: Grosset & Dunlap, 1940)
Bound in red cloth with black lettering on the front cover and spine, this 1940 reprint can be distinguished from the earlier reprints by the fact that the black-and-white interior illustrations have been omitted completely (except for the map by ERB and the St. John title page drawing). The tops of the pages are dyed green. Price: 75¢. 377 numbered pages.

687. *Tarzan, Lord of the Jungle* (New York: Grosset & Dunlap, 1943)
This is the cheap wartime edition bound in maroon cloth with black lettering on the front cover and spine. The dust jacket and small title page drawing are by J. Allen St. John. Besides its thin size (fewer pages and thinner brown brittle paper), it can be identified by the "Madison Square" label on the dust jacket. The book sold for 50¢ until 1945, when the price was dropped to 49¢. 309 numbered pages.

688. *Tarzan, Lord of the Jungle* (Racine, WI: Whitman Publishing Company, 1946)
This Better Little Book is a small yet thick illustrated children's book bound in paper boards. The cover is by an unknown artist who is copying Rex Maxon, and interior art is by Rex Maxon, containing 173 illustrations from the 1931 newspaper strip. Book number 1407. 352 pages. For more information on this series, see #932–968.

689. *Tarzan, Lord of the Jungle* (New York: Grosset & Dunlap, April 1948)

This, the first post-war reprinting, is bound in green decorated *cloth* with dark green lettering on the spine. It sold for $1.00. The dust jacket art is by C. Edmund Monroe, with a decorated title page and an end-paper map of Africa by Rafael Palacios. The next reprinting of this title had paperbound boards in tan with brown decorations and lettering and sold for $1.25. The later 1958 reprinting omitted the end-paper map, and the price was raised to $1.50. 309 numbered pages.

690. *Tarzan, Lord of the Jungle* (New York: Ballantine Books, September 1963)

The first paperback edition has a front cover illustration by Richard Powers. Stock No. F 772, price 50¢. 191 numbered pages.

691. *Tarzan, Lord of the Jungle* (New York: Grosset & Dunlap, 1967)

This hardback is bound in pictorial boards with front cover art by C. E. Monroe. There is a decorated title page by Rafael Palacios. The book has the number 2637 on the spine. 309 numbered pages.

692. *Tarzan, Lord of the Jungle* (New York: Ballantine Books, October 1969)

The third paperback printing has a new front cover illustration by Robert Abbett. Stock No. 01753, price 50¢. 191 numbered pages.

693. *Tarzan, Lord of the Jungle* (New York: Ballantine Books, November 1976)

The sixth Ballantine paperback printing has a new front cover illustration by Boris Vallejo. Stock No. 24170, price $1.25. 191 numbered pages.

Tarzan of the Apes

694. "Tarzan of the Apes" (THE ALL-STORY, October 1912)

This is the second published story by Edgar Rice Burroughs (although it is the third story written by ERB, not counting two early stories written for family members). It is the first appearance of Burroughs' greatest and most enduring literary creation, *Tarzan of the Apes*. Unlike so many other ERB stories, this was not serialized. The entire novel was published in the single October issue of the pulp magazine and sold for 15¢. There are subtle differences in the content of the first magazine appearance of "Tarzan of the Apes" and the hardback

BY EDGAR RICE BURROUGHS

first edition published a year-and-a-half later (the original magazine text has been reprinted in the 1988 Avenel anthology of four Tarzan titles; see item #724). The front cover by Clinton Pettee illustrates Tarzan, knife in left hand, straddling a lion, holding it by the throat as it rears back off the ground. Tarzan's cousin, Cecil Clayton, watches apprehensively in the background. Jungle creepers and vines fill the foreground. There is a black-and-white headpiece designed and executed by Fred W. Small. This certainly counts as one of the rarest and most desirable of all the Burroughs items. When he finished writing and selling *Tarzan of the Apes*, Burroughs began work on a second tale of John Carter entitled *The Gods of Mars*. It too is a favorite among many fans.

695. *Tarzan of the Apes* (Chicago: A.C. McClurg & Co., 1914)
Even rarer than the first edition hardback is the prepublication paperback review copy, of which there were probably only a few dozen published. The wraparound dust jacket illustration used on the first edition has been printed on heavy papercovers. The interior seems identical with the first edition described in detail below. There are only two copies known to exist.

——————————— FIRST EDITION ———————————
696. *Tarzan of the Apes* (Chicago: A.C. McClurg & Co., June 17, 1914)
Tarzan of the Apes is the third story Burroughs wrote, but is the first hardback book Burroughs published. This is the first appearance of the Lord of the Jungle in hardback. There were about 5,000 copies of the first state of the first edition printed; it is bound in dark red cloth with gold lettering on the front cover and spine. There is *no* acorn on the spine.* The wrap-around dust jacket was done

There has been a great deal of controversy over the first state and the second state of the first edition of Tarzan of the Apes. *For many years it was believed that the A.C. McClurg acorn device on the spine was the true first because it was obviously rarer than the other variety. Henry Hardy Heins'* A Golden Anniversary Bibliography of Edgar Rice Burroughs *lists the acorn as the true first (he has photographs of both variants on page 32). It seemed a reasonable assumption that McClurg, not realizing how popular the title would be, printed a small number of books with an acorn, and then when it sold out quickly, McClurg would have ordered a larger printing, and this one was without the acorn device. However, this is* not *what happened.*

In 1965 and 1966, George Fowler published an article, "The Case Against the Acorn," and in the second installment (ERB-DOM #19), Mr. Fowler relates that the inscribed copy which Burroughs presented to his wife was dated two weeks before *the official release date, June 17, 1914, and the book lacks an acorn. In addition, a second copy has been found, inscribed to the author's brother and dated about a week before the official release date, and it too lacks the acorn device. As George McWhorter explained in his interview with Heins, published in* McWhorter's *excellent publication, the* EDGAR RICE BURROUGHS QUARTERLY, *vol. I, no. 1 (fall 1982), making the very reasonable assumption that the proud ERB would have given his wife one of the very first copies ever printed, it followed that the acorn was* not *the earliest printing, i.e., it was not the first state of the first edition. Agreeing with the reasoning, Heins revised his opinion as a result.*

So, where does the acorn variant fit in? According to Alan M. Freedman, writing in a booklet entitled The 75th Anniversary Dinner Celebrating the First Publication of a Hardcover

I. BIBLIOGRAPHY OF BOOKS

The first appearance of Tarzan of the Apes, THE ALL-STORY, October 1912

by Fred J. Arting. It is primarily black with dark green and gold used sparingly. There is a price of $1.30 on the spine of the dust jacket. The title page for this book is the dust jacket's black-and-white silhouette of Tarzan seated on the branch of a tree, with the full moon behind his head, also by Fred J. Arting. The publisher's imprint is in a small box in the lower left of the illustrated silhouette. The most important indication of the true first edition is the appearance of "𝔚. 𝔍. ℌ𝔞𝔩𝔩" in Old English script on the copyright page. The dedication is to Burroughs' first wife, Emma Hulbert Burroughs. There are 400 (+1) numbered pages. According to Henry Heins, McClurg first printed 5,000 copies, and there were additional printings (the last in December 1914) which brought the total to about 10,000 printed. These findings were corroborated by Alan Freedman, who discovered the pertinent original McClurg documentation (see the BURROUGHS BULLETIN, New Series, Number 3 [July 1990], pp. 3–10, for more information).

697. *Tarzan of the Apes* (Chicago: A.C. McClurg & Co., 1914)
   First edition, second state; this is identical to #696 above, except there is a small gold acorn on the spine directly above the publisher's "McClurg" imprint. The acorn edition is very desirable to collectors, and it is even rarer than the first state described above, inasmuch as there were probably only 2,500 copies printed. The dust jacket is identical with the entry above.

698. *Tarzan of the Apes* (Chicago: A.C. McClurg & Co., 1914)
   First edition, third state, probably published in early 1915. It is believed that there were approximately 2,500 printed. The third state is different from the first two. Mitchell Harrison describes it as an A.L. Burt body with a McClurg cover. The covers are known to have been in different colors, some dark red, some green, and even an orange cover exists. There are two important differences between these and the first two McClurg printings. The paper on this third state is lighter and thinner (just like the Burt reprint copy printed in 1915). The second important difference is the appearance of the "W. F. Hall" imprint on the copyright page in Gothic type instead of Old English. The dust jacket is identical with #696 above.

699. *Tarzan of the Apes* (New York: A. L. Burt, 1915)
   The five *Tarzan* titles which A.L. Burt reprinted are generally much earlier than the G&Ds. The first reprint of *Tarzan of the Apes* is bound in dark green

---

[continued] Novel by Edgar Rice Burroughs *(October 21, 1989), Samuel A. Peeples obtained the following explanation in 1929 from A.C. McClurg: it is very probable that the initial demand for Tarzan of the Apes exceeded the 5,000 that the A.C. McClurg bindery had printed, and so they contracted with a different bindery which was occasionally hired to handle the overload demand. That bindery used the A.C. McClurg slug with the acorn on it for the extra 2,500 copies it bound for McClurg. Thus the acorn is listed as the "second state."*

quality cloth, with the bright white lettering on the front deeply embossed into the cloth, with a white embossed border, and white lettering on the spine. It was made to sell for 50¢. As with the first edition dust jacket, the design is by Fred J. Arting, and the earliest A.L. Burt dust jacket is virtually identical with the McClurg jacket: Tarzan, the tree trunks and branches, and the lions are in black silhouette, the leaves are dark green. The sun and ground are yellow, and the rear flyleaf is blank (note that Burt dust jackets seem more prone to fade over the years than the McClurg and G&D jackets). On some jackets, the bottom half of the artist's name, "Fred J. Arting," is cut off by the bottom of the page. The black-and-white title page from the first edition is adapted to serve as a frontispiece (the A.C. McClurg & Co. name is removed). The dedication page is present. 400 (+1) numbered pages.

700. *Tarzan of the Apes* (New York: A.L. Burt Company, 1915–1928)
There are numerous binding variants of *Tarzan of the Apes* published by A.L. Burt between 1915 and 1928 (however, all carry the same "1914" date on the copyright page). They are bound in various shades of less expensive green cloth (dark green, pale green, olive green, light green) and blue-gray, but the later reprintings all have black lettering, some with the embossed letters and border, and others without the embossed cover used on the earliest reprint edition. The pagination is the same for all reprints. A close guess as to the actual date of the reprint can be determined by a careful examination of the advertisements for A.L. Burt books found at the back of the book; these vary from year to year depending upon which books were published that year. The dust jackets occur in at least two variations: (1) Tarzan, trees, trunks, branches, and lion are all in dark green ink, with leaves and lettering in a very pale green, with a yellow sun; back flyleaf is blank; (2) Tarzan, trees, trunks, branches and lion are black, but leaves and lettering are pale green and the sun is red; back flyleaf has an advertisement. The 1915 printings sold for 50¢, then the price was raised to 60¢ in 1917, and raised again to 75¢ in 1919.

701. *Tarzan of the Apes* (New York: Grosset & Dunlap, 1927)
The first Grosset & Dunlap reprint (12 years later than the earliest Burt reprint) was bound in red cloth with black lettering on both the front cover and the spine. Even though the earliest Grosset & Dunlap reprint was 13 years after the first edition, the book carries the "1914" date, with no internal evidence of the fact that it was published so much later. The first reprint, from 1927, can be identified by the presence of the original silhouette of Tarzan in the tree, again used as a frontispiece, as in the A.L. Burt variants described above. The wrap-around dust jacket art was based upon and freely adapted from the Fred J. Arting green-and-black silhouette used by McClurg. However, it was repainted, changed from a moonlit scene to full daylight. In addition, the posture of Tarzan on the tree is not quite the same in the original dust jacket. Color has been added, details of leaves, grass, vines, rocks and trees have been added. Tarzan's face has

BY EDGAR RICE BURROUGHS

A dust jacket for *Tarzan of the Apes* (1914)

been filled in with rather unprepossessing features, and now he is wearing a loin cloth. In the McClurg jacket, Tarzan's locket swings free from his body and is seen in silhouette. In this G&D jacket, the locket is delineated against his chest. The name "Fred J. Arting" is gone. Robert R. Barrett, expert on Burroughs artists, believes that the artist Paul Stahr did the repainting. In at least one 1930s variant, the tops of the pages were dyed yellow, and then green. The dedication page is present. On the reverse of the earliest dust jacket, there are 24 ERB titles listed. Price: 75¢. The number of pages has been reset to 392 numbered pages.

702. "Tarzan of the Apes" (BEST STORIES OF ALL TIME magazine, August/September, October, November, December 1926; January, February, March, April 1927).

The story was reprinted in eight installments. There was no cover illustration and no interior illustrations. Each issue sold for 25¢.

703. *Tarzan of the Apes* (Racine, WI: Whitman Publishing Company, 1933)

This is the Whitman Big Little Book, the equivalent of the inexpensive comic book, illustrated and aimed at children. The books in this series generally measure 3½" wide by 4⅜" high, and average about 1¼" in width. The cover and 307 interior drawings are by Juanita Bennett (who later illustrated the 1936 Big Big Book, *Tarzan and the Tarzan Twins with Jad-Bal-Ja, the Golden Lion*, page 172 and entry #657 of this book). This Big Little Book carries the Whitman identification number 744. 320 pages. For more information on these books, see #932–968.

704. *Tarzan of the Apes* (Racine, WI: Whitman Publishing Company, 1935).

A much abridged version of the story was reprinted again, probably in 1935. It uses 23 illustrations from the 1933 Big Little Book, but has just 48 stapled pages. It is 3½" × 5¾" and was a free give-away.

705. *Tarzan of the Apes* (New York: Grosset & Dunlap, 1940)

The 1940 reprint has red cloth with black lettering on the front cover and spine. The dust jacket is the same G&D color adaptation of Fred J. Arting's silhouette described on the previous page. The 1940 printings are identified by the absence of the Arting frontispiece described above. As with the other reprints, the dedication page is present, and it has 392 numbered pages. This seems to have been reprinted several times. An examination of the back flap of the dust jacket reveals differences; it may carry an advertisement for a Burroughs book or a listing of the complete novels of ERB up to about 1938. Grosset & Dunlap apparently did not get reprint rights for any *new* Burroughs books after about 1939. Price: 75¢.

BY EDGAR RICE BURROUGHS

706. *Tarzan of the Apes* ("Armed Services Edition #M-16," Editions for the Armed Services, Inc., "Copyright 1940")
This is an unusual paperback edition (4" × 5½") issued 1940-1941 for the Council on Books in Wartime, and distributed to military camps, ships, hospitals, and airbases (cf. Heins, *A Golden Anniversary Bibliography*, p. 36). Despite the small pocket size, the paperback is complete and unabridged. The cover has a cartoonish drawing of a (non-existent) hardback of the book with an illustration of Tarzan running through the jungle. The cover has the following information: "Overseas edition for the Armed Forces. Distributed by the Special Services Division, A.S.F., for the Army, and by the Bureau of Naval Personnel for the Navy. U. S. Government property. Not for sale. Published by Editions for the Armed Services, Inc., a non-profit organization established by the Council on Books in Wartime." There are no interior illustrations. These were given away free to the libraries of ships, hospitals, military bases, etc., for the use of members of the armed forces. 351 (+1) numbered pages.

707. *Tarzan of the Apes* (New York: Grosset & Dunlap, 1943)
This is the "Madison Square" wartime edition. These were bound in maroon cloth with black lettering on the front cover and spine. Very thin paper with high acid content was used, making the book appear much thinner than the previous printings. There is a title page decoration by J. Allen St. John of "Tarzan and the Golden Lion." The dust jacket is the same color adaptation of the original dust jacket art by Fred J. Arting described above as #701. The main difference is a "Madison Square" logo on the spine of the dust jacket. Reset to 314 numbered pages. Price: 50¢ until 1945, 49¢ thereafter.

708. *Tarzan of the Apes* (New York: Grosset & Dunlap, 1960)
Bound in tan decorated boards with dark brown cover design and dark brown lettering on spine. The number "2638" appears on the spine of the jacket. Gerald McCann is the artist for the dust jacket illustration. The title page is not decorated and there is no map of Africa on the end pages (as found on the eight other G&D reprints from the 1950s). Price: $1.50. 314 numbered pages.

709. *Tarzan of the Apes* (New York: Ballantine Books, July 1963)
The first standard paperback edition of *Tarzan of the Apes* has a front cover painting by Richard Powers. Different places in the 1912 story have been revised to better accord with 1960s sensibilities, and there are some minor omissions as well. The alterations are numerous, but mostly they involve grammatical refinements and modifications of ERB's rather quaint attempts to reproduce British English of 1888. The most significant changes occur in chapter 15, with Jane Porter and Esmeralda in the cabin under siege by a lioness. Ballantine continues to reprint this modified version year after year. Stock No. F 745, price 50¢. 219 numbered pages.

710. *Tarzan of the Apes* (Racine, WI: Whitman, 1964)
Illustrated laminated pictorial boards by Al Anderson. Interior illustrations by Al Anderson and Jesse Marsh. Unabridged. The book was reprinted at least once. Book number 1507. 285 pages.

711. *Tarzan of the Apes* (New York: Ballantine Books, August 1966)
The third Ballantine paperback edition of *Tarzan of the Apes* has a new front cover with a photograph of Ron Ely (who was playing Tarzan on the television series during that time). Stock No. U2001, price 50¢. 219 numbered pages.

712. *Tarzan of the Apes* (New York: Grosset & Dunlap, 1967)
This is like the 1960 hardback edition with the Gerald McCann dust jacket illustration of Tarzan holding a spear, but this is printed onto a pictorial front cover. No dust jacket was issued. A decorated title page has been added, but no other interior illustrations. Book number 2638. 314 numbered pages.

713. *Tarzan of the Apes* (New York: Ballantine Books, April 1969)
The fifth Ballantine paperback printing was reset and has new front cover art by Robert Abbett. Stock No. 01591, price 50¢. 245 numbered pages.

714. *Tarzan of the Apes* (New York: Grosset & Dunlap, 1973)
This is like the 1967 hardback edition but with a different illustration. Artist George Gross illustrated the pictorial front cover (Tarzan holds a boulder). There is a decorated title page. There are two variants: (1) a trade edition with #11572 on the spine, and (2) a library edition with #13161 on the spine. 314 numbered pages.

715. *Tarzan of the Apes* (New York: Ballantine Books, April 1975)
The ninth Ballantine paperback printing has new front cover art by Neal Adams. Stock No. 24159, price $1.25. 245 numbered pages.

716. *Tarzan of the Apes* (New York: Ballantine Books, January 1976)
This special paperback edition (probably the eleventh) of *Tarzan of the Apes* is labeled "A Ballantine Special Book Club Edition." It lacks the Ballantine stock number and has no price. The Neal Adams cover art is unchanged. 245 numbered pages.

717. *Tarzan of the Apes* (New York: Buccaneer Books, 1977)
This printing is bound in gray cloth with yellow lettering on the spine (later printings have silver letters on the spine). The book never had a dust jacket. There are no interior illustrations. Stock No. 046-0. Price $17.95. 245 numbered pages.

BY EDGAR RICE BURROUGHS

718. *Tarzan of the Apes* (New York: Random House, 1982)
This, the most popular of all ERB books, is bound in pictorial boards with front cover art and numerous interior illustrations by Tim Gaydos. This is a Random House "Step-up Adventures" series abridgment, adapted by Harold and Geraldine Woods. Stock No. 394-95089-5. 94 (+1) numbered pages.

719. *Tarzan of the Apes* (New York: Random House, 1982)
Paperback edition of the 1982 Random House book described directly above. Stock No. 394-85089-0.

720. *Tarzan, King of the Apes* (New York: Random House, December 1983)
This new Random House adaptation is bound in pictorial boards with front cover art by Charles Ren (the same cover illustration used on Ballantine's twentieth reprinting). The "adaptation" was done by Joan D. Vinge. There are no interior illustrations. ISBN 0-394-96212-5. 104 numbered pages.

721. *Tarzan, King of the Apes* (New York: Random House, 1983)
Paperback version of the 1983 Random House adaptation described directly above. ISBN 0-394-86212-0. Price $1.95.

722. *Tarzan of the Apes* (New York: Ballantine Books, December 1983)
The twentieth Ballantine paperback printing has new front cover art by Charles Ren. The book is a movie tie-in with the film *Greystoke*. Stock No. 31531, price $2.50. 245 numbered pages.

723. *Tarzan of the Apes* (Ballantine, May 1988).
This twenty-fifth Ballantine reprint is a curiosity of interest for two reasons: (1) Tarzan's Peerage name ("Lord Greystoke") is misprinted on the cover as "Greystone"; (2) the cover has returned to the old Neal Adams cover art. The number is 31977. Price $3.50. 245 numbered pages.

724. *Tarzan of the Apes* (New York: Avenel, 1988)
This anthology of four titles is bound in maroon cloth with gold lettering on the spine. The beautiful dust jacket design is the one which J. Allen St. John painted for the first hardback appearance of *Tarzan at the Earth's Core*. This book is of special interest because its contents include the *original magazine* version of *Tarzan of the Apes*, in addition to *The Son of Tarzan, Tarzan at the Earth's Core* and *Tarzan Triumphant*. The interior black-and-white illustrations are reproductions of the original J. Allen St. John and Studley Burroughs art, but there are four original works by Esteban Maroto. The four novels are consecutively paginated with 848 numbered pages.

I. BIBLIOGRAPHY OF BOOKS

725. *Tarzan of the Apes* (New York: New American Library, March 1990).
This Signet Classic paperback has an introduction by Gore Vidal ("Tarzan Revisited" from 1963) and the cover illustration is a reproduction of a painting by Thomas Baines. Price $2.45. Stock No. 451-CE2423. 288 numbered pages.

726. *Tarzan of the Apes* (New York: Penguin Books, 1990).
This larger quality paperback has a striking black-and-white reproduction of the McClurg frontispiece (Tarzan silhouette) on the cover and used again as a frontispiece), and a 21 page introduction by John Seelye plus eight pages of notes for readers not familiar with some of the terminology and situations portrayed in the book. Price $6.95. 286 (+ xxx) pages.

727. *Tarzan of the Apes* (New York: Random House, 1991)
A fourth paperback printing with a new cover illustration by Kenneth E. Laager. Stock No. 394-85089-0.

728. *Tarzan of the Apes / The Return of Tarzan* (New York: Book-of-the-Month-Club, July 1995)
This special Book-of-the-Month Club edition was first advertised in the July 1995 BOMC bulletin. It is photographic reproductions of the early Grosset & Dunlap printings of the first two Tarzan books combined into one volume. Bound in green cloth spine and dark green boards with a dust jacket by Michael Samuel. Original price: $17.95. Stock No. 94-8541. 784 numbered pages.

729. *Tarzan of the Apes / The Return of Tarzan* (New York: Book-of-the-Month-Club, July 1995)
This is a paperback version for a paperback book club. It is photographic reproductions of the early Grosset & Dunlap editions of the first two Tarzan books combined into one volume. Original price: $7.95. 784 numbered pages.

730. *Tarzan of the Apes* (Norwalk, CT: The Easton Press, 1995)
The Easton Press published this book as volume #121 of the "Masterpieces of Science Fiction" series. It is bound in a quality leather binding with a color frontispiece by Kent Bash. It includes a four-page introduction by George T. McWhorter. Original price: $38.50. 252 (+x) pages.

731. *Tarzan of the Apes* (Shelton, CT: The First Edition Library)
In late 1995, an announcement was made of the intent to publish an almost exact reproduction of the original 1914 A.C. McClurg & Co. first edition, including a duplicate of the attractive first edition dust jacket. The book will be in a handsome slipcase, and is expected to be published in 1998.

BY EDGAR RICE BURROUGHS

Tarzan the Invincible

732. "Tarzan, Guard of the Jungle" (THE BLUE BOOK MAGAZINE, October 1930 through April 1931)
About two months after he completed *Jungle Girl*, Burroughs began work on another Tarzan novel in March of 1930. Originally entitled "Tarzan and the Man Things," this was first published as a seven-part serial with front cover illustrations on the first six installments by Laurence Herndon. Frank Hoban, another prolific BLUE BOOK illustrator, did numerous interior black-and-white illustrations. Each issue sold for 25¢. A week after finishing this tale, he began writing *The Deputy Sheriff of Comanche County*.

———————FIRST EDITION———————
733. *Tarzan the Invincible* (Tarzana: Edgar Rice Burroughs, Inc., November 20, 1931)
The thirty-sixth hardback by ERB, this was the very first hardback published by Burroughs' own publishing company. The first edition is bound in smooth blue cloth with red lettering on the front cover and spine. The first four titles published by ERB, Inc. were not marked "First Edition." Thus, this book does *not* have the usual "First Edition" imprint on the copyright page. The dust jacket art and black-and-white frontispiece are by Studley Burroughs, Burroughs' nephew. Price: $2.00. 318 numbered pages.

734. *Tarzan the Invincible* (New York: Grosset & Dunlap, 1933)
The first reprint is bound in the usual G&D red cloth with black lettering on the front cover and spine, and the tops of the pages are dyed green. The earliest printing has 33 ERB books listed in the page of advertising at the back of the book. Just like the first edition, the dust jacket and frontispiece are by Studley Burroughs. A reprinting from 1937 or 1938 has only 29 ERB books listed at the back. There is a decorated title page (elephant head). The earliest jacket lists 32 ERB titles on the inner reverse of the jacket. Later jackets are blank on the inside. Price: 75¢. 318 numbered pages.

735. *Tarzan the Invincible* (New York: Grosset & Dunlap, 1940)
The second G&D reprint is bound in red cloth with black lettering on the front cover and spine. It uses the dust jacket design by Studley Burroughs. It can be distinguished from the earlier reprint by its total absence of interior illustrations. There are only 22 ERB titles listed in the advertising at the back of the book. The title page is decorated with the head of an elephant. Price: 75¢. 318 numbered pages.

736. *Tarzan the Invincible* (Tarzana: Edgar Rice Burroughs, Inc., March 26, 1948)
Typical of the ERB, Inc. 1948 reprints, this is bound in tan-gray cloth with blue lettering on the front cover and spine. The dust jacket and black-and-white frontispiece are by Studley O. Burroughs. Price: $1.00. 318 numbered pages.

737. *Tarzan the Invincible* (New York: Ace Books, Inc., March 1963)
The first paperback printing has front cover art and a title page drawing by Frank Frazetta. Stock No. F-189, price 40¢. 220 numbered pages.

738. *Tarzan the Invincible* (New York: Ballantine Books, March 1964)
The first Ballantine paperback printing has front cover art by Richard Powers. Stock No. U2014, price 50¢. 192 numbered pages.

739. *Tarzan the Invincible* (New York: Ballantine Books, April 1970)
The second Ballantine paperback printing has a new front cover illustration by Robert Abbett. Stock No. 01908, price 75¢. 192 numbered pages.

740. *Tarzan the Invincible* (New York: Ballantine Books, November 1975)
The fourth Ballantine paperback printing has a new front cover illustration by Neal Adams. Stock No. 24484, price $1.25. 192 numbered pages.

Tarzan: The Lost Adventure

This title is a curiosity for several reasons. Burroughs began an untitled Tarzan novel on September 7, 1946, but because of ill health, set it aside uncompleted. At his death in March 1950, Burroughs left just 83 typewritten pages recounting the beginning of one last adventure of Tarzan of the Apes. The Burroughs corporation simply ignored the manuscript for the next 45 years. However, in late 1994, arrangements were made for the story to be published by Dark Horse comics. Dark Horse hired another writer to finish the story, Joe. R. Lansdale, and published it in a format which echoed the pulp magazines of the 1920s and 1930s. Four artists were hired to do illustrations for the four separate 64-page installments. Mr. Lansdale did not merely complete the manuscript; ERB's original story has been restructured and rewritten from the very earliest pages. Dark Horse announced plans to continue Tarzan's adventures in a series of comic book tales.

BY EDGAR RICE BURROUGHS

A limited hardback version of this book was published in December 1995.

741. *Tarzan: The Lost Adventure* (Milwaukie, OR: Dark Horse Comics, vol. 1, no. 1, January 24, 1995)
   The first magazine appearance of Burroughs' last Tarzan story was published as a pulp serial in four separate issues composed of four separate pulp-sized quality editions. The first installment was illustrated by the excellent Burroughs artist, Thomas Yeates. The painted cover illustration, against a white background, is by Arthur Suydam. The issue also contains a reprinting of John Coleman Burroughs' original comic-format retelling of *A Princess of Mars*. Price $2.95. 64 numbered pages.

742. *Tarzan: The Lost Adventure* (Milwaukie, OR: Dark Horse Comics, vol. 1, no. 2, February 1995)
   Burroughs' last Tarzan story is continued in the second installment of four pulp-sized editions. This is illustrated by Charles Vess, and the painted cover illustration against a black background is by Arthur Suydam. This issue also contains the second installment of the reprinting of John Coleman Burroughs' original retelling of *A Princess of Mars*. This issue has 28 pages of the Tarzan story supplemented by an interview with Danton Burroughs (with the assistance of George T. McWhorter) and illustrated by classic pictures and photographs. $2.95. 64 numbered pages.

743. *Tarzan: The Lost Adventure* (Milwaukie, OR: Dark Horse Comics, vol. 1, no. 3, March 1995)
   The third part of Burroughs' last Tarzan story was illustrated by Gary Gianni in a style which echoes the classic illustrations of J. Allen St. John. The painted cover illustration on a white background is by Arthur Suydam. This volume also contains the third installment of the reprinting of John Coleman Burroughs' original comic-format retelling of *A Princess of Mars*. $2.95. 64 numbered pages.

744. *Tarzan: The Lost Adventure* (Milwaukie, OR: Dark Horse Comics, vol. 1, no. 4, April 1995)
   The fourth and final installment of the first magazine appearance of Burroughs' last Tarzan story was illustrated by Michael William Kaluta. The painted cover illustration by Arthur Suydam is against a green background. Joe Lansdale finished his story with a traditional open ending in the style of ERB; the story concludes as Tarzan begins his descent into the inner world of Pellucidar. This issue also contains the final installment of the reprinting of John Coleman Burroughs' *A Princess of Mars*. In addition, there is "A Tarzan Chronology" by Henning Kure, and a letters-to-the-editor section entitled "Ape Language." $2.95. 64 numbered pages.

I. BIBLIOGRAPHY OF BOOKS

---FIRST EDITION---

745. *Tarzan: The Lost Adventure* (Milwaukie, OR: Dark Horse, December 5, 1995)
The hardback first edition of the Lansdale-Burroughs Tarzan story has a new foreword by George T. McWhorter and includes a reproduction of Burroughs' own book plate, and the autograph of Danton Burroughs, the grandson of ERB. In addition to the art used in the pulp-comic editions, there is new art by Monty Sheldon and a new dust jacket cover painting by Dean Williams. The book is large format, 7" × 10" and is bound in leather. Price: $99.95. 208 numbered pages.

746. *Tarzan: The Lost Adventure* (Milwaukie, OR: Dark Horse, April 1996).
This is the mass-market trade edition of the Lansdale-Burroughs Tarzan. Most of its contents are identical with the limited edition, including the foreword by George T. McWhorter and reproduction of Burroughs' own book plate. However, it does not have the Danton Burroughs autograph, and it is bound in dark green cloth instead of leather. It uses the same dust jacket cover painting by Dean Williams, but the right side of the front of the dust jacket includes a gold seal "FIRST TIME IN PRINT." The book is large format, 7" × 10". Price: $19.95. 208 numbered pages.

Tarzan the Magnificent

747. "**Tarzan and the Magic Men**" (ARGOSY WEEKLY, September 19, 26; October 3, 1936)
After finishing *Back to the Stone Age* in September of 1935, Burroughs began work on this story, which was published as a three-part serial with a front cover illustration (September 19th issue) by Hubert Rogers. In addition there is one interior black-and-white illustration, each installment, by Samuel Cahan. Each issue sold for 10¢.

748. "**Tarzan and the Elephant Men**" (BLUE BOOK OF FICTION AND ADVENTURE, November, December 1937; January 1938)
Eight months after he finished "**The Resurrection of Jimber-Jaw**," Burroughs began work on a new Tarzan story in December of 1936. It was published as a three-part serial with a front cover illustration (November issue) by Herbert Morton Stoops. Using the pseudonym "Jeremy Cannon," Stoops did many interior black-and-white (and one sepia tone) illustrations for each installment. Each issue sold for 15¢. Four months after finishing this, he began work on *Carson of Venus*.

BY EDGAR RICE BURROUGHS

――――――――― FIRST EDITION ―――――――――

749. *Tarzan the Magnificent* (Tarzana: Edgar Rice Burroughs, Inc., September 25, 1939)
 This first edition was Burroughs' fifty-third hardback book. It is bound in the usual pebbled blue cloth with red lettering on the front cover and spine. It has the "First Edition" imprint on the copyright page. The dust jacket art and five interior black-and-white plates are by John Coleman Burroughs. The volume is dedicated to Cyril Ralph Rothmund (ERB's secretary and close friend). The first half of the hardback has some deletions when compared with the magazine serial. Price: $2.00. 318 numbered pages.

750. *Tarzan the Magnificent* (Tarzana: Edgar Rice Burroughs, Inc., 1948)
 Like the other 1948 reprints, this is bound in tan-gray cloth with blue lettering on the front cover and the spine. Dust jacket and frontispiece are by John Coleman Burroughs. Price: $1.00. 318 numbered pages.

751. *Tarzan the Magnificent* (New York: Ballantine Books, March 1964)
 The first paperback edition has front cover art by Richard Powers. Stock No. U2021, price 50¢. 192 numbered pages.

752. *Tarzan the Magnificent* (New York: Ballantine Books, September 1977)
 The fourth Ballantine printing has new front cover art by Boris Vallejo. Stock No. 25961, price $1.75. 192 numbered pages.

Tarzan the Terrible

753. "Tarzan the Terrible" (ARGOSY ALL-STORY WEEKLY, February 12, 19, 26; March 5, 12, 19, 26, 1921)
 Begun in August of 1920, this powerfully written seven-part serial reflected Burroughs's strongly negative attitude towards Germany as a result of World War I, and continues Tarzan's battle against the Germans in Africa, begun with the apparent murder of Jane in *Tarzan the Untamed* in 1919. It has a front cover illustration on the first installment by P. J. Monahan. There are no interior illustrations. Each issue sold for 10¢. Finishing this, ERB began writing *The Chessmen of Mars*.

――――――――― FIRST EDITION ―――――――――

754. *Tarzan the Terrible* (Chicago: A.C. McClurg & Co., June 20, 1921)
 The first edition of the twelfth hardback by ERB is bound in red decorated

I. BIBLIOGRAPHY OF BOOKS

Original McClurg first edition dust jacket for *Tarzan the Terrible* (1921)

cloth with black lettering on the front cover and spine. The dust jacket art and nine interior sepia plates are by J. Allen St. John, plus a map of Pal-ul-don by Burroughs and a glossary. One can find an "M. A. Donohue" printer's imprint on the copyright page. The title page clearly states "1921." The illustration facing page 248 uses the incorrect name "Ko-tan." 45,000 copies of the first, and one reprinting, were printed by A.C. McClurg in 1921 and 1922. Price: $1.90. 408 numbered pages.

755. *Tarzan the Terrible* (Chicago: A.C. McClurg & Co., 1922)
The first reprint has two points of difference compared to the first edition. First, the date "1922" appears on the title page. Secondly, an error in the illustration caption has been corrected: the first uses the name "Ko-tan" for the illustration facing page 248; it has been corrected to read "Mo-sar." This does have the M.A. Donohue printer's imprint on the copyright page. Price: $1.90. 408 numbered pages.

756. *Tarzan the Terrible* (New York: Grosset & Dunlap, 1923)
The second reprint, and the first G&D printing, is bound in red decorated cloth with black lettering on the front cover and spine. There is a dust jacket and *four* interior black-and-white illustrations by J. Allen St. John, plus a map of Pal-ul-don and glossary. The erroneous illustration has been corrected to read "Mo-sar" and moved facing page 234 (illustrations are facing pages 106, 170, and 234). For the earliest G&D printing, there are no ERB books mentioned in the advertisements in the back. In the next reprinting, the illustrations have been moved to pages 98, 162, and 242, and 6 ERB titles are listed in the back. A variant exists in a dull pink cover, with illustrations facing pages 98, 170, and 250, and 6 ERB titles listed in the ads at the back. In the 1924 printing, 11 ERB titles are listed at the back; in 1926 there are 15 titles. Subsequent printings list 28 titles (1930), 29 titles (this variant has yellow dye on the tops of the pages), and 33 titles (1934). The earliest dust jacket has ERB's photo in a blue oval device, with 3 ERB books listed inside a fancy red border. After 1924, the jackets have 8 ERB titles listed in the back in black print, and then 16 titles. After 1927, the jacket has a rectangular photo of ERB on the back. Price: 75¢. 408 numbered pages.

757. *Tarzan the Terrible* (New York: Grosset & Dunlap, 1934)
There are two later G&D variants, both bound in red decorated cloth with black lettering on the front cover and spine, but they have a green dye on the top of the pages. There are no illustrations. There are 33 titles in the ads in the back of the book in the 1934 variant, and only 22 titles in the 1939 printing. Sometime after 1933, the dust jacket has a yellow background with a sketch of ERB and different ERB titles advertised on the back flap. Price: 75¢. 408 numbered pages.

I. BIBLIOGRAPHY OF BOOKS

758. *Tarzan the Terrible* (New York: Grosset & Dunlap, 1940)
This reprinting, bound in red decorated cloth with black lettering on the front cover and spine, is distinguished from the earlier reprint by the total absence of interior illustrations. It does have the map by ERB and the glossary. Price: 75¢. 408 numbered pages.

759. *Tarzan the Terrible* (Racine, WI: Whitman Publishing Company, 1942).
This is one of the series of children's Better Little Books published by Whitman. These were small, thick, and aimed at children. They were completely illustrated, and printed on inexpensive paper. This series of books measures 3½" wide by 4⅜" high. The cover art is by John Coleman Burroughs, and the 209 interior illustrations were abridged from the 1931-1932 daily newspaper comic strip by Rex Maxon. This has one small illustration by John Coleman Burroughs in the upper corner of each page, which created the illusion of movement when the pages were flipped. Whitman number 1453. 432 pages. For more information on these, see #932–968.

760. *Tarzan the Terrible* (New York: Grosset & Dunlap, 1943)
The thin and inexpensive World War II wartime edition bound in maroon decorated cloth with black lettering on the front cover and spine. The dust jacket and decorated title page are by J. Allen St. John. There are no interior illustrations. The glossary is included. "Madison Square" imprint is on the dust jacket. Price: 50¢ until 1945, 49¢ thereafter. 305 numbered pages.

761. *Tarzan the Terrible* (New York: Grosset & Dunlap, July 1949)
The first time this title was reprinted in this post-war series, it was bound in green decorated *cloth* with dark lettering on the spine and sold for $1.00. The illustrated endpapers are a map of Africa done by Rafael Palacios. The dust jacket art is by C. Edmund Monroe. The book includes a glossary. The next 1955 reprinting of this title used tan paperbound boards with dark brown decorations and lettering. It included the endpaper map of Africa and sold for $1.25. The subsequent 1958 reprinting omitted the endpaper map by Palacios, and the price was raised to $1.50. 305 numbered pages.

762. *Tarzan the Terrible* (New York: Ballantine Books, July 1963)
The first paperback edition has a front cover illustration by Dick Powers. Stock No. F 752, price 50¢. A glossary is included. 220 numbered pages. Ballantine printed the first ten Tarzan stories in July, and they were almost immediately sold out. The titles were all reprinted in November 1963.

BY EDGAR RICE BURROUGHS

763. *Tarzan the Terrible* (New York: Grosset & Dunlap, 1967)
This is a reprint of the 1949 edition. It is bound in pictorial boards with front cover art by C. Edmund Monroe. The number 2635 is on the spine. 305 numbered pages.

764. *Tarzan the Terrible* (New York: Ballantine Books, October 1969)
The third Ballantine paperback printing has a new front cover illustration by Robert Abbett. Stock No. 01750, price 50¢. Includes glossary. 220 numbered pages.

765. *Tarzan the Terrible* (New York: Ballantine Books, November 1976)
The sixth Ballantine reprint has a new front cover illustration by Boris Vallejo. Stock No. 24167, price $1.25. Includes glossary. 220 numbered pages.

Tarzan the Untamed

766. "Tarzan the Untamed" (THE RED BOOK MAGAZINE, March, April, May, June, July, August 1919)
This powerfully written Tarzan novel begins with the apparent death of Jane at the hands of German army officers. Burroughs began work on it in September 1918, and the book reflected America's strong anti–German sentiments as a result of World War I, as is obvious in its original title, "**Tarzan and the Huns.**" It was started about a month after ERB completed "**Out of Time's Abyss.**" It was first published as a six-part serial with 25 black-and-white illustrations by Charles Livingston Bull. Each issue sold for 20¢.

767. "Tarzan and the Valley of Luna" (ALL-STORY WEEKLY, March 20, 27; April 3, 10, 17, 1920)
This five-part serial, which continues Tarzan's savage revenge against the German military, has a front cover illustration on the March 20th issue by P. J. Monahan. There were no interior illustrations. Each issue sold for 10¢. Finishing this book, Burroughs brought the saga to completion and resurrected Jane in *Tarzan the Terrible*.

─────────────── FIRST EDITION ───────────────

768. *Tarzan the Untamed* (Chicago: A.C. McClurg & Co., April 30, 1920)
This was the tenth novel published by ERB, and the first edition is bound in a light olive-green cloth with brown lettering on the front cover and spine. The dust jacket and nine interior sepia plates are by J. Allen St. John. There is

I. BIBLIOGRAPHY OF BOOKS

"Tarzan and the Valley of Luna" (part of *Tarzan the Untamed*) March 20, 1920

an "M. A. Donohue" imprint on the copyright page, and it is clearly marked 1920 on the title page. This must have been the period of peak popularity for Burroughs, as McClurg printed a combined total of 77,000 copies of the first and one subsequent reprinting. The second largest printing is 63,000 copies for *Jungle Tales of Tarzan* in four printings. Price: $1.90. At 428 numbered pages, this is the lengthiest ERB hardback novel.

769. *Tarzan the Untamed* (Chicago: A.C. McClurg & Co., 1921)
This McClurg reprint is identical with the first edition described above, except that it is clearly marked 1921 on the title page and is bound in brighter green cloth with brown lettering on the front cover and spine. The dust jacket and nine interior sepia plates are by J. Allen St. John. There is an "M. A. Donohue" imprint on the copyright page. Price: $1.90. 428 numbered pages.

770. *Tarzan the Untamed* (New York: Grosset & Dunlap, 1922)
The first G&D reprint is bound in light red cloth cover with black lettering on the front cover and spine. The dust jacket and *four* (not nine) interior black-and-white plates are by J. Allen St. John. The illustrations face pages 128, 232 and 352. The earliest G&D jacket has a photograph of ERB in an oval device and lists three ERB titles with six ERB titles listed on the reverse side of the jacket. The next jacket version also has the ERB photo in an oval design, but lists eight ERB titles on the back. Price: 75¢. 428 numbered pages.

771. *Tarzan the Untamed* (New York: Grosset & Dunlap, 1926)
A subsequent G&D reprint is bound in the standard red cloth cover with black lettering on the front cover and spine. The dust jacket and four interior black-and-white plates are by J. Allen St. John. The illustrations face pages 136, 232 and 360. Advertisements at the back of the book include 15 ERB titles. Price: 75¢. 428 numbered pages.

772. *Tarzan the Untamed* (New York: Grosset & Dunlap, 1928)
Subsequent G&D reprintings are bound in the standard red cloth cover with black lettering on the front cover and spine. The dust jacket and four interior black-and-white plates are by J. Allen St. John. The illustrations face pages 136, 264 and 360, and then 136, 256, and 360. There are nine pages of advertisements at the back of the book, including 25 ERB titles. A 1929 reprinting lists 28 ERB titles in the ads at the back; in the 1931 reprinting, 29 ERB titles are listed; 33 ERB titles appear in the back of the 1934 reprint, and 37 titles are in the ads for the 1936 reprinting. The later jackets for *Tarzan the Untamed* have ERB's photo in a rectangular design, and list 28 titles (in black letters), then 32 titles (in blue letters). After 1933, the back of the jacket has a yellow background and 34 titles (printed in green letters). Price: 75¢. 428 numbered pages.

773. Tarzan the Untamed (New York: Grosset & Dunlap, 1940)
This reprint, bound in red cloth with dark green lettering on the front cover and spine, is distinguished by the total absence of interior illustrations (as is typical of the 1940s G&D reprint series). Dust jacket by J. Allen St. John. Price: 75¢. 428 numbered pages.

774. Tarzan the Untamed (Racine, WI: Whitman Publishing Company, 1941)
This is one of the series of Better Little Books published by Whitman in paper boards. Its small size and cheap paper made it appropriate for children. The book measures 3½" × 4⅜". The cover illustration is by John Coleman Burroughs, while the interior art is adapted from Rex Maxon's 1932-1933 daily Tarzan comic strip. Whitman number 1452. 432 pages. For more information on these, see #932–968.

775. Tarzan the Untamed (New York: Grosset & Dunlap, 1943)
The cheap World War II wartime edition is bound in maroon cloth with black lettering on the front cover and spine. There are no interior illustrations. The book has the "Madison Square" identifying mark on the dust jacket and the small St. John decoration on the title page. The book sold for 50¢ until 1945, when the price was dropped to 49¢. 309 numbered pages.

776. Tarzan the Untamed (New York: Grosset & Dunlap, April 1948)
The first time G&D reprinted this title after World War II, it was bound in red cloth and sold for $1.00. The dust jacket illustration is by C. Edmund Monroe. There are illustrated endpapers with a map of Africa and a title page decoration by Rafael Palacios. The next time G&D reprinted this title (1955), it appeared in tan paperbound boards with brown decoration and lettering, but it included the endpaper map of Africa. It sold for $1.25. When reprinted in 1958, the endpaper map was omitted, and the price was raised to $1.50. 309 numbered pages.

777. Tarzan the Untamed (New York: Ballantine Books, July 1963)
The first paperback printing of *Tarzan the Untamed* has a front cover by Richard Powers. Stock No. F 751, price 50¢. 254 numbered pages. Ballantine printed the first ten Tarzan stories in July, and they sold out almost immediately. A second printing appeared in November 1963.

778. Tarzan the Untamed (New York: Grosset & Dunlap, 1967)
This hardback was bound in pictorial boards with a front cover illustration by C. E. Monroe, Jr. (it is the same illustration as the dust wrapper in the previous 1948 G&D edition). There is a decorated title page. The book number, 2636, is on the spine. 309 numbered pages.

779. *Tarzan the Untamed* (New York: Ballantine Books, October 1969)
The third paperback printing has a new front cover by Robert Abbett. Stock No. 01749, price 50¢. 254 numbered pages.

780. *Tarzan the Untamed* (New York: Ballantine Books, November 1976)
The sixth paperback printing has a new front cover illustration by Boris Vallejo. Stock No. 24166, price $1.25. 254 numbered pages.

781. *Tarzan the Untamed* (New York: Ballantine–Del Rey, June 1991)
The sixteenth paperback printing uses the Boris Vallejo front cover illustration but it has a white border around it (earlier printings have a yellow border). Stock No. 32391, price $3.95. 254 numbered pages.

Tarzan Triumphant

782. "The Triumph of Tarzan" (THE BLUE BOOK MAGAZINE, October, November, December 1931; January, February, March 1932)
This six-part serial whose original title was "**Tarzan and the Raiders,**" had front cover illustrations, first and third issues, by Laurence Herndon. Frank Hoban provided many black-and-white interior illustrations for each issue. Each issue sold for 25¢. The Tarzan tale was started in February of 1931, after Burroughs completed *The Deputy Sheriff of Comanche County*, but not until after Burroughs had spent seven frustrating months trying to market his western story.

──────────────── FIRST EDITION ────────────────

783. *Tarzan Triumphant* (Tarzana: Edgar Rice Burroughs, Inc., September 1, 1932)
Burroughs' thirty-eighth hardback appeared in first edition bound in the usual pebbled blue cloth with red lettering on the front cover and spine. It is the third hardback published by Burroughs' own publishing company, and does *not* have the "First Edition" imprint on the copyright page. There is a dust jacket and five interior black-and-white plates by Studley Burroughs (ERB's nephew). Price: $2.00. 318 numbered pages.

784. *Tarzan Triumphant* (New York: "Mixed Edition," 1934)
This reprint is bound in red cloth with black lettering on the front cover and the G&D imprint on the spine. However, inside it is identical with #783 above and has an ERB, Inc. title page. The dust jacket and four interior black-and-white plates are by Studley Burroughs. Price: 75¢. 318 numbered pages.

I. BIBLIOGRAPHY OF BOOKS

785. *Tarzan Triumphant* (New York: Grosset & Dunlap, 1934)
The first G&D reprint is bound in red cloth with black lettering on the front cover and spine and the page tops are dyed green. The earliest printing has three pages of advertisements at the end of the book; a subsequent printing has four pages of ads. It has a dust jacket and four interior black-and-white plates by Studley Burroughs. The earliest jacket has 34 ERB books listed in the inside reverse of the jacket. Later jackets are blank on the inside. Price: 75¢. 318 numbered pages.

786. *Tarzan Triumphant* (New York: Grosset & Dunlap, 1940)
The 1940 reprint is bound in red cloth with black lettering on the front cover and spine. The page tops are dyed green. It can be distinguished from the previous reprint by its total absence of interior illustrations. The dust jacket is by Studley Burroughs. Price: 75¢. 318 numbered pages.

787. *Tarzan Triumphant* (Tarzana: Edgar Rice Burroughs, Inc., 1940)
The ERB, Inc. reprint is one of seven titles bound in red cloth with blue lettering on the front cover and spine. The Studley Burroughs dust jacket is identical with the first edition dust jacket. The book also includes the frontispiece by Studley Burroughs. Price: 75¢. 318 numbered pages.

788. *Tarzan Triumphant* (Tarzana: Edgar Rice Burroughs, Inc., March 26, 1948)
The second reprint series is bound in the usual 1948 tan-gray boards with blue lettering on the front cover and spine. It has the dust jacket and black-and-white frontispiece by Studley Burroughs. Price: $1.00. 318 numbered pages.

789. *Tarzan Triumphant* (New York: Ace Books, Inc., April 1963)
This is the first paperback edition with front cover art and title page drawing by Roy G. Krenkel. The cover was completed with the assistance of Frank Frazetta. Stock No. F-194, price 40¢. 222 numbered pages.

790. *Tarzan Triumphant* (New York: Ballantine Books, March 1964)
The first Ballantine paperback edition has front cover art by Richard Powers. Stock No. U2015, price 50¢. 192 numbered pages.

791. *Tarzan Triumphant* (New York: Ballantine Books, April 1970)
The second Ballantine paperback printing has new front cover art by Robert Abbett. Stock No. 01909, price 75¢. 192 numbered pages.

792. *Tarzan Triumphant* (New York: Ballantine Books, November 1975)
The fourth Ballantine paperback printing has new front cover art by Neal Adams. Stock No. 24485, price $1.25. 192 numbered pages.

BY EDGAR RICE BURROUGHS

Tarzan's Quest

793. "**Tarzan and the Immortal Men**" (THE BLUE BOOK MAGAZINE, October, November, December 1935; January, February, March 1936)
This six-part serial, written directly after *Swords of Mars*, was begun in May of 1934 and was not completed until January 1935. It has a front cover illustration on the first installment by Herbert Morton Stoops. Frank Hoban provided numerous interior black-and-white illustrations for each installment. Each issue sold for 15¢. This story is important because it marks the final appearance of Jane as a major character in the Tarzan series. Rather than a pure Tarzan story, it stresses Jane's resourcefulness and strength dealing with jungle situations. One working title was "**Tarzan and Jane.**"

---FIRST EDITION---

794. *Tarzan's Quest* (Tarzana: Edgar Rice Burroughs, Inc., September 1, 1936)
The first edition of Burroughs's forty-seventh hardback is bound in blue cloth with red lettering on the front cover and spine. The back of the copyright page says "First Edition." There is a wrap-around dust jacket and five black-and-white plates by J. Allen St. John. As with several other of the ERB first editions, the dust jacket appears in (1) a laminated state, and (2) an unlaminated state. Price: $2.00. 318 numbered pages.

795. *Tarzan's Quest* (New York: Grosset & Dunlap, 1938)
The first reprint is bound in red cloth with black lettering on the front cover and spine. The dust jacket and one black-and-white frontispiece are by J. Allen St. John. Price: 75¢. 318 numbered pages.

796. *Tarzan's Quest* (Tarzana: Edgar Rice Burroughs, Inc., 1940)
This reprint is one of the seven ERB, Inc. reprints bound in red cloth with blue lettering on the front cover and spine. There is a binding variant with red textured cloth (a pattern imprinted on the material instead of woven). The dust jacket by J. Allen St. John is the first edition jacket put on a reprint book. This reprinting also includes the black-and-white frontispiece by J. Allen St. John. Price: 75¢. 318 numbered pages.

797. *Tarzan's Quest* (Tarzana: Grosset & Dunlap, 1940)
This reprint is distinguished from the 1938 G&D reprint by the absence of the frontispiece, and by the fact that the page tops were dyed black. In fact, the 1940 G&D reprints are easily distinguished because they were all printed with-

out the original frontispiece art work. The dust jacket is by J. Allen St. John. Price: 75¢. 318 numbered pages.

798. *Tarzan's Quest* (Tarzana: Edgar Rice Burroughs, Inc., March 26, 1948)
This reprint, like the other 1948 reprints, is bound in tan-gray boards with blue lettering on the front cover and spine. The jacket and black-and-white frontispiece are by J. Allen St. John. Price: $1.00. 318 numbered pages.

799. *Tarzan's Quest* (New York: Ballantine Books, March 1964)
The first paperback printing is illustrated with front cover art by Richard Powers. Stock No. U2019, price 50¢. 191 numbered pages.

800. *Tarzan's Quest* (New York: Ballantine Books, September 1977)
The fourth Ballantine paperback printing has a new front cover illustration by Boris Vallejo. Stock No. 25959, price $1.75. 191 numbered pages.

Thuvia, Maid of Mars

801. "Thuvia, Maid of Mars" (ALL-STORY WEEKLY, April 8, 15, 22, 1916)
This three-part serial, originally entitled **"Carthoris,"** was Burroughs' sixteenth story. ERB began work on it in April 1914, about three weeks after completing **"The Girl from Farris's."** When published in ALL-STORY WEEKLY, it had an exquisite front cover illustration on the first installment by P. J. Monahan. The same illustration was used four years later for the dust jacket of the McClurg first edition. There are no interior illustrations. Each issue sold for 10¢. Finishing this, Burroughs returned to complete his story of an island romance with **"The Cave Man."**

───────────── FIRST EDITION ─────────────

802. *Thuvia, Maid of Mars* (Chicago: A.C. McClurg & Co., October 30, 1920)
This is the eleventh hardback by Burroughs, and the fourth Mars book. The first edition is bound in olive green decorated cloth with black lettering on the front cover and spine. The dust jacket art by P. J. Monahan is reproduced from the magazine cover. J. Allen St. John provided ten interior sepia plates. The book includes a glossary of names and terms at the back, added so that the book would reach minimum length for hardback publication. A.C. McClurg records indicate that a total of 17,000 copies were printed of the first and one reprinting. Price: $1.75. 256 numbered pages.

803. *Thuvia, Maid of Mars* (Chicago: A.C. McClurg & Co., 1921)
The first reprint is the same in content as the first edition described above, except the title page date is clearly marked 1921. This edition is noticeably thicker than the relatively thin first edition described above. Price: $1.75. 256 numbered pages.

804. *Thuvia, Maid of Mars* ("Mixed edition," McClurg and Grosset & Dunlap, 1921)
There is also a darker olive green version of *Thuvia, Maid of Mars* with a McClurg binding and text, and a Grosset & Dunlap title page tipped in. The thickness of the books may vary. 256 numbered pages.

805. *Thuvia, Maid of Mars* (New York: Grosset & Dunlap, 1921)
This G&D reprint is bound in pink cloth with the same decoration as the first edition, and with black lettering on the front cover and spine. The next reprinting has a red-brown cover. There are only *four* (not ten) interior black-and-white plates by J. Allen St. John, facing pages 82, 130, and 242. The next reprinting has a flat brown cover, and illustrations facing pages 90, 138, and 234. These all have six pages of advertisements at the back of the book. The earliest jackets use the P.J. Monahan illustration, but have only three ERB titles listed on the back and a photo of ERB in an oval shaped design. The 1922 dust jacket has six ERB titles listed, with the oval design around the photo. Original price: $1.00. In 1922, the price was dropped to 75¢. 256 numbered pages.

806. *Thuvia, Maid of Mars* (New York: Grosset & Dunlap, 1922–1934).
At the end of 1921 or early 1922, G&D reprinted this title bound in the traditional red cloth with black lettering on the front cover and spine. It has 10 pages of ads at the back of the book, but none of them are for ERB books. The four illustrations face pages 82, 124, and 250. The next reprinting has a pink-brown cover with six ERB titles listed among the ads. It is probably after 1922. The illustrations face pages 74, 122, and 250, and remain anchored here for subsequent reprints. The next reprinting is again in red, listing 11 ERB titles among the 9 pages of ads at the back. The probable date is after 1924. The 1927 reprinting lists 15 ERB titles at the back ads. In 1928, there are 23 ERB titles in the ads. The 1934 reprinting lists 33 ERB titles among its 10 pages of ads. The earliest jackets use the P.J. Monahan illustration, but the backs of the 1924 jackets use a rectangular design around ERB's photo, and list 12 titles. Jackets exist with 16 titles (1926), 24 titles (1929), or 28 titles (after 1929). Although the earliest price was $1.00, after 1922, the price was dropped to 75¢. 256 numbered pages.

807. *Thuvia, Maid of Mars* (New York: Grosset & Dunlap, 1940)
This G&D reprint is bound in red cloth with the same decoration as first edition, and with black lettering on the front cover and spine. It uses the P.J. Mon-

ahan dust jacket. There are *no* interior black-and-white plates. Price: 75¢. 256 numbered pages.

808. *Thuvia, Maid of Mars* (Tarzana: Edgar Rice Burroughs, Inc., March 26, 1948)
Like the other 1948 reprints, this is bound in tan-gray boards with dark red lettering on the front cover and spine. The P. J. Monahan dust jacket remains unchanged. There is *one* black-and-white frontispiece by J. Allen St. John. This reprint includes the glossary of names. Price: $1.00. 256 numbered pages.

809. *Three Martian Novels: Thuvia, Maid of Mars / The Chessmen of Mars / The Master Mind of Mars* (New York: Dover Publications, Inc., April 1962, October 1963, and again at least seven different times)
This compilation volume was one of the very first Burroughs books available in the early 1960s, and presaged the Burroughs revival dominated by the Ace paperbacks and the Canaveral hardbacks. It is a large size (5⅜" × 8½"), thick paperback with cover and 16 interior black-and-white illustrations by J. Allen St. John. The stories are continuously paginated. Stock No. T39, price $1.75, raised to $1.85 in October, 1963. There are 499 numbered pages.

810. *Thuvia, Maid of Mars* (New York: Ace Books, Inc., November 1962)
The first paperback edition has front cover art and a title page drawing by Roy G. Krenkel. Stock No. F-168, price 40¢. 143 numbered pages.

811. *Three Martian Novels: Thuvia, Maid of Mars / The Chessmen of Mars / The Master Mind of Mars* (New York: Peter Smith, 1963).
This is the Dover volume (listed above) bound in a red cloth hardback (with black lettering on the spine only) for the use of libraries. It has 16 St. John illustrations. The book sold for $3.75. 499 numbered pages.

812. *Thuvia, Maid of Mars* (New York: Ballantine Books, September 1963)
The first Ballantine paperback edition has a front cover illustration by Robert Abbett. Stock No. F 770, price 50¢. Includes the glossary of names. 158 numbered pages.

813. *Thuvia, Maid of Mars* (New York: Ballantine Books, February 1969)
This third Ballantine paperback printing has new front cover art by Robert Abbett. Stock No. 01524, price 50¢. 158 numbered pages.

814. *Thuvia, Maid of Mars* and *The Chessmen of Mars* (New York: Doubleday, 1972)

BY *EDGAR RICE BURROUGHS*

The Science-Fiction Book Club edition is bound in green boards with gold lettering on the spine. A beautiful wrap-around dust jacket illustration and six interior black-and-white illustrations are by Frank Frazetta. The two stories are consecutively paginated. 341 numbered pages.

815. *Thuvia, Maid of Mars* (New York: Ballantine Books, October 1973)
This fourth Ballantine paperback printing has new front cover art by Gino D'Achille. The attractive cover illustration was also issued separately as a large 24" × 36" poster ($3.50) with "Welcome to Barsoom" in large letters on the bottom. Stock No. 23581, price $1.25. 158 numbered pages.

816. *Thuvia, Maid of Mars* (New York: Ballantine–Del Rey, May 1979)
This eleventh Ballantine paperback printing has new front cover art by Michael Whelan. Stock No. 27837, price $1.95. 158 numbered pages.

817. *Science Fiction Classics by Edgar Rice Burroughs* (Secaucus, NJ: Castle, 1982)
This anthology volume is bound in orange boards with black lettering on spine. The dust jacket design is inspired by the J. Allen St. John original, and the 26 interior black-and-white illustrations are photographs of the originals by St. John. In addition there is one black-and-white illustration by Paul F. Berdanier. This volume contains five novels: *Pellucidar; Thuvia, Maid of Mars; Tanar of Pellucidar; The Chessmen of Mars;* and *The Master Mind of Mars.* The specific Castle printing can be determined from the numbers on the copyright page. The five novels are continuously paginated. ISBN 0-89009-582-5. 451 numbered pages.

818. *Science Fiction Classics by Edgar Rice Burroughs* (Secaucus, NJ: Castle, 1982)
The second printing of this anthology volume (bound in orange boards with black lettering on spine) has a new dust jacket illustration by Kevin Johnson. The interior illustrations are unchanged. This volume contains the same five novels described above. The specific Castle printing can be determined from the numbers on the copyright page. The five novels are continuously paginated. ISBN 0-89009-582-5. 451 numbered pages.

819. *Science Fiction Classics by Edgar Rice Burroughs* (Secaucus, NJ: Castle, 1982)
The third printing of this anthology volume is bound in maroon boards with gold lettering on spine. This volume contains the same five novels: *Pellucidar; Thuvia, Maid of Mars; Tanar of Pellucidar; The Chessmen of Mars;* and *The Master Mind of Mars.* The specific Castle printing can be determined from the

numbers on the copyright page. The five novels are continuously paginated. ISBN 0-89009-582-5. 451 numbered pages.

820. *Three Martian Novels: Thuvia, Maid of Mars / The Chessmen of Mars / The Master Mind of Mars* (New York: Dover Publications, Inc.)
This compilation volume was reprinted with a different cover by J. Allen St. John from *The Gods of Mars*. It is a thick paperback with 16 interior black-and-white illustrations by J. Allen St. John. The stories are continuously paginated. Stock No. 486-20039-6. The price is $9.95. There are 499 numbered pages.

The War Chief

821. "The War Chief" (ARGOSY ALL-STORY WEEKLY, April 16, 23, 30; May 7, 14, 1927)
In August 1926, nine months after completing *The Master Mind of Mars*, Burroughs began work on this western tale, originally entitled "**The War Chief of the Apaches**," which reflected ERB's deep and abiding respect for the Apaches gained during his experiences when he was a young man with the 7th U.S. Cavalry in Arizona in 1896-1897. It was first published as a five-part serial with a front cover illustration for the first installment by Paul Stahr. In addition, there is one interior black-and-white illustration, each installment, by Roger B. Morrison. Each issue sold for 10¢. Four days after finishing this western, he began work on a new Tarzan tale, *The Tarzan Twins* (first published by Volland in 1927).

———————— FIRST EDITION ————————
822. *The War Chief* (Chicago: A.C. McClurg & Co., September 15, 1927)
The first edition of Burroughs's twenty-seventh hardback is bound in orange cloth with dark brown lettering on the front cover and spine. A profile drawing of the Apache hero is underneath the title on the front cover and spine. The dust jacket illustration by Paul Stahr is the same as the initial magazine appearance (April 16th, 1927). There is also a decorated title page by an unidentified artist (an Indian on the top of a tall cliff, overlooking a valley), but no frontispiece or other illustrations. There is a glossary at the end of the book. A.C. McClurg records indicate that 6,000 copies of the first edition were printed. Price: $2.00. 382 numbered pages.

BY EDGAR RICE BURROUGHS

823. *The War Chief* (New York: Grosset & Dunlap, 1928)
The first reprint is bound in red cloth with black lettering on the front cover and spine. All other points are the same as the first, including the drawing of the Apache hero underneath the title on the front cover and spine, the dust jacket by Paul Stahr, and the decorated title page. This reprint does include the glossary. Price: 75¢. 383 numbered pages.

824. *The War Chief* (New York: Ballantine Books, June 1964)
The first paperback edition has front cover art by Ronnie M. Lessor. Stock No. U2045, price 50¢. The book includes a glossary. 190 numbered pages.

825. *The War Chief* (Boston, Gregg, 1978)
This reprint is bound in dark brown cloth with gold lettering on the spine. The dust jacket is obviously adapted from the Paul Stahr title page (the Indian on a cliff) of the first edition. There are no interior illustrations. Includes the glossary. 382 numbered pages.

826. *The War Chief* (New York: Ballantine Books, February 1973)
The second Ballantine edition has new front cover art by Frank McCarthy. Stock No. 03082, price 95¢. The book includes a glossary. 190 numbered pages.

827. *The War Chief* (New York: Ballantine Books, October 1975)
The third Ballantine edition was reset and has new front cover art by Greg and Tim Hildebrandt. Stock No. 24634, price $1.25. The book includes a glossary. 215 numbered pages.

The Warlord of Mars

828. "Warlord of Mars" (THE ALL-STORY, December 1913; January–March 1914)
After he finished *The Monster Men*, Burroughs set to work on his third story of Mars, and his ninth novel. Begun in June of 1913, the entire book took just one month to complete. The ending of the second Mars tale (*The Gods of Mars*) had left Dejah Thoris in a very serious predicament, and it was time to extricate her. The original title which ERB had used was **"Yellow Men of Barsoom"** and then **"The Fighting Prince of Mars."** Then he toyed with **"Across Savage Mars."** The title he used when he sent it in to the editor at THE ALL-STORY was **"The Prince of Helium"** although he also suggested **"The War Lord of Mars."** It was published as a four-part serial, 15¢ each issue, with an interesting front cover illustration for the Christmas 1913 issue by F. W. Small. The same Fred W. Small

I. BIBLIOGRAPHY OF BOOKS

"The Warlord of Mars" December 1913

The Warlord of Mars

black-and-white headpiece appears in each installment. The three novels, *A Princess of Mars*, *The Gods of Mars*, and this, *The Warlord of Mars*, comprise a classic trilogy which was profoundly important in shaping the history of science-fiction. A month after completing this, ERB began to write a serious novel focusing upon social inequity in Chicago: *The Mucker*.

———————————— FIRST EDITION ————————————

829. *The Warlord of Mars* (Chicago: A.C. McClurg & Co., September 27, 1919)

The first edition of Burroughs' ninth hardback is bound in dark red cloth with gold lettering on the front cover and spine. The dust jacket cover illustration is by J. Allen St. John, with same illustration used for the sepia frontispiece. The copyright has a "W.F. Hall" imprint. This title had the largest print run of all the McClurg "Mars" books. A.C. McClurg records indicate that 20,000 copies of the first and one subsequent reprinting were printed. Price: $1.40. 296 numbered pages.

830. *The Warlord of Mars* (Chicago: A.C. McClurg & Co., 1919)

The first reprint is by McClurg, and is virtually identical to the first edition. The only difference is the *absence* of the "W. F. Hall" imprint on the copyright page. Price: $1.40.

831. *The Warlord of Mars* (New York: Grosset & Dunlap, 1920)

The G&D reprint comes bound in many different colors of cloth. The earliest has a dark maroon cover with black letters and, in the back, has ads for Zane Grey and B.M. Bower. What is probably the next reprinting has ads for Zane Grey and Jack London, and appears with the same maroon cover and then with a brown cover with orange letters. It was reprinted, perhaps in 1921, with the same two pages of ads and either a tan or dark blue cover. A 1924 reprinting has a pale green cover, and has a one-page ad listing eleven ERB titles. A medium green cover has 13 pages of ads (11 ERB titles). A light green cover with black letters has 15 ERB titles listed (probably 1926). The 1927 reprinting lists 23 ERB titles. A gray-green cover lists 28 ERB titles (probably 1930). These are all listed in the Heins bibliography. The St. John dust jacket and black-and-white frontispiece are the same illustrations as the first edition. The earliest dust jacket has a photo of ERB on the rear and lists three ERB titles. The 1923 jacket lists eight ERB titles on the rear. The 1925 jacket lists 12 ERB titles. The next has 24 ERB titles (probably 1928), and a 1932 jacket lists 32 titles on the rear. The 1920 printing sold for $1.00; after 1922 they were all 75¢ each. 296 numbered pages.

832. *The Warlord of Mars* (New York: Grosset & Dunlap, 1940)

The 1940 G&D reprint can be easily identified by the absence of all interior illustrations, including the frontispiece. It is bound with red cloth (perhaps other colors too), with black lettering on the front cover and spine. Price: 75¢. 296 numbered pages.

833. *The Warlord of Mars* (Tarzana: Edgar Rice Burroughs, Inc., March 26, 1948)
Like the other 1948 ERB, Inc. reprints, this is bound in tan-gray boards with dark brown lettering on the front cover and spine. The dust jacket and frontispiece, like the others, are by J. Allen St. John. The copyright page says "Copyright ERB 1947." Price: $1.00. 296 numbered pages.

834. *The Warlord of Mars* (New York: Ballantine Books, March 1963)
The first paperback printing has a front cover illustration by Robert Abbett. Stock No. F 711. The price 50¢. 158 numbered pages.

835. *The Warlord of Mars* and *Thuvia, Maid of Mars* (New York: Doubleday, 1971)
The black covered Science-Fiction Book Club edition has a very attractive wrap-around dust jacket and interior illustrations by Frank Frazetta. 336 pages.

836. *The Warlord of Mars* (New York: Ballantine Books, October 1973)
The sixth paperback printing has a new front cover illustration by Gino D'Achille. Stock No. 23580. The price is $1.25. 158 numbered pages.

837. *The Warlord of Mars* (New York: Ballantine–Del Rey, May 1979)
The thirteenth paperback printing has a new front cover illustration by Michael Whelan. Stock No. 27836. The price is $1.95. 158 numbered pages.

838. *The Warlord of Mars* (New York: Buccaneer Books, 1983)
This hardback is bound in black cloth with red and yellow lettering on its spine. The book never had a dust wrapper. There are no illustrations. 158 numbered pages.

The Wizard of Venus

FIRST EDITION

839. *Tales of Three Planets* (New York: Canaveral Press, Inc., April 27, 1964)
The first edition of this, the sixty-second Burroughs hardback, is bound with two different color bindings: blue cloth and tan cloth with black lettering

on the front cover and spine. Roy G. Krenkel provided the dust jacket art, the illustrated endpages, and ten interior black-and-white illustrations. In addition, there are several maps and an alphabet by Arlene Williamson. Richard A. Lupoff, the editor, provides an eight-page introduction. This anthology contains "**Beyond the Farthest Star**," "**The Resurrection of Jimber-Jaw**," "**Tangor Returns**," and "**The Wizard of Venus**." The four stories are consecutively paginated; 282 numbered pages.

840. *The Wizard of Venus* (Idaho Falls, ID: Habblitz & Broadhurst, summer 1964)
This nicely done illustrated fanzine was produced as a souvenir of the twenty-second World Science Fiction Convention held in Los Angeles. It is bound in paper wrappers with front and back cover illustrations by Harry Habblitz. The story was adapted from ERB's 1941 short story (completed three months before the bombing of Pearl Harbor) by Dale Broadhurst and illustrated by Mike Royer. 36 numbered pages.

841. *The Wizard of Venus* (New York: Ace Books, Inc., August 1970)
This first Ace printing has front cover art by Roy G. Krenkel but does not have a title page sketch. Advertising the fact that the book included "**Pirate Blood**," which was a new ERB story, the cover has: "Including the first publication anywhere of PIRATE BLOOD Burroughs' last great adventure novel." Stock No. 90190, price 60¢. Consecutively paginated; 158 numbered pages.

842. *The Wizard of Venus* (New York: Ace Books, Inc., January 1973)
Second paperback printing with front cover art and title page drawing by Roy G. Krenkel. Stock No. 90191, price 75¢. Contains "**Pirate Blood**." 158 pages.

843. *Tales of Three Planets* (New York: Canaveral Press, Inc., 1974)
Canaveral reprinted this title in 1974. It has the same interior as the first edition. In addition to "**The Wizard of Venus**," this anthology contains "**Beyond the Farthest Star**," "**The Resurrection of Jimber-Jaw**," and "**Tangor Returns**." The four stories are consecutively paginated; 282 numbered pages.

844. *The Wizard of Venus and Pirate Blood* (New York: Ace Books, Inc., June 1979)
Although the copyright page states that this is the third printing (the third printing is Stock No. 90192), actually this is the *fourth* Ace reprinting. The front cover art is by Esteban Maroto. Stock No. 90193, price $1.95. Contains "**Pirate Blood**." 248 pages.

845. *The Wizard of Venus and Pirate Blood* (New York: Ballantine–Del Rey, July 1991)

I. BIBLIOGRAPHY OF BOOKS

The first authorized Ballantine–Del Rey printing has a cover illustration by Richard Hescox. Stock No. 37012, price $3.95. 186 pages.

You Lucky Girl!

NOTE: The 1994 announcement that ERB, Inc. would allow the publication of two hitherto unpublished manuscripts by Burroughs was welcome news for his numerous fans. It is very probable that the 1927 "You Lucky Girl!," a 23,000-word play, was written by Burroughs as a vehicle for his daughter Joan (pronounced "Jo-ann"), who wanted to be an actress. One of Joan's best friends was Florence Gilbert, who had been a popular movie actress in many silent films of the 1920s, and she may have been an influence upon Joan. Joan attended a private school which taught stage acting, and she landed a few small and unimportant roles in a stock company in Ogden, Utah, for a few weeks. Then she had several roles in the Glendale Playhouse, Glendale, California (near Tarzana). One year later Joan Burroughs became Mrs. Jim Pierce (James Pierce played the role of Tarzan in a 1927 film and in a radio series), and it is very likely that the play written by her father was put away and forgotten. Although not in ERB's notebook, it is likely that *You Lucky Girl!* was written between *The Tarzan Twins* and *Tarzan the Invincible*. *You Lucky Girl!* received its world premiere performance in April and May, 1997, at the Palmdale Playhouse, Palmdale, California. Guided into production and directed by Hugh Munro Neely, the play received glowing reviews.

──────────── FIRST EDITION ────────────

846. *You Lucky Girl!* (Hampton Falls, NH: Donald M. Grant, Publishers, 1997)

In 1995, Donald M. Grant, Publishers, announced that they intended to publish this Burroughs rarity in 1997. The book will be published in two versions: a limited deluxe edition ($60) and a regular trade edition ($30). The story has never appeared in any form previous to the Grant publication. Illustrated by Ned Dameron. The number of pages is unknown.

© 1993, Thomas Yeates

II
Other Bibliographies

II. OTHER BIBLIOGRAPHIES

Unpublished and Miscellaneous Short Works by Burroughs

(Alphabetical by title)

The titles on the following list were obtained from many different sources. One was a shorter list compiled by Hulbert Burroughs in 1972, and shared with the readers of ERB-DOM (#56). I have also used the list in Heins, *A Golden Anniversary Bibliography of Edgar Rice Burroughs*, pp. 230-231, and included various titles described throughout Porges, *Edgar Rice Burroughs: The Man Who Created Tarzan*. Some of these smaller pieces have been reprinted in Burroughs fanzines. Each piece is unpublished unless otherwise indicated. The texts whose dates can be established are included on the list found in Appendix G of this book.

847. "The Absurd Quarantine" (for a Los Angeles newspaper on hoof and mouth disease in the San Fernando Valley, probably early 1920s)
848. "Angel's Serenade" (1939; 24,000 words)
849. "Author-Publisher" (for WRITER'S DIGEST, 1937)
850. *An Auto-Biography* (Republic Motor Truck Company, 1916; 150 were reprinted in 1996 by Robert Zeuschner for attendees of the 1996 Tarzana Dum-Dum)
851. *Autobiography of Edgar Rice Burroughs* (incomplete; 15,000–20,000 words)
852. "The Avenger" (approx. 3,600 words from 1912)
853. "Ballad of the B's" (unpublished poem from 1937; Burroughs referred to himself as "Big B" and to his wife, Florence Gilbert Burroughs, as "Lil' B")
854. "The Bank Murder" (unpublished mystery story)
855. "The Birth of Tarzan, by His Poppa" (ROB WAGNER'S SCRIPT MAGAZINE, 1932)
856. "Black Man's Burden" (poem published in the POCATELLO TRIBUNE)
857. "BMTCers Can Shoot" (HONOLULU ADVERTISER, 1942)
858. "Calling All Cars" (1931 crime story, 6,531 words)
859. "Came the War [World War II]" (December, 1941, 2,700 words)
860. "The Citizen and the Police" (published in POLICE REPORTER, 1929; 1,500 words)
861. "The Climate and the View" (poem from 1914)
862. "Clubs Like the Edgewater" (1926 article on leisure)
863. "Creator of Tarzan Speaks" (1923, LOS ANGELES SUNDAY TIMES)

II. OTHER BIBLIOGRAPHIES

864. "Dear Old Eighty Two-Three" (unpublished poem)
865. "The Death Valley Expedition of the Intrepid 33ers" (1933, 2,700 words)
866. "Diary of a Confused Old Man, or Buck Burroughs Rides Again" (unpublished travelogue)
867. "Diary of an Automobile Camping Trip Undertaken by the Burroughs Family in 1916"
868. "Do Boys Make Good Soldiers" (1918, unpublished)
869. "Don't Let 'Em Kid You, Joe" (HONOLULU ADVERTISER, 1942)
870. "Edgar Rice Burroughs Tells All" (published in ROB WAGNER'S SCRIPT, 7/9/32; reprinted by George McWhorter & Bob Zeuschner for the 1989 Burroughs Dum-Dum in Louisville)
871. "The Eleven Year Itch" (ROB WAGNER'S SCRIPT, 1927, 5,500 words)
872. "Entertainment Is Fiction's Purpose" (WRITER'S DIGEST, June, 1930)

II. OTHER BIBLIOGRAPHIES

873. "Even Apes Fight for It" (ROB WAGNER'S SCRIPT, 1939)
874. "Fall of a Democracy" (1941, 2,100 words)
875. "Famous Living Americans and Their Homes" (1942, unpublished)
876. "For the Fool's Mother" (1912, 3,600 words; Western film scenario)
877. "For the Victory Loan" (1919, unpublished poem)
878. "Ghenghis Khan" (1930, 10 page poem)
879. "The Ghostly Script" (1920, 31 pages, unfinished ghost story)
880. "Go to Pershing" (1918, WWI article)
881. "Heil Hitler" (1938, film scenario)
882. "His Majesty, the Janitor" (1915, 2,100 word comedy film scenario)
883. "Hollywood" (1925, unpublished poem)
884. "How I Wrote the Tarzan Books" (NEW YORK WORLD newspaper, October 27, 1929, 1,650 words)
885. "I See a New Race" (1920s, 1,800 words)
886. "The Illustrator and the Author" (AUTHOR'S LEAGUE BULLETIN, October 1927)
887. "It's Ants" (1937, unpublished poem)
888. "Laughs at Sea" (HONOLULU ADVERTISER, June 9, 1945)
889. "The Lion Hunter" (an outline for a comedy from 1915; 1,500 words)
890. "The Little Door" (1917, 2,800 words; an anti–German short story)
891. "Little Lessons for Little Learners—1: Jonathan's Patience, or How Fortune Came Through Faith" (a Sunday School story, date unknown)
892. "Little Ol' Buck Private" (1919, unpublished poem)
893. "Man-Eaters" (LOS ANGELES TIMES SUNDAY MAGAZINE, August 22, 1937; lion behavior)
894. *Marcia of the Doorstep* (1924, 125,000 words, scheduled to be published by Donald M. Grant, Publishers, in 1996)
895. "Meet the Authors: Edgar Rice Burroughs" (AMAZING STORIES, June 1941)
896. "Men Who Make the Argosy" (ARGOSY magazine, March 12, 1932)
897. "Minidoka 937th Earl of One Mile Series M" (written around 1903)
898. "Misogynists Preferred" (1940, approx. 4,000 words)
899. "More Fun! More People Killed!" (1943, 20,727 words)
900. "Murder: A Collection of Short Murder Mystery Puzzles" (unpublished unless otherwise noted): "Murder at Midnight," "Bank Murder," "The Terrace Drive Murder" (published in ROB WAGNER'S SCRIPT MAGAZINE, 1932), "The Gang Murder," "The Lightship Murder" (published in ROB WAGNER'S SCRIPT MAGAZINE, 1935), "The Dark Lake Murder," "Who Murdered Mr. Thomas?" (published in ROB WAGNER'S SCRIPT MAGAZINE, 1932), "The Red Necktie" (ROB WAGNER'S SCRIPT MAGAZINE, 1932), "The Dupuyster Case."
901. "A National Reserve Army" (published in the ARMY-NAVY JOURNAL, 8/31/18)

II. OTHER BIBLIOGRAPHIES

902. "Night of Terror" (approx. 18,000 words)
903. "Oahu: Singapore or Wake" (HONOLULU ADVERTISER, May 19, 1942)
904. "Our Japanese Problem" (Hawaii, June 30, 1944)
905. "Out of Time's Abyss" (article for the school paper of the Urban Military Academy, where Hulbert and John Coleman Burroughs attended school, 1924-1925)
906. "Patriotism by Proxy" (published in OAK LEAVES, 5/25/18, Oak Park, Ill., 1,700 words)
907. "Peace and the Militia" (article for THE OAK PARKER, 11/16/18)
908. "The Prospector" (a Western film scenario; 3,300 words)
909. "Quiet Please!" (nine articles for a 1939 proposed newspaper column by ERB but never published)
910. "The Saddle Horse in Southern California" (LOS ANGELES TIMES, January 1, 1925)
911. "The Savage Breast" (1921?, film scenario)
912. "Selling Satisfaction: An Anecdote by Normal Bean" (900 words)
913. "The Strange Adventures of Mr. Dinwiddie" (1940, approx. 5,700 words)
914. "Symbol of a New Day" (ROB WAGNER'S SCRIPT MAGAZINE, February 17, 1934)
915. "Tarzan's Seven Lives" (1934, screenplay)
916. "The Tarzan Theme" (WRITER'S DIGEST, June 1932)
917. "Them Thar Papers" (script for a home movie on the Tarzana ranch, using friends and family as actors)
918. "Two-Gun Doak Flies South" (1937-1938, approx. 26,700 words)
919. "Uncle Bill" (1944, 1,787 words, unpublished horror story)
920. "Uncle Miner and Other Relatives" (22,800 words, fiction)
921. "The Violet Veil: A Treely True Story" (between 1904 and 1907)
922. "Wanted—Good Citizens" (a call for volunteers for the Illinois Reserve Militia, Oak Park, Illinois, 1918).
923. "What Every Young Couple Should Know" (1908, 3,300 words on infant care)
924. "What Is the Matter with the U.S. Army" (2,196 words)
925. *You Lucky Girl!: A Play in Three Acts* (1927, 23,000 words, to be published in 1996)
926. "The Zealots" (1915, medical film scenario)
927. Untitled play (29 pages)
928. 83-page manuscript of an unfinished Tarzan story (revised and completed by Joe R. Lansdale as *Tarzan: The Lost Adventure*, published by Dark Horse, 1995)
929. A 600-word piece on the Scopes trial for the International Press Bureau
930. Speech (delivered at Flag Day exercises, Oak Park, Illinois, 6/14/18)
931. Radio Interview for the Texaco Star Theatre (Ken Murray, 10/18/39)

II. OTHER BIBLIOGRAPHIES

Big Little Books Based on Burroughs' Plots or Characters

(Chronological by publisher or series)

Many Burroughs novels were abridged and pictorialized in a small size, using cardboard covers and very cheap paper. These were the 1930s equivalent of comic books, the so-called "Better Little Books" or "Big Little Books" published by Whitman, and the Dell "Fast Action Books." Most of the early ones were merely adaptations of the Rex Maxon daily Tarzan comic strips which began in 1929 (the color Sunday Tarzan comic strip started in 1931). Although many of the "Big Little Book" stories were based on Burroughs' original plots, most were not. The Big Little Book series of books generally measure 3½" wide by 4⅜" high, and average about 1¼" in width. The books were inexpensively made, cheaply printed and fall apart easily. In addition to the "Better Little Books," there were several items which were free "Premiums" or "give-aways," generally based on the Whitman and Dell books; these are listed below. Whitman used several different series numbers, and often titles with earlier numbers were printed after titles with higher numbers. The reason behind this remains unclear. My profound thanks to Robert R. Barrett who provided many of the details in the following list. (NOTE: Many of the Whitman Big Little titles were reprinted in Spanish translations. For example, you can find *Tarzan y los Hombres Hormigas* published by Editorial Abril in Buenos Aires in 1946 just one year after the original *Tarzan and the Ant Men* was published as Whitman 1444.)

The "700" Series, 1932–1936 (Big Little Books)

932. Whitman 744
Tarzan of the Apes, 1933. 320 pages. The cover art of this Big Little Book, and 307 interior illustrations are by Juanita Bennett, and are indebted to the artwork of Hal Foster. The book is 3½" x 4⅜".

933. Whitman
Tarzan of the Apes. 48 pages. This same title was reprinted in 1935 (no number) with the Juanita Bennett cover and 23 illustrations reprinted from the Big Little Book; it is 3½" x 5¾" and was a free give-away. The cover is not cardboard, and was stapled.

II. OTHER BIBLIOGRAPHIES

934. Whitman
Tarzan of the Apes. 48 pages. This same title was reprinted again, probably in 1935. It is identical to the reprint above, except that this one has added advertising pages. It is 3½" × 5¾" and was a free giveaway. The cover is stapled.

935. Whitman 769
Tarzan the Fearless, 1934. 240 pages. The cover has a colored still from the 1933 Buster Crabbe film, with 50 more stills from the movie interspersed within the text. It is 3½" wide by 4⅜" high.

936. Whitman 778
Tarzan of the Screen, 1934. 240 pages. Cover and 111 stills from the Johnny Weissmuller films interspersed in the text; 52 from "Tarzan the Ape Man" (1932) and 59 from "Tarzan and His Mate" (1934). The book also has a brief story of the life of Johnny Weissmuller. There are two printings. At the back of the book, the first printing has 15 titles listed in an ad; the second printing has 16 titles listed.

937. Whitman 770
The Tarzan Twins, 1934. 432 pages. The cover art on this Big Little Book is by Hal Arbo, with 189 interior illustrations by Juanita Bennett, and is a condensed and slightly revised version of book #657. The book is 3½" × 4⅜".

938. Whitman
The Tarzan Twins, 1935. 432 pages (variant of #770 above [no number]). The cover is a reprint of the illustration on p. 409 and the back cover reprints the illustration from p. 83; same 189 interior illustrations by Juanita Bennett.

939. Whitman
The Tarzan Twins, 1935. 48 pages. This is a third version of this title, but this one has a soft cover illustrated by Juanita Bennett, and only 23 interior illustrations by Bennett reprinted from the Big Little Book. It is stapled together. This variant was an unusual size, 3½" × 5¾" and was another of the free give-aways.

First "1100" Series, 1934–1936 (Big Little Books)

940. Whitman 1180
New Adventures of Tarzan, 1935. 160 pages. Cover is colored stills from the 1935 Herman Brix (later known as Bruce Bennett) film, with interior art of 66 more scenes from the movie. The book is an unusual size, measuring 4½" wide by 5" high, and 1" in width. There are three variants. One has a paper spine, another has a hard spine. A third is a softcover book with a blank "Big Little Book" logo on the front cover.

941. Whitman 1182
Tarzan Escapes, 1936. 240 pages. Cover is a colored still from the 1936 Weismuller movie, illustrated with 76 stills from the MGM film, which follows the original script titled "The Capture of Tarzan."

Second "1100" Series, 1936–1937 (Big Little Books)

942. Whitman 1102
Return of Tarzan, 1936. 432 pages. Cover by Hugh Hutton; 209 interior illustrations by Rex Maxon, abridged from his 1929 newspaper daily Tarzan comic strips.

First "1400" Series, 1937–1938 (Big Little Books)

943. Whitman 1410
Beasts of Tarzan, 1937. 432 pages. The cover art of this Big Little Book is by Hal Arbo, with 218 interior illustrations by Rex Maxon abridged from the 1929 daily comic strip. It is the standard size of 3½" wide by 4⅜" high. The first printing is identified by the presence of a handwritten #425 on page 425; obviously an editor's mark which was left on the page by error.

944. Whitman 1410
Beasts of Tarzan, 1937. 432 pages. This is a variant of the Big Little Book above. The second printing has a standard #425 on page 425 (the error noted above was fixed and the book reprinted). It is the same standard size of 3½" wide by 4⅜" high.

II. OTHER BIBLIOGRAPHIES

945. Whitman 1488
Tarzan's Revenge, 1938. 432 pages. Cover art by Robert Weisman; 207 interior illustrations by Juanita Bennett. This is an adaptation of the 1938 Tarzan film of the same title starring Glenn Morris and Eleanor Holm.

946. Whitman 1488
Tarzan's Revenge, 1938. This is a variant of the book described above. Unlike the above title, the black circle on the front cover is solid; it omits "The Big Little Book" inside the circle.

Third "1400" Series, 1939–1941 (Better Little Books)

947. Whitman 1477
Son of Tarzan, 1939. 432 pages. Cover art by Henry Vallely, 209 interior illustrations by Rex Maxon adapted from the 1929-1930 daily comic strip; this was referred to as a "Better Little Book."

948. Whitman 1495
Tarzan and the Jewels of Opar, 1940. 432 pages. Cover by Robert Weisman, 214 interior illustrations by Rex Maxon adapted from the 1930 daily newspaper comic strip; this is a "Better Little Book." It measures 3¾" wide by 4½" high.

949. Whitman 1402
John Carter of Mars, 1940. 432 pages. The cover of this "Better Little Book" and 209 interior illustrations are by John Coleman Burroughs; the story is a shorter version of the first 7½ chapters of "John Carter & the Giant of Mars" item #192 in this volume, while the last 15 pages are original material not in the AMAZING STORIES appearance.

950. Whitman 1452
Tarzan the Untamed, 1941. 432 pages. John Coleman Burroughs cover, 209 interior illustrations adapted from the several hundred Rex Maxon drew for the 1932-1933 daily comic strip. It has a flip-cartoon by John Coleman Burroughs.

Fourth "1400" Series, 1941–1943 (Better Little Books)

951. Whitman 1453
Tarzan the Terrible, 1942. 432 pages. John Coleman Burroughs cover, 209 interior illustrations abridged from the 1931-1932 Rex Maxon

daily Tarzan comic strip. This "Better Little Book" also has a flip-cartoon drawn by John Coleman Burroughs.

952. Whitman 1448
Tarzan and the Golden Lion, 1943. 432 pages. This "Better Little Book" has a John Coleman Burroughs cover, and 209 interior illustrations abridged from the 1930-1931 Rex Maxon comic strip; Robert R. Barrett notes that the first five illustrations of this title were not from the comic strip but were new to this book. It is 3½" × 4⅜".

Fifth "1400" Series, 1943–1946 (Better Little Books)

953. Whitman 1444
Tarzan and the Ant Men, 1945. 352 pages. First printing. This "Better Little Book" has a John Coleman Burroughs cover, and 171 interior illustrations abridged from the 1932 Rex Maxon newspaper comic strip. It is 3½" × 4⅜". The first printing is identified by the spine. Against a red color, there is a white rectangle at the top with the words "and the Ant Men" inside. The second box on the bottom of the spine has "Edgar Rice Burroughs" and "1444" inside.

954. Whitman 1444
Tarzan and the Ant Men, 1945. 352 pages. Second printing. On the second printing, the spine is red and the white boxes have been filled in. The second printing is easier to find than the first.

Sixth "1400" Series, 1946–1949 (Better Little Books)

955. Whitman 1407
Tarzan, Lord of the Jungle, 1946. 352 pages. Cover by an unknown artist imitating Rex Maxon, and interior art by Rex Maxon, containing 173 illustrations abridged from the 1931 newspaper strip.

956. Whitman 1442
Tarzan and the Lost Empire, 1948. 288 pages. The cover of this "Better Little Book" is a copy of a panel by Jesse Marsh from the Dell one-shot #134, 'Tarzan and the Devil Ogre," with 141 illustrations by Rex Maxon abridged from the 1930 newspaper strip.

957. Whitman 1467
Tarzan and the Land of the Giant Apes, 1949. 288 pages. Cover and inte-

rior by Jesse Marsh, 140 illustrations from the 1947 Dell one-shot #134, "Tarzan and the Devil Ogre."

The "700-10" Series, 1949–1950 (New Better Little Books)

958. Whitman 709-10
Tarzan and the Journey of Terror, 1949/50. 200 pages. Cover and interior by Jesse Marsh, including 186 illustrations from the Dell Tarzan Comic #7, Jan-Feb 1949, "Tarzan In the Valley of Monsters" and from comic #8, "Tarzan and the White Pygmies." 3⅛" × 5½".

The "2000" Series, 1967–1969 (A Big Little Book)

959. Whitman 2005
Tarzan: The Mark of The Red Hyena, 1967. 256 pages. Written by George S. Elrick; cover and 122 interior illustrations by Jerry Pellini, many of which are close copies of Russ Manning's Tarzan comic work. The endpapers inside the cover on the first printing are blue with white circular BLB logos. They are grey circles on white endpapers for the second. The third printing is just plain white without any circular BLB logos. 3⅞" × 5".

Tarzan Ice Cream Cup Give-Aways

960. Whitman
Tarzan, 1936. 144 pages. Cover by Juanita Bennett and 36 interior 3¾" × 4" illustrations by Bennett. This ice-cream cup give-away is an abridgment of the first half of the *Tarzan of the Apes* Big Little Book.

961. Whitman
Tarzan and His Jungle Friends, 1936. 128 pages. The cover artist is unknown but there are 62 interior illustrations by Juanita Bennett. This ice-cream cup give-away is an abridgment of the last half of the *Tarzan of the Apes* Big Little Book, in the unusual size of 3½" × 3½".

Pan-Am Oil Give-Aways

962. Whitman Premium
Tarzan and a Daring Rescue, 1938. 64 pages. The front cover is by Juanita Bennett, while the back cover is a reproduction of the Tarzan billboard ad for Pan-Am Oil Co. Inside covers are also reprints of Pan-

II. OTHER BIBLIOGRAPHIES

Am ads. There are 31 illustrations taken from the several hundred Rex Maxon drew for the 1929 newspaper strip "Return of Tarzan." This version comprises only one incident from the lengthy newspaper story, and the names and places have been changed. It was a free give-away.

963. Whitman Premium
Tarzan and a Daring Rescue, 1938. 64 pages. Identical to the premium described above, except this one has additional advertising.

964. Whitman Premium
Tarzan in the Golden City, 1938. 64 pages. A Whitman Premium Book; this booklet was given away as a free premium; the front cover is soft, and the illustration is a copy of a Hogarth panel. The back cover and inside covers are reprints of Pan-Am Oil Co. ads. There are 31 interior illustrations taken from the several hundred Rex Maxon drew for the 1929 newspaper strip of "The Return of Tarzan." The story is rewritten.

965. Whitman Premium
Tarzan in the Golden City, 1938. 64 pages. Identical to the stapled soft cover described above, except this one has additional advertising.

Dell Fast Action Books

966. Dell
Tarzan and the Tarzan Twins in the Jungle, 1938. 192 pages. A Dell Fast Action Book, which is a condensation of the Whitman #770 *Tarzan Twins* with 95 illustrations; Doc and Dick become Bob and Don. 4" x 5½".

967. Dell
Tarzan the Avenger, 1939. 192 pages. This Dell Fast-Action Book has a soft cover illustrated by Dick Moores, with 95 interior illustrations by Rex Maxon abridged and revised from his 1929-1930 "Son of Tarzan" newspaper comic strip. Korak becomes Tarzan, and Meriem becomes Amine.

968. Dell
John Carter of Mars, 1940. 192 pages. A Dell Fast-Action Book, with its cover copied from a Flash Gordon drawing by Alex Raymond and 95 interior illustrations reprinted from Dell's *The Funnies* and story

II. OTHER BIBLIOGRAPHIES

adapted from the first 19 chapters of ERB's *"A Princess of Mars."* 48 illustrations by Jim Gary and 47 illustrations by John Coleman Burroughs.

Published and Unpublished Books Based on Burroughs' Plots or Characters
(Alphabetical by Author)

The fantasy realms of Edgar Rice Burroughs have continued to inspire and intrigue his readers long after the death of Burroughs in 1950.

II. OTHER BIBLIOGRAPHIES

Many amateur and professional authors have written pastiches, that is, novels and short stories which continue the adventures of Tarzan, John Carter, David Innes, and others, or stories set in the realms created by Burroughs. There have been many authorized and unauthorized Tarzan books published in Spanish, Chinese and other languages. Numerous screenplays have been written over the years, only a few of which were actually produced. In addition, many ERB short-story pastiches have been published in various small fanzines, including ERBANIA, ERB-DOM, and the BURROUGHS BULLETIN. The screenplays, fanzine poems and short stories are *not* included in the titles and authors mentioned below. The following list is by no means complete, but includes a broad sampling stressing full book-length stories (thus omitting most of the shorter stories and the game-oriented booklets). This will suggest the range of materials, published and unpublished, devoted to the creations of Edgar Rice Burroughs.

969. "John Bloodstone" (Stuart J. Byrne)

Tarzan on Mars. In 1955, Raymond Palmer, editor of *Other Worlds* magazine, advocated naming a successor to Burroughs, and suggested Stuart J. Byrne. Bryne, using the pseudonym "John Bloodstone," had written a fairly good novel entitled *Tarzan on Mars,* but the ERB, Inc. offices had absolutely no desire to do anything new with Burroughs' creations. The book was never printed, although the original manuscript of the book has been retyped and xeroxed many times and passed between ERB collectors; a quality hardback version of the book was published in Germany (in English) around 1990.

970. Elizabeth Beecher

Tarzan of the Apes and Little Konga (1954); from The Golden Digest for Boys and Girls, NY: Simon and Schuster, 1954. Illustrated in color by Mo Gollub.

971. Frank Castle

Tarzan and the Lost Safari, a novelization of the 1957 Tarzan film, published by Whitman.

972. A. Bertram Chandler

The Alternate Martians (New York: Ace Books, 1965); an Ace Double, M-129.

973. L. Sprague De Camp

"Sir Harold of Zodanga," in de Camp, L. Sprague, and Christopher Stasheff, *The Exotic Enchanter* (Riverdale, NY: Baen Books, 1995)

II. OTHER BIBLIOGRAPHIES

974. George S. Elrick
Tarzan and the Mark of the Red Hyena, a 1967 Whitman Big Little Book.

975. Philip José Farmer
Philip José Farmer has been one of the most creative and successful authors who have written novels inspired by ERB. Mr. Farmer has written many stories (some quite controversial because of Farmer's willingness to explore the personal and sexual life of Tarzan) using the ERB characters and realms, including: *A Feast Unknown* (1969), *Lord of the Trees* (1970), *Lord Tyger* (1970), *Time's Last Gift* (1972), *Tarzan Alive* (1972), *Hadon of Ancient Opar* (1974), *The Adventure of the Peerless Peer* (1974), *Mother Was a Lovely Beast* (1974), *Flight to Opar* (1976). Many fans consider Farmer's *Time's Last Gift* to be one of the best Tarzan pastiches ever written.

976. Henry G. Franke III
Snowmen of Jupiter (1993)

977. William Gilmour
Back to the Earth's Core (1971), *Lost on Jupiter* (1962); a sequel to ERB's "Skeleton Men of Jupiter," *Tarzan and the Lightning Man*

978. Alan Howard Gross
Farewell Pellucidar (Baltimore, MD: A. Philistine & Co., 1991).

979. Robert Heinlein
The Number of the Beast (Fawcett, 1980)

980. Edward Hirschman
Tarzan at Mars's Core (1975; reprinted February 1977 in a limited edition of 2,000 copies), *Tarzan, Jane and Jungle Lust* (1983)

981. John Eric Holmes
Mahars of Pellucidar (1976) (published), *Red Axe of Pellucidar* (1980) (unpublished)

982. David J. Lake
The Gods of Xuma or Barsoom Revisited (1978)

983. Alex Lewis
Mars in Her Ashen Glory (1976)

984. Fritz Leiber
Tarzan and the Valley of Gold (1966); a novelization of the film of the same title.

II. OTHER BIBLIOGRAPHIES

985. John and Thomas McGeehan
The Adventures of Lord Blackstoke (1962)

986. Michael D. Resnick
The Forgotten Sea of Mars (1965); an authorized supplement to *Llana of Gathol*; free supplement to the ERB fanzine, ERB-DOM.

987. Conrad H. Rupert
The Vikings in Pellucidar (*Science Fiction Digest*, 11/32).

988. Frank P. Shonfeld
Tarzan's Tribute (1978 and 1990), *The Bridge of Life* (1965).

989. Barry E. Stubbersfield
Tarzan the Valiant (1982) 130 pages, *Tarzan the Furious* (1985) 133 pages.

II. OTHER BIBLIOGRAPHIES

Mr. Stubbersfield is the author of numerous smaller (5 pages to 40 pages) stories including: "Tarzan and the Jungle Invaders," "Tarzan's Timeless Journey," "Tarzan and the Beast of Kerchak," "John Carter's Quest," "Tarzan Downunder," "Ships in the Night," "John Carter and the Secret of Mars," "Charade on Mars," "Kra Gan of Mars," "Nightmare on Mars," "John Carter on Trisurn," "The Glory of Mars," "The Sword of Karramar," "The Search for John Carter," "Brendara of Mars," "The Return of the Jasoomian," "Pirates of Mars," "Isandora," "The Red Sword of Mars," and "Kardus Kur of Mars."

990. Jean-Luc Triolo
Les Insurgés de Mars (Editions Antares, 1988); 48 pages.

991. J.D. Van der Merwe
Tarzan (The Wide World, 7/46; reprinted in ERBANIA #16, 17, 18)

992. Gina Ingoglia Weiner
Tarzan (Whitman Little Golden Book, 1964)

993. "Barton Werper" (Peter and Peggy Scott)
In the early 1960s, there was a mistaken belief that ERB, Inc. had allowed all of the Burroughs works to fall into the public domain, and some publishers assumed that the Tarzan character and novels were no longer protected under copyright law. A small paperback publishing company, Gold Star Books, hired a husband and wife writing team, Peter T. and Peggy O'Neil Scott, to quickly turn out several novels to capitalize on the Burroughs boom. The books were published under the pseudonym "Barton Werper," the name of a character in *Tarzan and the Jewels of Opar*. Gold Star was sued by ERB, Inc. and the series stopped with the fifth title in 1965.

The Gold Star Tarzan books have little value to those who like to read the Burroughs books, because they are poorly written, badly plotted, and have little coherency or continuity. The best parts are mostly plagiarized from authentic ERB works, but rearranged enough to be confusing. However, the cover artwork by Jack Endeweldt was very interesting.

The following titles were published in paperback: *Tarzan and the Silver Globe* (1964), *Tarzan and the Cave City* (1964), *Tarzan and the Snake People* (1965), *Tarzan and the Abominable Snowman* (1965), *Tarzan and the Winged Invaders* (1965)

994. Dennis Wilcutt
Tarzan and Jane in The Collector (ERBAPA 1995-1996)

995. Gene Wolfe
Tarzan of the Grapes (*Magazine of Fantasy and Science Fiction*, 1972)

II. OTHER BIBLIOGRAPHIES

996. Robert F. Young
"The Blonde from Barsoom" (AMAZING STORIES, July 1962, pp. 62–70). "The Tarks were attacking, the bosomy princess was clinging to him in terror, and Harold Smith realized he was at the end of his plot line."

A Selected Bibliography of Works About Burroughs
(Alphabetical by author)

997. Adkins, P. H. *Edgar Rice Burroughs: Bibliography and Price Guide.* New Orleans: P.D.A. Enterprises, 1974. 25 pages.
998. Aldiss, Brian. *Billion Year Spree: The True History of Science Fiction.* Garden City, NY: Doubleday, 1973.
999. Altrocchi, Rudolph. *Sleuthing in the Stacks.* Cambridge, MA: Harvard University Press, 1944; reprinted Port Washington, NY: Kennikat Press, 1968.
1000. Anderson, Poul. "Apes and Martians." BOY'S LIFE MAGAZINE, September 1, 1972.
1001. *Antiquarian Bookman*, November 25, 1963 (an issue devoted to Burroughs with a biography and other remarks by Richard A. Lupoff, a brief "ERB on Edgar Rice Burroughs" taken from the 6/41 issue of AMAZING STORIES magazine, a brief piece by Edmund Fuller, and a piece by Camille "Caz" Cazedessus, Jr.).
1002. ANTIQUES JOURNAL. "The Enduring Novels of Edgar Rice Burroughs." June 1, 1975.
1003. "Ape-man Business." FORTUNE, March, 1938, p. 18.
1004. ARGOSY MAGAZINE. "Tarzan and the City of Gold," part 1, March 12, 1932, has an autobiographical sketch of ERB plus a photograph.
1005. Bailey, J.O. *Pilgrims Through Space and Time.* New York: Argus Books, 1947.
1006. Behlmer, Rudy. "Tarzan, Hollywood's Greatest Jungle Hero." AMERICAN CINEMATOGRAPHER. January and February, 1987.
1007. Bergen, James A., Jr. *Edgar Rice Burroughs Reference Guide: Prices.* Beaverton, OR: Golden Lion Press, August, 1996. This is an update of the same author's *Price and Reference Guide* described below.
1008. _____. *Price and Reference Guide to Books Written by Edgar Rice Burroughs.* Beaverton, OR: Golden Lion Press, 1991; this useful

II. OTHER BIBLIOGRAPHIES

reference book lists suggested prices for Burroughs books as of the end of 1991. The paperback version was 2,000 copies; fifty copies were bound in hardback under the title *Edgar Rice Burroughs Reference Guide*.

1009. BIG LITTLE TIMES, volume 3, no. 1, January-February 1984. Lengthy article on the ERB "Big Little Books."
1010. Bleiler, Ev. *Science Fiction: The Early Years*. Kent, OH: Kent State University Press, 1991.
1011. *Blue Book*. "A Fighting Man of Mars." Part 6, September 1930, has a biography of ERB plus photograph.
1012. Boatz, Darrel L. "Burroughs Bibliophile: George McWhorter"; "Fan in the Know: Bob Hyde." COMICS INTERVIEW #109, 110, 1992.
1013. Bradbury, Ray. "Tarzan, John Carter, Mr. Burroughs, and the Long Mad Summer of 1930," introduction to Irwin Porges, *Edgar Rice Burroughs: The Man Who Created Tarzan*, Provo, UT: Brigham Young University Press, 1975.
1014. Brady, Clark A. *The Burroughs Cyclopædia: Characters, Places, Fauna, Flora, Technologies, Languages, Ideas and Terminologies Found in the Works of Edgar Rice Burroughs*. Jefferson, NC: McFarland, 1996.
1015. Burroughs, Edgar Rice. "Entertainment Is Fiction's Purpose." WRITER'S DIGEST. June 1930, pp. 5-6.
1016. _____. "How I Wrote the Tarzan Books." NEW YORK WORLD. October 27, 1929.
1017. _____. "The Illustrator and the Author." AUTHOR'S LEAGUE BULLETIN. October 1927, pp. 7-8.
1018. _____. "Letter from an Author Who Publishes His Own Books." WRITER'S DIGEST. May 1937, pp. 33-34.
1019. _____. "Meet the Authors." AMAZING STORIES. June 1941, p. 138-139.
1020. _____. "Protecting the Author's Rights." WRITER'S YEARBOOK. 1932.
1021. _____. "The Tarzan Theme." WRITER'S DIGEST 12. June 1932, pp. 29–32.
1022. Carter, John T. "Back to Barsoom: Remembering Edgar Rice Burroughs." THE WORLD & I. April 1995, vol. 10, no. 4, pp. 160–169. An article on the ERB collection at the University of Louisville.
1023. Cheatwood, Derral. "The Tarzan Films: An Analysis of Determinants of Maintenance and Change in Conventions." JOURNAL OF POPULAR CULTURE 16. No. 2, Fall 1982, pp. 127–142.
1024. Clemens, Cyril. "Edgar Rice Burroughs: Multimillionaire Author." HOBBIES. May 1950, p. 121.

II. OTHER BIBLIOGRAPHIES

II. OTHER BIBLIOGRAPHIES

1025. Clute, John. *Science Fiction: The Illustrated Encyclopedia*. New York: Dorling Kindersley, 1995.
1026. Clute, John and Peter Nichols. *The Encyclopedia of Science Fiction*. New York: Orbit, 1993.
1027. Cohen, Joel H. "Hollywood and Vines: Edgar Rice Burroughs Climbed to the Top Building His Own Empire Estate." JOE FRANKLIN'S NOSTALGIA. Vol. 1, no. 2, May 1990.
1028. Cook, John F. "An Index to the Magazines and Newspaper Stories of Edgar Rice Burroughs." Bradford, Pennsylvania; n.d., 8 pages.
1029. Couperie, Pierre. *Tarzan*. Paris: PHENIX REVUE INTERNATIONALE DE LA BANDE DESSINÉE, 1970; a paper-covered reprint of the *Illustrated Tarzan Book No. 1* with several additional essays, all in French.
1030. Cowart, David. "The Tarzan Myth and Jung's Genesis of the Self." JOURNAL OF AMERICAN CULTURE 2. n.d., p. 220.
1031. Cowley, Robert H. *The Magic of Literature: A Miscellany for Boys and Girls, Book 1*. London: Blackie & Sons, Ltd., 1940. Includes excerpts from *Tarzan of the Apes* plus an introduction.
1032. Cullinan, Bernice and M. Jerry Weiss, eds. *Books I Read When I Was Young*. New York: Avon, 1980. Arthur C. Clarke refers to ERB on p. 32.
1033. Cummings, David G. (pseudonym for Harold R. Peters). "An Edgar Rice Burroughs Checklist." Savage Press Publication, 1974, 32 pages.
1034. Davis, Robert H. "How Burroughs Wrote the Tarzan Tales," in *Tarzan and the Ant Men*. Chicago: A.C. McClurg & Co., 1924.
1035. Day, Bradford M. "Edgar Rice Burroughs: A Bit of His Life," in E.R. Burroughs, *Beyond Thirty and the Man-Eater*. New York: Science-Fiction and Fantasy Publications, 1957.
1036. _____. *Edgar Rice Burroughs Biblio*. New York: Science-Fiction and Fantasy Publications, 1956. An 8½ × 11 bibliography, 28 + 1 pages. Mimeographed, stapled in red covers; price 50¢.
1037. _____. *Edgar Rice Burroughs: A Bibliography*. New York: Science-Fiction and Fantasy Publications, 1962, 45 + 2 pages, photo-offset booklet; blue covers with a cover drawing by Gilbert Kane; price $1.10.
1038. Day, David. *The Burroughs Bestiary*. London: New English Library, 1978, 150 pages.
1039. Del Rey, Lester. *The World of Science Fiction: The History of a Subculture*. New York: Ballantine 25452, 1979.
1040. "Edgar Rice Burroughs, Rex Maxon and Harold Foster." NEW OUTLOOK. May 1935, p. 44.

II. OTHER BIBLIOGRAPHIES

1041. Eney, Dick, ed. *21st World Science Fiction Convention: The Proceedings*. Chicago: Advent, 1965 [contains a transcript of a panel discussion on the writings of Burroughs].
1042. Essoe, Gabe. *Tarzan of the Movies*. Secaucus: Citadel Press, 1968; 2nd. edition, 1973.
1043. Farmer, Philip José. *Mother Was a Lovely Beast*. Chilton Book Co., 1974, includes ERB's "The God of Tarzan."
1044. _____. *Tarzan Alive*. Garden City, NY: Doubleday & Co., 1972.
1045. _____. "Tarzan Lives! An Interview with Tarzan." ESQUIRE, vol. 78, no. 4, 4/72; especially interesting for the very arresting oil painting of Lord Greystoke.
1046. Fenton, Robert W. *The Big Swingers*. Englewood Cliffs, NJ: Prentice-Hall, 1967.
1047. Fick, Alvin, ed. *The Dream Weaver*. Fort Johnson, NY: Pinion Private Press, 1962.
1048. Fiedler, Leslie. "Lord of the Absolute Elsewhere." NEW YORK TIMES BOOK REVIEW. 6/9/ 74, 10, 12, 14, 17.
1049. Flautz, John T. "An American Demagogue in Barsoom." JOURNAL OF POPULAR CULTURE 1. 1967, pp. 263–275.
1050. Fuller, Edmund. "Return of Tarzan." WALL STREET JOURNAL. November 21, 1963.
1051. Fury, David. *Kings of the Jungle: An Illustrated Reference to "Tarzan" on Screen and Television*. Jefferson, NC: McFarland, 1993.
1052. Galloway, Stan. "The Greystoke Connection: Medievalism in Two Edgar Rice Burroughs Novels." STUDIES IN MEDIEVALISM, vol. VI, 1994.
1053. Goodstone, Tony. *The Pulps*. New York: Chelsea House, 1970. A photographic reprinting of the 1937 "The Resurrection of Jimber-Jaw."
1054. Goulart, Ron. *Cheap Thrills: The Amazing! Thrilling! Astonishing! History of Pulp Fiction*. New Rochelles, NJ: Arlington House, 1972. A chapter is devoted to ERB and his imitators.
1055. Green, Roger L. *Into Other Worlds: Space-Flight in Fiction, from Lucian to Lewis*. London: Abelard-Schuman, 1957.
1056. Griswold, Jerry. *Audacious Kids: Coming of Age in America's Classic Children's Books*. Oxford University Press, 1992 (includes a chapter analyzing the Tarzan story in a psychological framework).
1057. _____. "Young [Ronald] Reagan's Reading." NEW YORK TIMES BOOK REVIEW. 8/30/91, 1,21 (mentions Tarzan as a book Reagan read as a child).
1058. Gunn, James. *Alternate Worlds: The Illustrated History of Science Fiction*. Englewood Cliffs, NJ: Prentice-Hall, 1975. Chapter 7

II. OTHER BIBLIOGRAPHIES

©1993, Thomas Yeates.

devotes six pages to the place of Burroughs in the history of science-fiction.
1059. Hanson, Alan. A CHRONO-LOG OF E.R.B.'S TARZAN SERIES. Spokane, Washington: Waziri Publications, 1990; a fan publication.
1060. Harrison, Mitchell. "Building an Edgar Rice Burroughs Collection." FIRSTS: COLLECTING MODERN FIRST EDITIONS. Vol. 1, no. 10, 1991.
1061. Harwood, John. *The Literature of Burroughsiana*. Baton Rouge, LA: Camille Cazedessus, Jr., 1963.
1062. _____. "The Master of Adventure." Baton Rouge, LA: Camille Cazedessus, Jr., 1967; 8 pages, a bibliography of ERB's books combined with a brief biography by Harwood.
1063. Heins, Henry Hardy. *A Golden Anniversary Bibliography of Edgar Rice Burroughs*. Albany, NY, 1962. Mimeographed on 8½" × 11" green vellum, including 22 pages of illustrations reproduced by photo-offset. The cover is gray with 122 + 3 pages. Heins reports that he produced 148 copies, 98 distributed as loose sheets and covers punched for 3-hole binders; 50 in a white plastic comb binding for special friends and for libraries. This was the precursor to the remarkable volume described below.

II. Other Bibliographies

1064. _____. *A Golden Anniversary Bibliography of Edgar Rice Burroughs.* Rhode Island: Donald M. Grant, 1964. A groundbreaking bibliography.
1065. Henighan, Tom. "Tarzan and Rima." RIVERSIDE QUARTERLY, March 1969, pp. 256–265.
1066. Hill, Roger. *The Fantastic Worlds of P. J. Monahan.* Wichita, KS: Preservation Press, 1988 (a paper-covered beautifully illustrated 60-page study of this artist who did many of the ERB covers for the pulp magazines).
1067. Hollow, John. "Rereading *Tarzan of the Apes*; or 'What Is it,' Lady Alice Whispered, 'A Man?' " DALHOUSIE REVIEW 56, 1976, pp. 83–92.
1068. Holtsmark, Erling B. *Edgar Rice Burroughs.* Boston: Twayne Publishers, 1986.
1069. _____. *Tarzan and Tradition: Classical Myth in Popular Literature.* Westport, CT: Greenwood Press, 1981.
1070. Horn, Maurice. *Tarzan, Seigneur de la Jungle.* Paris: Azur, 1967.
1071. Horvath, Robert. *Amtorian Dictionary*, 1960.
1072. "How Tarzan Kept the Wolf from the Door." THE LITERARY DIGEST. November 30, 1929, p. 41.
1073. "I Am a Barbarian." LIBRARY JOURNAL. March 1, 1968, p. 1018.
1074. Johnson, Alva. "How to Become a Great Writer." THE SATURDAY EVENING POST. July 29, 1939, p. 5.
1075. Julius, Kevin C. "A Pocket Bibliography of Edgar Rice Bur-roughs." Edgar Rice Burroughs Appreciation Society, 1980, 36 pages.
1076. Kudley, Robert R. and Joan Leiby. "Burroughs' Science Fiction with an Analytical Subject and Name Index." School of Library and Information Science, State University College of Arts and Sciences, Geneseo, NY, 1973, 236 pages.
1077. Kyle, Richard. "Out of Time's Abyss: The Martian Stories of Edgar Rice Burroughs, A Speculation." RIVERSIDE QUARTERLY 4.2, January 1970, pp. 110–122.
1078. Lacassin, Francis. *Tarzan, ou le Chevalier Crispé* ["Tarzan, or the Constricted Knight"]. Paris, France: Union Générale d'Editions, Christian Bourgois, 1971.
1079. Lacon-Watson, E. H. "'Tarzan' and Literature." FORTNIGHTLY 119. June 23, 1923, pp. 1035–1045.
1080. LaFleur, Laurence. "Marvelous Voyages—II: The Scientific Romances of Edgar Rice Burroughs." POPULAR ASTRONOMY. February 1942, pp. 69–73.
1081. Lee, Ray and Vernell Coriell. *A Pictorial History of the Tarzan Movies.* Los Angeles, CA: Golden State News, 1966.

II. OTHER BIBLIOGRAPHIES

1082. Levin, Martin, ed. *Love Stories.* New York: Quadrangle-New York Times Book Co., 1975. Uses the chapter "Tarzan's First Love" from *Jungle Tales of Tarzan.*
1083. Levinsen, Henrik. "'Vildmanden Tarzan' af Edgar R. Burroughs," in *Børne- og ungdomsbøger: Problemer og analyser.* Copenhagen: Gyldendal, 1969, pp. 139-147.
1084. LIBRARY REVIEW #30, University of Louisville, 5/1/80, the issue is devoted to the ERB collection at the University of Louisville, including an article by the curator, George McWhorter, entitled "ERB: King of Dreams."
1085. LIFE magazine, details on the Tarzan movies in the issue of June 14, 1963; follow-up letters on July 5, 1963.
1086. Lowndes, A. W. *Three Faces of Science Fiction.* NESFA Press, 1973, several brief mentions of ERB as a type of S.F.
1087. Lowery, Larry and Brian Bohnett. *A Guide to TARZAN Big Little Books and Other Related Books.* Williamston, MI, Mad Kings Publishing Company, 1966. This is a very useful 187-page small paperback book the approximate size of the Big Little Books, with a great deal of information about Big Little Books and related toys and premiums.
1088. Lupoff, Richard A., *Barsoom: Edgar Rice Burroughs and the Martian Vision.* Baltimore: Mirage Press, 1976.
1089. _____. *Edgar Rice Burroughs: Master of Adventure.* Canaveral Press, 1964 (this is also available as a 1969 paperback from Ace #N-6 or #18771).
1090. _____. *The Reader's Guide to Barsoom and Amtor.* New York: Richard A. Lupoff, 1963.
1091. Lupoff, Richard A. and Donald Thompson, eds. *The Comic Book Book.* New Rochelle, NJ: Arlington House, 1973 (contains a history of the Tarzan comics by Camille "Caz" Cazedessus, Jr.).
1092. McGreal, Dorothy. "The Burroughs No One Knows." THE WORLD OF COMIC ART 1.2. Fall 1966, pp. 12-15.
1093. McQuade, Donald and Robert Atwan. "Edgar Rice Burroughs/Tarzan of the Apes: Tarzan Meets Jane, or Girl Goes Ape," in *Popular Writing in America: The Interaction of Style and Audience.* New York: Oxford University Press, 1988.
1094. McWhorter, George T. *Burroughs Dictionary: An Alphabetical List of Proper Names, Words, Phrases and Concepts Contained in the Published Works of Edgar Rice Burroughs.* Lanham, MD: University Press of America, 1987.
1095. _____. *Edgar Rice Burroughs: A Biographical Sketch.* Sierra Madre, CA: Bottleneck Blues Press, 1992 (this small paperback book of

II. OTHER BIBLIOGRAPHIES

40 pages was given away as a free souvenir to attendees of the 1992 Dum-Dum held in Louisville).
1096. _____. *Edgar Rice Burroughs Memorial Collection: A Catalog.* House of Greystoke, University of Louisville Library, Burroughs Memorial Collection, Louisville, KY, 1991.
1097. Malkin, Sol M., ed. "Edgar Rice Burroughs: Life and Work." ANTIQUARIAN BOOKMAN, November 25, 1963.
1098. Maloff, Saul. "Speaking of Books: Tarzan's First Love." NEW YORK TIMES BOOK REVIEW, December 22, 1968, p. 2.
1099. Mandel, Paul. "Tarzan of the Paperbacks." LIFE. November 29, 1963, pp. 11-12.
1100. Manson, Cynthia and Charles Ardai. *High Adventure: Stories by Arthur Conan Doyle, Ian Fleming, Edgar Allan Poe, Jack London, James M. Cain, Edgar Rice Burroughs, and Others.* New York: Barnes and Noble, 1992. Contains "Tarzan's First Love" from *Jungle Tales of Tarzan.*
1101. Michel, Jacques. "Tarzan ou le Mythe perdu." LE MONDE. Paris, March 11, 1965.
1102. Miller, Joseph W. "Information on the Publication of Burroughs First Editions." Fond du Lac, Wisconsin: Mafia Press, October 1954, 4 pages mimeographed.
1103. Morsberger, Robert E. "Edgar Rice Burroughs' Apache Epic." JOURNAL OF POPULAR CULTURE 7, 1973. pp. 280–287.
1104. Moskowitz, Sam. "The Amazing Edgar Rice Burroughs" in *Satellite Science Fiction.* October 1958.
1105. _____. *Explorers of the Infinite: Shapers of Science Fiction.* New York: World Publishing, 1963.
1106. _____. *Under the Moons of Mars: A History and Anthology of "The Scientific Romance" in the Munsey Magazines, 1912–1920.* New York: Holt, Rinehart & Winston, 1970.
1107. Mullen, Richard D. "Edgar Rice Burroughs and the Fate Worse Than Death." RIVERSIDE QUARTERLY 4. June 1970, pp. 187ff.
1108. _____. "The Undisciplined Imagination: Edgar Rice Burroughs and Lowellian Mars," in *SF: The Other Side of Realism: Essays on Modern Fantasy and Science Fiction,* ed. by Thomas D. Clareson. Bowling Green: Bowling Green University Popular Press, 1971, pp. 229–247 (a detailed and critical attack on Burroughs' writing style and technical errors in astronomy).
1109. Nesterby, James R. "The Tenuous Vine of Tarzan of the Apes." JOURNAL OF POPULAR CULTURE 13. 1980, pp. 483-87.
1110. Nye, Russell. *The Unembarrassed Muse.* New York: Dial Press, 1970. "Tarzan remains the greatest popular creation of all time," p. 272.

II. OTHER BIBLIOGRAPHIES

1111. Onyx, Narda. *Water, World & Weissmuller*. New York: Vion Publishing Company, 1964.
1112. Orth, Michael. "The Vaults of Opar: Through the American Mind with Camera, Gun, and Knife." ERB-DOM, #81-86, April 1975-April 1976 (original title: "Tarzan's Revenge: A Literary Biography of Edgar Rice Burroughs").
1113. Peters, Harold R. "An Edgar Rice Burroughs Collector's Notebook," Grindstone, Pa., Silver Sun Press, 1995 (an 8½" × 11" spiral bound collector's bibliography providing for each title a place to check off ownership of a book and the condition of book and jacket; 125 were printed.
1114. Pierce, James H. *The Battle of Hollywood: James H. Pierce, Oldest Living Tarzan*. Kansas City, MO: House of Greystoke, 1978.
1115. "Place to Play In." BETTER HOMES AND GARDENS. August, 1931, p. 18.
1116. Porges, Irwin. *Edgar Rice Burroughs: The Man Who Created Tarzan*. Provo, UT: Brigham Young University Press, 1975. This profusely illustrated altogether amazing and monumental biography and bibliography was revised and reissued in September 1976 as a two-volume Ballantine paperback boxed set, with revisions by Hulbert Burroughs; the page numbers are *not* the same.
1117. Post, J. B. *An Atlas of Fantasy*. Baltimore, MD: 1973. A chapter of this book is devoted to a large collection of maps of ERB's fantasy worlds, most drawn by Burroughs himself.
1118. Randall, David A., Sigmund C. Fredericks and Tim Mitchell. "An Exhibition of Science Fiction and Fantasy." *Catalog of the Lilly Library Exhibit*. Indiana University Library, 1/1/75.
1119. Resnick, Michael. *The Official Guide to Fantastic Literature*. Florence, AL: House of Collectibles, 1976.
1120. Romer, Margaret. "Edgar Rice Burroughs, Creator of Tarzan." OVERLAND MONTHLY. March 1934, p. 67.
1121. Roy, John Flint. *A Guide to Barsoom: The Mars of Edgar Rice Burroughs*. New York: Ballantine Books #24722, October 1976.
1122. Rubanowice, Robert J. "The Tarzan Series: A Twentieth Century Case Against Civilization," in *Proceedings of the Sixth National Convention of the Popular Culture Association*, ed. Michael T. Marsden. Bowling Green: Bowling Green University Press, 1976, pp. 563-80.
1123. Sampson, Robert. *Yesterday's Faces: Volume II: Strange Days*. Bowling Green: Bowling Green University, 1984.
1124. Samuelson, David Norman. "Studies in the Contemporary American and British Science Fiction Novel." Unpublished Ph.D. dissertation, University of Southern California, 1969.

1125. Sanders, Jacquin. "Tarzan on the Upswing." NEWSWEEK. July 29, 1963, p. 70.
1126. Sharp, Dolph. "Edgar Rice Burroughs, Inc." WRITER'S DIGEST. August, 1949.
1127. Shepard, Richard F. "For Tarzan Fans, New Adventures." NEW YORK TIMES. November 26, 1963, p. 43.
1128. Simon, Seymour. *Creatures from Lost Worlds*. Firefly Paperbacks, Scholastic Book Service: J. B. Lippincott, 1979 (brief discussion of Pellucidar and other Hollow Earth stories).
1129. Slate, Tom. "ERB and the Heroic Epic." RIVERSIDE QUARTERLY 3. March 1968, pp. 118–123.
1130. Sorel, Stephen. *Tarzan de Deutschenfresser*. Berlin: C. Stephenson Verlag, 1925.
1131. "They Stand Out from the Crowd." LITERARY DIGEST. September 15, 1934, p. 12.
1132. "Tips." PUBLISHER'S WEEKLY. December 16, 1963, p. 34.
1133. Topping, Gary. "The Pastoral Ideal in Popular American Literature: Zane Grey and Edgar Rice Burroughs." RENDEVOUS: IDAHO STATE UNIVERSITY JOURNAL OF ARTS AND LETTERS 12, no. 2, 1977, pp. 11– 25.
1134. Van Arnam, Dave. *The Reader's Guide to Barsoom and Amtor*. New York: Richard Lupoff, 1963.
1135. Van Hise, James. *Pulp Masters*. Yucca Valley, CA: Midnight Graffiti, Pubs. 1996 (contains "Edgar Rice Burroughs: Pulp Master" by James Van Hise).
1136. _____. *Edgar Rice Burroughs' Fantastic Worlds*. Yucca Valley, CA: Midnight Graffiti Publications, 1996.
1137. Vidal, Gore. *Reflections Upon a Sinking Ship*. Boston: Little Brown, 1969.
1138. _____. "Tarzan Revisited." ESQUIRE. Vol. 60, December 1963, pp. 281–83, 484-85.
1139. Waters, William P. *Essays on Mars: Exploring the Red Planet of Edgar Rice Burroughs*. W. P. Waters, publisher, 1989 (a paperback chapbook with contributions by several fans, plus illustrations).
1140. _____. *Jungle of Dreams: The Tarzan Mythos of Edgar Rice Burroughs*. W. P. Waters, publisher, 1990 (a nicely done paperback chapbook with contributions by several fans and numerous illustrations).
1141. Watson, E. H. L. "Tarzan and Literature." FORTNIGHTLY REVIEW. June, 1923, pp. 1035–1045.
1142. "Wax Recording by Creator of Tarzan Discovered." NEW YORK TIMES. August 6, 1968, p. 34.
1143. Wood, Thomas. "He Tarzan—You Fan." COLLIER'S. May 9, 1953;

II. OTHER BIBLIOGRAPHIES

also note the detailed letter from Vern Coriell which was published in the July 4, 1953 issue.

1144. Zinman, David. *Saturday Afternoon at the Bijou.* New Rochelle, NY: Arlington House, 1973.

A Selected Bibliography of Works About Burroughs Artists
(Alphabetical by artist)

Arting, Fred J., and Clinton Pette:
1145. Barrett, Robert R. "In the Shadow of the Sun: Fred J. Arting and Clinton Pettee," THE BURROUGHS BULLETIN, New Series, #3, July 1990.
Blackbeard, Bill:
1146. Blackbeard, Bill, editor. *Tarzan: In Color.* New York: NBM—Flying Buttress Classics Library, 1992. A series projected to take 18 volumes dedicated to the accurate reproduction of the Sunday "Funnies" artwork of the Hal Foster and Burne Hogarth Tarzan comic strip, which were begun in 1931.
Bull, Charles Livingston:
1147. Barrett, Robert R. "Animal Fashion Plates: Charles Livingston Bull," THE BURROUGHS BULLETIN, New Series, #15, July 1993.
Cochran, Russ:
1148. Cochran, Russ. *The Edgar Rice Burroughs Library of Illustration.* Three Volumes. Russ Cochran, West Plains, MO, 1976, 1977, 1984. An amazing labor of love reproducing a great many of the fine illustrations associated with Burroughs' books and magazines.
Fortunino Matania:
1149. Barrett, Robert R. "Fortunino Matania," THE BURROUGHS BULLETIN, New Series, #10, July 1992.
Foster, Harold:
1150. Barrett, Robert R. "Harold Foster: Artist Adventurer," #48, ERB-ANIA, winter 1981.
Frazetta, Frank:
1151. Frazetta, Frank. *The Fantastic Art of Frank Frazetta.* Five Volumes. New York: Peacock Press/Ballantine Books & Charles Scribner's Sons, 1975-1985. Although not all Burroughs art, these books include numerous paintings Frazetta did for the early ERB Ace paperbacks, and several black line drawings and sketches, sometimes rather

II. OTHER BIBLIOGRAPHIES

poorly reproduced. Along with J. Allen St. John, Frank Frazetta is unquestionably one of the greatest of all the Burroughs illustrators.

1152. Barrett, Robert R. "Frank Frazetta: History of a Burroughs Artist." THE BURROUGHS BULLETIN Original Series, #29, spring 1973.

1153. *Frank Frazetta: The Living Legend.* Marshall's Creek, PA: Sun Litho-Print / Frazetta Prints, 1981.

1154. Barrett, Robert R. "Frank Frazetta and ERB." ERBANIA #45, summer 1980.

II. OTHER BIBLIOGRAPHIES

1155. *Frazetta: A Retrospective.* New York: Alexander Gallery, 1994. A 200 page coffee table book which is actually a show and sale catalog issued in conjunction with a Frazetta exhibition at the end of 1994. It has numerous ERB illustrations.
Hescox, Richard:
1156. Barrett, Robert R. "Richard Hescox: Penetrating the Cloud Cover," THE BURROUGHS BULLETIN, New Series, #9, January 1992.
Hogarth, Burne:
1157. Hogarth, Burne. *Tarzan of the Apes.* New York: Watson-Guptill Publications, 1972. Burne Hogarth began illustrating the Tarzan comic strip in May, 1937, and continued until 1950. This art book is a brand new Hogarth re-drawing of *Tarzan of the Apes.*
Krenkel, Roy:
1158. Krenkel, Roy. *Cities and Scenes from the Ancient World.* Philadelphia, PA: Owlswick Press, 1974.
1159. Barrett, Robert R. "Roy G. Krenkel," #50, ERBANIA, summer 1983.
1160. *Swordsmen and Saurians.* Forestville, CA: Eclipse Books, 1988.
Manning, Russ:
1161. Barrett, Robert R. *Russ Manning: A Bibliography.* Wichita, KS: H.O.B. and Co., 1993.
1162. Barrett, Robert R. "Tarzan's Third Great Comic Strip Artist: Russell G. Manning," #13, THE BURROUGHS BULLETIN, January 1993.
Mattingly, David:
1163. Barrett, Robert R. "David Mattingly: Visions of Pellucidar," THE BURROUGHS BULLETIN New Series, #2, April 1990.
Monahan, P.J.:
1164. Hill, Roger. *The Fantastic Worlds of P.J. Monahan.* Wichita, Kansas: Preservation Press, 1988 (a paper-covered beautifully illustrated 60-page study of this artist who did many of the ERB covers for the pulp magazines).
Monroe, C.E.:
1165. Barrett, Robert R. "The Story of C. E. Monroe, Jr.," THE BURROUGHS BULLETIN, New Series, #7, July 1991.
Mulford, Stockton:
1166. Barrett, Robert R. "Edgar Rice Burroughs to Zane Grey: Stockton Mulford," THE BURROUGHS BULLETIN, New Series, #16, October 1993.
Rubimor:
1167. Barrett, Robert R. "Rubimor: Forgotten Tarzan Artist," #66, ERBANIA, fall 1992.
St. John, J. Allen:
1168. Barrett, Robert and Henry Hardy Heins. *Addenda and Errata to*

II. OTHER BIBLIOGRAPHIES

"*J. Allen St. John: An Illustrated Bibliography by Darrell C. Richardson.*" Wichita, KS: H.O.B. and Co., 1991.
1169. Richardson, Darrell C. *J. Allen St. John: An Illustrated Bibliography.* Memphis, TN: Mid-America Publishers, Inc., 1991.
Schoonover, Frank E.:
1170. Barrett, Robert R. "Frank E. Schoonover: The Man Who Saw Barsoom," THE BURROUGHS BULLETIN, New Series, #4, October 1990.
Shaw, Barclay:
1171. Barrett, Robert R. "Barclay Shaw: Tarzan Artist of the 1990s," THE BURROUGHS BULLETIN, New Series, #5, January 1991.
Sperry, Armstrong:
1172. Barrett, Robert R. "The Story of Armstrong Sperry," THE BURROUGHS BULLETIN, New Series, #11, July 1992.
Stahr, Paul:
1173. Barrett, Robert R. "Paul Stahr: The Indian Is Not an Apache," THE BURROUGHS BULLETIN, New Series, #12, October 1992.
Stout, William:
1174. Barrett, Robert R. "William Stout: Burroughs Artist at Heart," THE BURROUGHS BULLETIN, New Series, #6, April 1991.
Whelan, Michael:
1175. Barrett, Robert R. "Michael Whelan: Burroughsian Wonderworks," #46, spring 1981.
Wyeth, N.C.:
1176. Barrett, Robert R. "N. C. Wyeth: An Essay on a Tarzan Artist, Pt. 1," #64, ERBANIA, fall 1991.
1177. Barrett, Robert R. "N. C. Wyeth: An Essay on a Tarzan Artist, Pt. 2," #65, ERBANIA, spring 1992.

Most of Mr. Barrett's articles are archived at the world's largest collection of material by and about Edgar Rice Burroughs—the Ekstrom Library of the University of Louisville, Louisville, Kentucky, 40292, George T. McWhorter, Curator of the Edgar Rice Burroughs Memorial Collection.

A Selected List of Burroughs Fanzines
(Alphabetical by title)

The number of fans who have created fan magazines ("fanzines") is truly enormous, and they occur all over the world. All the titles listed below are published in the United States unless otherwise noted. The following is just a sample:

II. OTHER BIBLIOGRAPHIES

1178. THE AMTORIAN (January–April, 1965); two issues.
1179. ANOTAR (1975). 3 issues (British).
1180. APE (1960–1961). 4 issues.
1181. THE AUSTRALIAN BURROUGHS COURIER (October, 1970).
1182. BARAMPOL (April 1986). 1 issue.
1183. BARAMPOL NEWSLETTER (April 1987–October 1989). 6 issues.
1184. BARSOOM! (November 1987–1989). 8 issues in French.
1185. THE BARSOOMIAN (August 1952–October 1969). 15 issues.
1186. THE BARSOOMIAN TIMES (August 1964–December 1965). 8 issues.
1187. BOREAL BULLETIN (January 1968–September 1968). 4 issues.
1188. BRITISH ERB SOCIETY NEWSLETTER (1974). 2 issues.
1189. BURI (1964). 2 issues.
1190. THE BURROUGHS BULLETIN (July 1947–present). Approximately 70 issues so far.
1191. BURROUGHS ILLUSTRATED (1964). 1 issue.
1192. THE BURROUGHS NEWSBEAT (December 1971–April 1977). 47 issues.
1193. THE BURROUGHS READER (Summer 1963–Spring 1965). 9 issues.
1194. BURROUGHSIANA (1956–1958). 18 issues (British).
1195. CAPRONA COURIER (June 1981). 1 issue.
1196. DREAM QUEST (1960). 2 issues.
1197. EDGAR RICE BURROUGHS AMATEUR PRESS ASSOCIATION (ERB-APA). (1982–present). 47 issues so far.
1198. EDGAR RICE BURROUGHS NEWS DATELINE (1979–present). 53 issues so far.
1199. EDGAR RICE BURROUGHS QUARTERLY (Fall, 1982). 1 issue.
1200. ERB COLLECTOR (January 1990–present). 10 issues.
1201. THE E.R.B. DIGEST (March 1967). 1 issue.
1202. ERBANIA (April 1956–present). Began in England, then moved to Canada, and then to USA (Florida). 74 issues.
1203. ERB-DOM (May 1960–June 1978). 90 issues. It has since resumed publication in 1993.
1204. ERB-FAN (September 1985–1988). 12 issues (German).
1205. ERBIVORE (September 1965–August 1973). 7 issues.
1206. FANTASTIC WORLDS OF EDGAR RICE BURROUGHS (1976–present). 37 issues so far (British).
1207. GREYSTOKER (1993). 5 issues.
1208. JASOOMIAN (1970–1974). 13 issues.
1209. JODADES (July–November 1965). 2 issues.
1210. JUNGLE TRAILS (Fall, 1981). 1 issue.
1211. THE LONG SWORD (1965–1968). 5 issues.

II. OTHER BIBLIOGRAPHIES

1212. NORMAL BEAN (1978–1985). 7 issues.
1213. ODWAR (September 1964). 1 issue.
1214. OPARIAN (September 1965). 1 issue.
1215. SARIAN (1971–1972). 3 issues
1216. TARZAN DRUM BEAT (Spring 1975–1978). 5 issues (published by ERB, Inc.).
1217. TARZINE (August 1981–1993). 82 issues.
1218. THURIA (1964). 1 issue (July 1964).
1219. ULSIO (June 1965). 1 issue.
1220. X-RAY DELTA ONE (January 1972) 1 issue devoted to Vern Coriell.
1221. ZOR (October 1969). 1 issue.

Appendices

Appendix A:
Values of Burroughs First Editions

It has been claimed that Edgar Rice Burroughs is one of the most avidly collected of all American authors. There is something about the compulsive thrust and excitement of his stories which many people find irresistible, especially if the stories were first encountered during the reader's adolescence. Certainly, his works seem particularly conducive to drawing out the rabid collector in many of us. Virtually anything with the name "Tarzan" or "Burroughs" on it, or an illustration of Tarzan, is collected by someone. Some of the items (like Tarzan buttons) might be worth $1 on a good day; other items are worth tens of thousands of dollars (if you can find the right wealthy collector).

Generally speaking, the earlier the title, the more difficult it is to find and the more valuable it is. The value of Burroughs's first editions from 1914 through the 1920s (in dust jacket) have gone from the $10 to $50 range in the 1950s, to the $1,000–$4,000 range for some of the rarest of the same titles today. For several years, the asking prices for the most desirable titles like a dust-jacketed first edition of *Tarzan of the Apes* showed surprising increases. The fact that ERB books vary in value makes any attempt to specify exact values potentially out-of-date within six months or less. Thus, the following remarks apply to values as of the end of 1995.

Several generalizations are possible. The first observation is that for serious Burroughs collectors, the presence of a good dust jacket on a particularly early book in fine condition can raise the value of the book by a factor of at least tenfold. And, the most desirable of all the ERB hardbacks are the twenty-nine A.C. McClurg first editions. The rarest of the rare would be the important American literary classic and single most important book by Burroughs, *Tarzan of the Apes*, in a fine dust jacket; an exceptional copy was offered by a dealer for $60,000 at a 1992 Book Fair. *A Princess of Mars* in an expertly restored dust jacket was offered

APPENDIX A

for $17,000 by the same dealer. Depending upon condition, *Tarzan of the Apes* without a dust jacket may be worth between $150 and $1,500.

Other A.C. McClurg titles in *fine* dust jackets can sell for as much as $1,000 to $4,000, depending upon their relative scarcity. Without a dust jacket, in fine condition the books are worth $100–$350.

On the other hand, the Edgar Rice Burroughs, Inc. titles from 1931 to 1967 in dust jackets are more recent and easier to find, and thus do not command anywhere near the same price range. In fine condition, most of them are available in the $300–$600 price range. *Tarzan and "The Foreign Legion"* and *Llana of Gathol* are the two easiest Edgar Rice Burroughs, Inc. titles and normally fall in the $75–$125 range in dust jacket. Among the rarer ERB, Inc. titles are *Jungle Girl, Oakdale Affair and the Rider, Tarzan's Quest, Tarzan and the City of Gold, Tarzan and the Lion Man, The Lad and the Lion, Apache Devil, Back to the Stone Age*, and *The Deputy Sheriff of Comanche County*. A fine copy in fine dust jacket of any of these is worth $400 to $650 as of 1995.

The Macaulay first edition of *The Girl from Hollywood* (1923) in dust jacket is rare, and could bring anywhere from $1,500 to $3,000 depending upon the condition of the book and the dust jacket. The second, third, and fourth issue of this book are not quite as valuable, although in dust jacket they are still sought after. Without a dust jacket, a fine copy of the book would be worth between $50 and $150.

The four ERB titles published by Metropolitan from 1929 to 1931 are only worth about $50–$100 without a dust jacket, but the presence of a particularly fine dust jacket could bring the value of the title to $1,000–$3,000.

An important factor in value is the presence of ERB's autograph or inscription. Burroughs signed his books freely upon request, and autographed titles are often available, but they are especially sought after by collectors. Even a dust jacketed reprint G&D or A.L. Burt Tarzan book in very good condition (which sells in the $30 to $80 range normally) could be worth $100 to $500 with an ERB inscription. An inscribed first edition in jacket can double the price of any Burroughs book; association copies of note will go much higher. In 1995, a complete collection of family copies, inscribed to ERB children and wives was offered recently for $550,000, roughly $10,000 each.

Burroughs stories in magazines are curious. The magazine appearances are earlier than the hardback books, and considerably more difficult to find, but their prices are not commensurate with the corresponding hardback first edition in jacket. The earliest magazines from 1913 to 1918 might be worth $40-$125 each in fine condition (especially if the cover illustration is for the ERB story). The later issues from the 1930s or 1940s might be worth $10-$50 each, depending upon the date and the presence of an ERB cover illustration. The rarest and most desirable of the ERB stories in magazines is clearly the first appearance of *Tarzan* in the October 1912 ALL-STORY magazine. Depending upon condition, with both front and back covers it is worth from $1,000 to $10,000. Magazines missing either of the covers are of little interest to serious collectors.

Appendix B: Chronological List (by Publication Date) of Burroughs Hardback First Editions

(The identificatory device of boldface has not been used here)

1914	Tarzan of the Apes		The War Chief
1915	The Return of Tarzan		The Tarzan Twins
1916	The Beasts of Tarzan	1928	The Master Mind of Mars
1917	The Son of Tarzan		Tarzan, Lord of the Jungle
	A Princess of Mars	1929	The Monster Men
1918	Tarzan and the Jewels of Opar		Tarzan and the Lost Empire
	The Gods of Mars		Tanar of Pellucidar
1919	Jungle Tales of Tarzan	1930	Tarzan at the Earth's Core
	The Warlord of Mars	1931	A Fighting Man of Mars
1920	Tarzan the Untamed		Tarzan the Invincible
	Thuvia, Maid of Mars	1932	Jungle Girl
1921	Tarzan the Terrible		Tarzan Triumphant
	The Mucker	1933	Apache Devil
1922	At the Earth's Core		Tarzan and the City of Gold
	The Chessmen of Mars	1934	Pirates of Venus
1923	Tarzan and the Golden Lion		Tarzan and the Lion Man
	Pellucidar	1935	Lost on Venus
	The Girl from Hollywood		Tarzan and the Leopard Men
1924	The Land That Time Forgot	1936	Swords of Mars
	Tarzan and the Ant Men		Tarzan and the Tarzan Twins
1925	The Cave Girl		with Jad-Bal-Ja, the Golden
	The Bandit of Hell's Bend		Lion (Whitman)
	The Eternal Lover		Tarzan's Quest
1926	The Moon Maid	1937	The Oakdale Affair and The
	The Mad King		Rider
1927	The Outlaw of Torn		Back to the Stone Age

APPENDIX C

1938	The Lad and the Lion		Tarzan and the Madman
	Tarzan and the Forbidden City		John Carter of Mars
1939	Carson of Venus	1965	Tarzan and the Castaways
	Tarzan the Magnificent	1967	I Am a Barbarian
1940	Synthetic Men of Mars	1996	Marcia of the Doorstep
	The Deputy Sheriff of Comanche County		You Lucky Girl!
1944	Land of Terror		
1946	Escape on Venus		NOTE: As of May 1995, these additional ERB works are available only in paper covers or as fan publications.
1947	Tarzan and "The Foreign Legion"		
1948	Llana of Gathol		
		1965	The Girl from Farris's
(Burroughs died in 1950)		1966	The Efficiency Expert
		1970	The Wizard of Venus and Pirate Blood
1957	Beyond Thirty and The Man-Eater		
		1971	The Scientists Revolt
1963	Savage Pellucidar	1995	Tarzan: The Lost Adventure (Dark Horse Comics)
1964	Tales of Three Planets		

Appendix C:
Companies That Published
Burroughs First Editions

A.C. McClurg   A. C. McClurg published twenty-nine first editions and occasional reprintings from 1914 to 1929. The fact that it is published by McClurg does *not* ensure that the book is a first edition.

Macaulay   Macaulay published only *one* Burroughs book, *The Girl from Hollywood*, 1923. However, in addition to the first edition of this title, there are numerous examples of later issues.

Metropolitan   Metropolitan published four first editions from 1929 to 1931:
Tarzan and the Lost Empire (1929)
Tanar of Pellucidar (1930)
Tarzan at the Earth's Core (1930)
A Fighting Man of Mars (1931)
Every book with a Metropolitan name on the spine

Burroughs First Editions Publishers

Appendix C

	is a first edition, although there are several "mixed editions" which have the Grosset & Dunlap name on the spine and Metropolitan's name on the title page.
Volland	Volland published the first edition of *The Tarzan Twins*, but also published at least seven reprintings of this title. Each is clearly marked.
Edgar Rice Burroughs, Inc.	Edgar Rice Burroughs, Inc. published twenty-three first editions from 1931 to 1948, and then *I Am a Barbarian* in 1967, making a total of twenty-four in all. ERB, Inc. also published reprints in 1948. The reprints are easily distinguished by tan-gray covers (and seven titles in red covers).
Canaveral Press	Canaveral published four first editions in 1964 when interest in Burroughs was very high. They are: *Tales of Three Planets* *Tarzan and the Madman* *John Carter of Mars* *Tarzan and the Castaways* Canaveral also published *Tarzan and the Tarzan Twins*, which is listed as a first edition in this bibliography, although the two stories which make up the book were published separately as first editions. In addition Canaveral published numerous reprints.
Science Fiction & Fantasy Publications	Bradford M. Day published *Beyond Thirty* and *The Man-Eater* in 1957
Donald M. Grant	Donald M. Grant Publishers were as of January 1996 scheduled to bring out two never before published manuscripts in 1996: *Marcia of the Doorstep* and *You Lucky Girl!* Grant also published Henry Hardy Heins' *A Golden Anniversary Bibliography of Edgar Rice Burroughs* in 1964.

One first edition appears only as a paperback (the August 1970 Ace *The Wizard of Venus and Pirate Blood*), and three other first editions were never available commercially. Two were published in 1965 and 1966 in a Burroughs fanzine from Vernell Coriell (BURROUGHS BULLETIN, including *The Girl from Farris's* and *The Efficiency Expert*). The third, *The Scientists Revolt*, first appeared in the Burroughs fanzine ERB-DOM in 1971. There is one other oddity: in 1959 several ERB fans published 250 copies of *The Girl from Farris's*, a tiny 48-page book bound in marble boards, which ERB, Inc. had allowed to fall out of copyright.

Appendix D: The Two Most Popular Burroughs Reprint Publishers

Grosset & Dunlap	Every one of the forty-five Burroughs titles which Grosset & Dunlap printed is a reprint, although there are several books which are hybrid publications with Grosset & Dunlap covers and dust jackets over interior pages by A.C. McClurg, Metropolitan, and ERB, Inc. G&D did publish a Hal Foster illustrated retelling of *Tarzan of the Apes* (see entry for *The Illustrated Tarzan Book No. 1*, page 70 in this bibliography), which counts as a first edition. However, it is not directly from the pen of ERB. Grosset & Dunlap printed quality reprints, which included original illustrations, until about 1935. A second series of G&D reprints was published between 1935 and 1940 with red covers, but with fewer or no illustrations. A third group of G&D reprints are the 1943 "Madison Square" editions, cheaply bound in maroon covers with very poor quality paper. The fourth phase occurred between 1948 and 1966, when the first nine *Tarzan* titles were printed in a uniform children's edition. The fifth phase began in 1967 when G&D reissued the same nine *Tarzan* titles without dust jackets, but with the jacket illustration printed directly on the cover.
A.L. Burt Company	The A.L. Burt Company reprinted the first five *Tarzan* titles between 1915 and 1928, and every Burt book is a reprint (although many were published very early, often less than a year after the McClurg first edition printings). They were made to sell for 50¢ apiece (the McClurg's generally sold in the higher price range, $1.30 to $2.00). They are not as sturdy, the paper is a less expensive weight, and the dust jackets have a distressing propensity toward fading. The five titles are:

APPENDIX E

Tarzan of the Apes   Son of Tarzan
The Return of Tarzan   Tarzan and the Jewels of Opar
The Beasts of Tarzan

Appendix E:
McClurg Print Run Records

Burroughs researcher Alan M. Freedman managed to unearth a treasure trove of information on actual print runs for the McClurg Burroughs books. His findings were published in the BURROUGHS BULLETIN #3 and #4 (New Series, July and October, 1990). Freedman explained that McClurg donated their records to the Newberry Library in Chicago in 1968, where he went through more than 5,000 pages of material to ferret out the information listed below.

The numbers are available only for the twenty-nine McClurg editions and are totals for ALL printings. Usually McClurg published just the first edition, but sometimes they published a second corrected state of the first, or even a second or third reprint edition (especially with the *Tarzan* series). For example, *Tarzan of the Apes* is thought to have had 5,000 copies in the first state, 2,500 in a third state, and an additional 2,500 using a McClurg Acorn colophon on the spine. This would explain the obvious rarity of the *Acorn* McClurg compared to the non-*Acorn* first edition. The work of Alan Freedman has clarified the rarity of many of the titles, and all Burroughs collectors owe him a great debt of gratitude.

Tarzan of the Apes (1st state, 2nd state, 3rd state)—10,000
Return of Tarzan (at least six McClurg printings)—15,000
Beasts of Tarzan (1st edition only)—19,500
Son of Tarzan (three McClurg printings)—32,000
Tarzan and the Jewels of Opar (one reprinting)—50,000
Jungle Tales of Tarzan (four printings)—63,000
Tarzan the Untamed (one reprinting)—77,000
Tarzan the Terrible (one reprinting)—45,000
Tarzan and the Golden Lion (1st edition only)—25,000
Tarzan and the Ant Men (1st edition only)—10,000
Tarzan, Lord of the Jungle (four printings)—7,500

A Princess of Mars (1st edition only)—10,200
Gods of Mars (one reprinting)—10,000
Warlord of Mars (one reprinting)—20,000
Thuvia, Maid of Mars (one reprinting)—17,000
Chessmen of Mars (1st edition only)—12,500
Master Mind of Mars (1st edition only)—5,000

At the Earth's Core (1st edition only)—17,000
Pellucidar (1st edition only)—10,000

The Mucker (one reprinting)—17,000
Land That Time Forgot (1st edition only)—10,000
Eternal Lover (1st edition only)—5,000
Bandit of Hell's Bend (1st edition only)—5,000
Cave Girl (1st edition only)—5,000
Moon Maid (1st edition only)—5,000
Mad King (first and second state)—5,000
Outlaw of Torn (one reprinting)—6,000
War Chief (1st edition only)—6,000
Monster Men (1st edition only)—5,000

Appendix F:
The House of Greystoke Publications

Vernell Coriell (1918–1987) devoted his life to the worlds created by Edgar Rice Burroughs, and originated the first Burroughs fan magazine, THE BURROUGHS BULLETIN, and the first noncommercial Burroughs fan organization, The Burroughs Bibliophiles. Originally, membership and fanzine were free. Vern published several titles, not to make a profit, but just because he loved the fantasy realms created by Edgar Rice Burroughs.

THE BURROUGHS BIBLIOPHILE #2: THE ILLUSTRATED TARZAN BOOK No. 1, Picturized from the novel TARZAN OF THE APES by Edgar Rice Burroughs (Kansas City, MO: House of Greystoke, 1967)
 This is a reprint of the original 1929 Grosset and Dunlap edition described in entry #191 of this book. There are two different colors for the paper wraps.

APPENDIX F

The regular edition is in yellow (gold) wraps. There was another variant with blue wraps, which Coriell sent to special friends. 8½" × 11".

THE ILLUSTRATED TARZAN BOOK No. 2 (Kansas City, MO: House of Greystoke, 1968)
Same format as No. 1 above, this is picturized from "The Return of Tarzan" with 239 illustrations by Rex Maxon. Yellow wraps, cover illustration by J. Allen St. John from chapter 24 of the novel.

THE ILLUSTRATED TARZAN BOOK No. 3 (Kansas City, MO: House of Greystoke, 1971)
Same format in yellow wraps as the previous two, this is picturized from "*The Beasts of Tarzan*" with 336 pictures by Rex Maxon. Cover illustration by J. Allen St. John from page 84 of the novel.

THE ILLUSTRATED TARZAN BOOK No. 13 (Wytheville, VA: House of Greystoke, n.d. [1981])
Like the ones described above, this follows the same 8½" × 11" format. It is in yellow wraps, picturized from the newspaper strip "Tarzan the Ape Man" with 552 pictures by Rex Maxon. The cover has a still from the movie, and the back cover has a publicity still of Johnny Weissmuller autographed to Rex Maxon.

ILLUSTRATED TARZAN BOOK No. 23 (Kansas City, MO: House of Greystoke, 1968)
Same format as those above; picturized from the newspaper strip "Tarzan Under Fire" (*Tarzan and the Tarzan Twins with Jad-Bal-Ja, the Golden Lion*) with 336 pictures by William Juhré. Cover illustration is a panel from Juhré's strip.

THE BURROUGHS BIBLIOPHILES PRESENTS "TARZAN AND THE JEWELS OF OPAR" (Kansas City, MO: House of Greystoke, 1964)
A reprint of the complete magazine serial from ALL-STORY WEEKLY, containing all of the first edition illustrations by J. Allen St. John, plus a separate folio of seventeen superb St. John ink illustrations drawn especially for the art director of the *Chicago Herald*, used to illustrate the 1918 newspaper appearance of this story. These illustrations were discovered in 1954 by Burroughs art enthusiast Robert R. Barrett. Some segments of the text are from THE VIRGINIA LEADER ("Virginia's Best Boy's Magazine" from 1920) and contain illustrations by Frank Parker. Mr. Coriell has provided a detailed pictorial bibliography at the end of the publication. 124 numbered pages.

House of Greystoke Publications

APPENDIX F

THE GIRL FROM FARRIS'S (Kansas City, MO: House of Greystoke, August 1965)
This attractive edition was advertised as an "*authorized* first edition" from the Burroughs Bibliophiles. It is bound in stiff yellow paper covers with cover art (repeated as frontispiece) by Frank Frazetta. This is an offprint of the serial described in entry #158 but Coriell has included a "Pictorial Bibliography" of the story at the end, reproducing two drawings by Sam Armstrong from the newspaper serial published in the TACOMA TRIBUNE in 1920. It also contains information on the earlier Wilma fan edition. Coriell had a few copies professionally bound in blue-cloth hard covers which he shared with close friends. The title and the author's name were stamped in silver on the front cover. It did not have a dust jacket. 70 (+6) numbered pages.

THE EFFICIENCY EXPERT (Kansas City, MO: House of Greystoke, BURROUGHS BULLETIN #57-58, 1976)
This title is a reprint of the 1966 first edition, described in more detail on page 52, and is a professionally printed wrapper edition for subscribers to the BURROUGHS BULLETIN. The front cover art is by Frank Frazetta. The same illustration serves as a frontispiece. In addition, there are four interior black-and-white illustrations by Roger B. Morrison. The interior is a photographic reprint of the ARGOSY ALL-STORY WEEKLY magazine story with added materials by Vern Coriell. 40 unnumbered pages.

THE BURROUGHS BIBLIOPHILE #3, DAVID INNES OF PELLUCIDAR (Kansas City, MO: House of Greystoke, 1968)
Wraps, cover by John Coleman Burroughs. 269 interior illustrations by John Coleman Burroughs, reprinted from *HI-SPOT COMICS* No. 1, 1940. This also prints all the chapter headings that John Coleman Burroughs drew for the first edition of *The Land of Terror* (see entry #240) but which were not used. Besides the pages from *HI-SPOT* comic book, this edition includes numerous other pages of *David Innes of Pellucidar* intended for further issues of the comic, but never used.

THE RED STAR OF TARZAN (Kansas City, MO: House of Greystoke, BURROUGHS BULLETIN #41-44, 1974)
This is a photographic reprint of the ARGOSY WEEKLY serial described in entry #568 of this book. Vern Coriell did his usual thorough job of providing relevant information in a brief preface. A very professional slim digest-sized fanzine publication in stiff paper covers. Size is 5½" × 7¾".

Appendix G: Chronological List (by Date of Authorship) of Burroughs' Stories

This list is only approximate. Burroughs wrote several unpublished manuscripts at various stages of his career, several of which are undated, and there are several titles listed on pages 222–225 in Part II which could not be accurately placed on this list. It is possible that not all of ERB's unpublished manuscripts are listed. (Note that the identificatory device of having ERB's major published works appear in boldface is not followed here.)

Minidoka 937th Earl of One Mile Series M (unpublished lengthy fairy tale, written around 1903)
The Violet Veil: A Treely True Story (between 1904–1907)
1911 A Princess of Mars
The Outlaw of Torn
Tarzan of the Apes
1912 The Gods of Mars
The Avenger (3,500 word short story, unpublished)
For the Fool's Mother (unpublished short story)
The Return of Tarzan
1913 At the Earth's Core
The Cave Girl (Part One)
The Monster Men
The Warlord of Mars
The Mucker (Part One)
The Mad King (Part One)
The Eternal Lover (Part One)
1914 The Beasts of Tarzan
The Lad and the Lion
The Girl from Farris's
Thuvia, Maid of Mars
The Cave Girl (Part Two)
The Eternal Lover (Part Two)
The Mad King (Part Two)
Pellucidar

1915 The Son of Tarzan
The Man-Eater
Beyond Thirty
Tarzan and the Jewels of Opar
The Rider
The Zealots (unpublished)
The Lion Hunter (unpublished outline)
1916 The Mucker (Part Two)
Jungle Tales of Tarzan (chapters 1–8)
1917 The Oakdale Affair
Jungle Tales of Tarzan (chapters 9–12)
The Land That Time Forgot (part 1)
The Little Door (unpublished)
The Land That Time Forgot (part 2)
1918 The Land That Time Forgot (part 3)
Tarzan the Untamed (chapters 1–13)
Patriotism by Proxy (Oak Leaves)
Peace and the Militia (Oak Parker)
A National Reserve Army (Army-Navy Journal)
Wanted—Good Citizens!

1919	The Moon Maid (Part Two)		Pirate Blood
	The Efficiency Expert		Lost on Venus
	The Ghostly Script (unpublished)		"Edgar Rice Burroughs Tells All" (*Rob Wagner's Script*)
1920	Tarzan the Terrible	1933	Tarzan and the Lion Man
1921	The Chessmen of Mars		Swords of Mars
	The Girl from Hollywood		The Death Valley Expedition of the Intrepid 33ers (automobile camping trip journal)
1922	Tarzan and the Golden Lion		
	The Moon Maid (Part One)		
	Beware!/The Scientists Revolt	1934	Tarzan's Quest
1923	The Bandit of Hell's Bend	1935	Back to the Stone Age
	Tarzan and the Ant Men		Tarzan the Magnificent (chapters 1–12)
1924	Marcia of the Doorstep		
	Out of Time's Abyss (article for Urban Military Academy school newspaper)	1936	The Resurrection of Jimber-Jaw
			Tarzan the Magnificent (chapters 13–25)
1925	The Moon Maid (Part Three)		
	The Master Mind of Mars	1937	Carson of Venus
1926	The War Chief		Tarzan and the Forbidden City
	"An Adventure in Plagiarism" (*The Bulletin of the Author's League*)		"Two Gun" Doak Flies South (unpublished)
		1938	Synthetic Men of Mars
	The Tarzan Twins		Land of Terror
1927	You Lucky Girl!	1939	Tarzan and the Jungle Murders (Tarzan and the Castaways)
	Tarzan, Lord of the Jungle		
	Apache Devil		
1928	Tarzan and the Tarzan Twins with Jad-Bal-Ja, the Golden Lion		Angel's Serenade (unpublished)
			Tarzan and the Champion (Tarzan and the Castaways)
	Tarzan and the Lost Empire	1940	Tarzan and the Madman
	Tanar of Pellucidar		Escape on Venus (chapters 1–16)
	Tarzan at the Earth's Core		
1929	A Fighting Man of Mars		Llana of Gathol (Part One)
	Jungle Girl		Savage Pellucidar (Part One)
	The Citizen and the Police (*Police Reporter*)		Escape on Venus (chapters 17–29)
1930	Tarzan the Invincible		Llana of Gathol (Part Two)
	The Deputy Sheriff of Comanche County		Savage Pellucidar (Part Two)
			Escape on Venus (chapters 30–42)
1931	Tarzan Triumphant		
	Calling All Cars (unpublished)		Llana of Gathol (Part Three)
	Tarzan and the Leopard Men		Beyond the Farthest Star (Tales of Three Planets)
	Pirates of Venus		
	Tarzan and the City of Gold		Savage Pellucidar (Part Three)
1932	Murder! (unpublished short mystery puzzles)		Escape on Venus (chapters 43–55)

APPENDIX G

Llana of Gathol (Part Four)
The Quest of Tarzan (Tarzan and the Castaways)
Tangor Returns (Tales of Three Planets)
The Strange Adventures of Mr. Dinwiddie (unpublished)
Mysogynists Preferred (unpublished)
1941 The Wizard of Venus (Tales of Three Planets)
Unfinished Venus story
I Am a Barbarian
Skeleton Men of Jupiter (John Carter of Mars)

1943 More Fun! More People Killed! (unpublished)
1944 Tarzan and "The Foreign Legion"
Savage Pellucidar (Part Four)
Uncle Bill (unpublished)
1946 An unfinished Tarzan novel (83 typewritten pages); revised and completed by Joe R. Lansdale as *The Lost Adventure*, published by Dark Horse Comics in four installments, January-April, 1995, and then in a limited hardback edition in December, 1995.

I have consulted many different sources in compiling this list, including Henry H. Heins, ERB-DOM No. 11 (August 1964), ERB-DOM No. 56, and Irwin Porges, Edgar Rice Burroughs: The Man Who Created Tarzan (Brigham Young, 1975), pp. 787–96.

Index

References are to entry numbers except where otherwise noted.

Abbett, Robert (ERB illustrator) 53, 100, 153, 182, 200, 228, 281, 321, 368, 428, 460, 497, 506, 513, 541, 548–549, 565, 595, 614, 624, 635, 647, 650, 677, 692, 713, 739, 764, 779, 791, 812–813, 834
"Absurd Quarantine" (ERB newspaper article) 847
acorn device (McClurg first edition) 697; *pages 186–187n*
"Across Savage Mars" (*The Warlord of Mars*) 828
Adams, Neal (ERB illustrator) 54, 230, 461, 498, 566–567, 615, 625, 636, 678, 715–716, 723, 740, 792
Adkins, Pat H. ("Edgar Rice Burroughs Bibliography and Price Guide") 997
"advance sheets" (pre-publication paperback editions issued for early McClurg titles) *Beasts of Tarzan* 41; *A Princess of Mars* 422; *Return of Tarzan* 445; *The Son of Tarzan* 483; *Tarzan of the Apes* 695
Adventures of Lord Blackstoke (John and Thomas McGeehan) 985
ALL-AROUND MAGAZINE 60; "Beyond Thirty" 61
THE ALL-STORY 380, 443; "The Cave Girl" 77; "The Gods of Mars" 174; "A Man Without a Soul" (*The Monster Men*) 328; "Tarzan of the Apes" 694; "Under the Moons of Mars" 421; "Warlord of Mars" 828
ALL-STORY CAVALIER WEEKLY: "Beasts of Tarzan" 40; "The Mucker" 357; "Pellucidar" 387; "Sweetheart Primeval" 134
ALL-STORY WEEKLY 612; "At the Earth's Core" 8; "Barney Custer of Beatrice" 300; "The Cave Man" 78; "The Eternal Lover" 134; "The Girl from Farris's" 158, 159, 161; "H.R.H. the Rider" 372, 462; "The Lad and the Lion" 233; "The Mad King" 299; "The Return of the Mucker" 358; "The Son of Tarzan" 482; "Tarzan and the Jewels of Opar" 597; "Tarzan and the Valley of Luna" 767; "Thuvia, Maid of Mars" 801
Alternate Martians (pastiche by A. Bertram Chandler) 972
AMAZING STORIES (magazine): "Black Pirates of Barsoom" 274; "The City of Mummies" 273; "Invisible Men of Mars" 276; "John Carter and the Giant of Mars" 192, 196; "The Land That Time Forgot" 252; "Men of the Bronze Age" 468; "Return to Pellucidar" 467; "Savage Pellucidar" 471; "Skeleton Men of Jupiter" 194, 197; "Tiger Girl" 469; "Yellow Men of Mars" 275
AMAZING STORIES ANNUAL: "The Master Mind of Mars" 314; reproduced again 323, 326
AMAZING STORIES QUARTERLY 314; "Black Pirates of Barsoom" 278; "The City of Mummies" 277; "Invisible Men of Mars" 279; "John Carter and the Giant of Mars" 193; "Return to Pelluci-

269

INDEX

dar/Men of the Bronze Age/Tiger Girl" 470; "Skeleton Men of Jupiter" 195; "Yellow Men of Mars" 279
Amtorian Dictionary (Robert Horvath) 1071
Anderson, Al (ERB illustrator) 458, 710
Anderson, Poul 1000
"Angel's Serenade" (an unpublished ERB story) 848
ANTIQUARIAN BOOKMAN 1001
ANTIQUES JOURNAL 1002
Apache Devil 4–7
"The Ape-Man" (*The Return of Tarzan*) 443
"Ape-Man Business" (FORTUNE MAGAZINE 1938) 1003
"Apes and Martians" (Poul Anderson) 1000
Arbo, Hal (Big Little Book artist) 48, 659, 937, 943
ARGOSY ALL-STORY WEEKLY: "Apache Devil" 1; "Bandit of Hell's Bend" 33; "Chessmen of Mars" 91; "The Efficiency Expert" 116; "The Moon Maid" 337; "The Moon Men" 338; "The Red Hawk" 339; "Tarzan and the Ant Men" 531; "Tarzan and the Golden Lion" 581; "Tarzan and the Jewels of Opar" 597; "Tarzan the Terrible" 753; "The War Chief" 821
ARGOSY WEEKLY 421, 439, 576; "Carson of Venus" 69; "Lost on Venus" 285; "Pirates of Venus" 405; "The Quest of Tarzan" 545; "The Red Star of Tarzan" 568; "The Resurrection of Jimber-Jaw" 436; "Seven Worlds to Conquer" 24; "Synthetic Men of Mars" 510; "Tarzan and the City of Gold" 553; "Tarzan and the Magic Men" 747
Armed Services Edition: *The Return of Tarzan* 453; *Tarzan of the Apes* 706
Armstrong, Sam (illustrator for "Girl from Farris's") 160–161
Arnold, Herb (illustrator for THE BURROUGHS BULLETIN, "The Scientists Revolt") 481

Arting, Fred J. (original artist for *Tarzan of the Apes* dust jacket) 696, 699, 701, 705, 707, 1145; *page 189*
At the Earth's Core 8–23, 77, 342, 387, 425, 435
"Author-Publisher" (in WRITER'S DIGEST) 849
AutoBiography by Edgar Rice Burroughs 850
Avenel Books 499, 724
"The Avenger" (an unpublished ERB article or story) 852

"Back to Barsoom: Remembering Edgar Rice Burroughs" (John T. Carter) 1022
Back to the Earth's Core (William Gilmour) 977
Back to the Stone Age 24–32, 747
"Back to the Stone Age: A Romance of the Inner World" 24
Baines, Thomas (Signet illustrator) 725
"Ballad of the Bs" (unpublished ERB poems and art) 853
Ballantine Special Book Club Edition of *Tarzan of the Apes* 716
The Bandit of Hell's Bend 33–39, 531
"The Bank Murder" (unpublished ERB mystery short story) 854
Bantam Books (*Tarzan in the Forbidden City*, first ERB paperback, from 1940) 570
Barker, J. Welford (publisher of THE VIRGINIA LEADER) 603
"Barney Custer of Beatrice" (*The Mad King*) 300
Barrett, Robert R. 120, 240, 371, 401, 568, 591, 612, 657, 701, 1145, 1147, 1149, 1150, 1152, 1154, 1156, 1159, 1161, 1162, 1163, 1165–1168, 1170–1177
Barsoom: Edgar Rice Burroughs and the Martian Vision (Richard A. Lupoff) 1088
Bartram, R. (ERB illustrator) 238
Bash, Kent (ERB illustrator) 730
"The Battle for Teeka" (*Jungle Tales of Tarzan*) 226, 229, 231

270

INDEX

Bean, Normal (Norman) (ERB pseudonym) 421, 912
The Beasts of Tarzan 11, 40–54, 233, 444, 484, 679; Big Little Book 48, 943–944
Beecher, Elizabeth (*Tarzan of the Apes and Little Konga*) 970
Belarski, Rudolph (ERB illustrator) 69, 510, 544, 568, 576
Bellew, Ruth (map illustrator): *Cave Girl* 84; *Tarzan and the Lost Empire* 644
"Ben, King of Beasts" (*The Man-Eater*) 309, 312, 482
Bennett, Juanita (ERB illustrator for Whitman) 657–661, 703, 932–934, 937–939, 945–946, 960–963; *page 174*
Berdanier, Paul F. (ERB illustrator) 15, 104, 394–396, 520–522, 525, 817
Bergen, James A., Jr. (*Price and Reference Guide to Books Written by Edgar Rice Burroughs*) 1007–1008
BEST STORIES OF ALL TIME (magazine) "Tarzan of the Apes" 702
Better Little Books *see* Big Little Books
"Beware!" (John Tyler McCulloch, pseudonym for ERB) *The Scientists Revolt* 478
"Beyond the Farthest Star" (*Tales of Three Planets*) 55–59, 437, 517–518, 545, 839, 843
"Beyond Thirty" 60–68, 309, 482, 597
Big Little Books (Whitman and Dell) 932–968
Billion Year Spree (Brian Aldiss) 998
"Birth of Tarzan by His Poppa" (published ERB article) 855
"Black Bear" (hero of *Apache Devil*) 1
"Black Coyote" (*The Bandit of Hell's Bend*) 33
"Black Man's Burden" (ERB poem) 856
Blackbeard, Bill (*Tarzan: In Color*) 1146
Blaine, Mahlon (ERB illustrator for Canaveral Press) 14, 151, 254, 331, 344, 393, 523

Bleiler, Ev (*Science Fiction: The Early Years*) 1010
"Blonde from Barsoom" (Robert F. Young) 996
"Bloodstone, John" (pseudonym for Stuart J. Byrne): *Tarzan on Mars* 969
BLUE BOOK MAGAZINE: "Beyond the Farthest Star" 55; "A Fighting Man of Mars" 145; "The Land of Hidden Men" 204; "The Land That Time Forgot" 247; "The New Stories of Tarzan" 213; "The Oakdale Affair" 371; "Out of Time's Abyss" 249; "The People That Time Forgot" 248; "Swords of Mars" 500; "Tanar of Pellucidar" 519; "Tarzan and the Champion" 543; "Tarzan and the Elephant Men" 748; "Tarzan and the Immortal Men" 793; "Tarzan and the Leopard Men" 617; "Tarzan and the Lost Empire" 637; "Tarzan at the Earth's Core" 664; "Tarzan, Guard of the Jungle" 732; "Tarzan, Lord of the Jungle" 681; "The Triumph of Tarzan" 782
"BMTCers Can Shoot" (ERB newspaper story from WWII) 857
Bohnett, Brian (*A Guide to the Tarzan Big Little Books*) 1087
Bonanza Books (a division of Crown Books) 439
Book-of-the-Month-Club 728, 729
Boris *see* Vallejo, Boris
Bottleneck Blues Press (Robert B. Zeuschner, publisher) 1095, 1096
Boucher, Anthony (an ERB illustration was mistakenly used on Boucher's *The Complete Werewolf*) 401
Bower, B. M. 831
Bradbury, Ray ("Tarzan, John Carter, Mr. Burroughs, and the Long Mad Summer of 1930") 1013
"The Brass Heart" (*The Deputy Sheriff of Comanche County*) 108
Bray, Joseph E. (editor at McClurg) 381

271

Brehm, George (ERB illustrator) 372, 462
"Bridge and the Oskaloosa Kid" (*The Oakdale Affair*) 371
Brigham, C. (ERB illustrator) 69
Broadhurst, Dale: "The Wizard of Venus" 840
Buccaneer Books, Publishers: *The Oakdale Affair* 378; *Tarzan of the Apes* 717; *The Warlord of Mars* 838
Bull, Charles Livingston (ERB illustrator) 766, 1147
Burroughs, Danton (grandson of ERB) 312, 745,
Burroughs, Emma Hulbert (ERB's first wife) 501, 696; *pages 7, 18*
Burroughs, Florence Gilbert (ERB's second wife) 70, 501; *pages 18, 220*
Burroughs, Hulbert (ERB's eldest son) 485, 486, 487, 489
Burroughs, Joan (daughter of ERB) 43, 373, 463, 846
Burroughs, John Coleman (ERB's younger son and illustrator) 25–26, 28, 70–72, 110, 112–114, 126, 127, 129, 192, 235–237, 240, 280, 373, 423, 463, 511, 512, 537, 569, 578, 591, 679, 741–744, 749–750, 759, 774; *pages 50, 82, 180; see also* #932–968 on Big Little Books
Burroughs, Studley O. (ERB's nephew and illustrator) 2, 3, 6, 206–208, 499, 724, 733–736, 741–744, 783–788; *page 27*
Burroughs Bestiary (David Day) 1038
Burroughs Bibliophiles (Burroughs literary society) 116, 117, 160, 161, 191, 192, 240, 323; 612; *see* Appendix F
Burroughs Bulletin (fan publication) 696; "Beware!" (*The Scientists Revolt*) 480, 481; "David Innes of Pellucidar" 240; "The Efficiency Expert" 116, 117; "The Girl from Farris's" 160, 161; "Master Mind of Mars" 323, 326; "The Red Star of Tarzan" (*Tarzan and the Forbidden City*) 576; "Tarzan and the Jewels of Opar" 612; "Tarzan Under Fire" 662; *page 132; see also* Appendix F
Burroughs Cyclopædia (Clark Brady) 1014
Burroughs Dictionary: An Alphabetical List of Proper Names, Words, Phrases and Concepts Contained in the Published Works of Edgar Rice Burroughs (George T. McWhorter) 1094
"The Burroughs No One Knows" (Dorothy McGreal) 1092
Burt, A. L. (publisher) *The Beasts of Tarzan* 44, 45; *The Return of Tarzan* 448, 449; *The Son of Tarzan* 489; *Tarzan and the Jewels of Opar* 600–602; *Tarzan of the Apes* 699–700; *pages 260–261*
Byrne, Stuart J. ("John Bloodstone") *Tarzan on Mars* 969

Cahan, Samuel (ERB illustrator) 24, 285, 405, 439, 510, 553, 568, 747
"Calling All Cars" (an unpublished ERB story) 858
"Came the War" (ERB article) 859
Canaveral Press 14, 28, 56, 72, 85, 127, 151, 181, 198, 199, 237, 254, 293, 331, 344, 367, 393, 412, 415, 437, 472, 517, 518, 523, 546, 547, 550, 649, 651, 658, 663, 670, 673, 839, 843
Cannon, Jeremy (pseudonym for Herbert Morton Stoops) 748
"**Captured on Venus**" (*Escape on Venus*) 119
Carroll & Graff, Publishers 434
Carson of Venus 69–76, 568, 748
"Carter of the Red Planet" (*A Princess of Mars*) 11, 425
"Carthoris" (*Thuvia, Maid of Mars*) 801
Castle, Frank (*Tarzan and the Lost Safari*) 971
Castle (publisher) 104–106, 396, 817–819
The Cave Girl 77–90, 328
"The Cave Man" 78, 801

INDEX

Cazedessus, Camille ("Caz," publisher of ERB-DOM): "The Scientists Revolt" 479; "The Terrible Tenderfoot" 111; *page 4*
Chandler, A. Bertram (*The Alternate Martians*) 972
Charter Books 39, 118
Chenoweth, Joseph (ERB illustrator) 500, 617
The Chessmen of Mars 91–107, 163, 396, 753, 809, 811, 814
Chicago Herald (newspaper) 612
"The Citizen and the Police" (an ERB article) 860
"City of Mummies" (*Llana of Gathol*) 273, 274, 277
"The Climate and the View" (an unpublished ERB poem) 861
"Clubs Like the Edgewater" (an unpublished ERB article) 862
Cochran, Russ: *The Edgar Rice Burroughs Library of Illustration* 1148
Cody, Mike (artist for "The Quest of Tarzan") 552
The Complete Werewolf (Anthony Boucher) 401
Condon, Grattan (ERB illustrator) 55
"Conquest of the Moon" (*The Moon Maid*) 11, 342
Conran, Michael: "The Quest of Tarzan" (*Tarzan and the Castaways*) 552; "Tarzan, Jr." 680; *pages 4, 180, 181*
"Cor Sva Jo" (*People That Time Forgot*) 248
Corben, Richard (science-fiction artist) 202, 282, 480
Coriell, Vern: "Beware!" (*The Scientists Revolt*) 480, 481; "David Innes of Pellucidar" 240; "The Efficiency Expert" 116, 117; "The Girl from Farris's" 160, 161; "Master Mind of Mars" 323, 326; *A Pictorial History of the Tarzan Movies* 1081; "The Red Star of Tarzan" (*Tarzan and the Forbidden City*) 576; "Tarzan and the Jewels of Opar" 612;

"Tarzan Under Fire" 662; *see also* House of Greystoke Publications in Appendix F
Council on Books in Wartime (Armed Services Editions): *The Return of Tarzan* 453; *Tarzan of the Apes* 706
Crandall, Reed (ERB illustrator for Canaveral) 198, 649
"Creator of Tarzan Speaks" (1923 *L.A. Times* article) 863
Cuneo-Henneberry printer's imprint: *Tarzan and the Jewels of Opar* 600–602
Cushing, Peter (star of film *At the Earth's Core*) 21

D'Achille, Gino (ERB illustrator) 102, 156, 184, 201, 283, 324, 432, 507, 514, 815, 836; poster "Welcome to Barsoom" 815
Dameron, Charles E. (ERB illustrator) 47
Dameron, Ned (ERB illustrator) 313, 846
"The Dancing Girl of the Leper King" (*Jungle Girl*) 204
Dark Horse Comics (*Tarzan: The Lost Adventure*) 741, 742, 743, 744, 745, 746; *page 196*
"David Innes of Pellucidar" (John Coleman Burroughs comic strip) *page 264*
Davis, Robert: author of "How Burroughs Wrote the Tarzan Tales" 532, 533, 597; editor of several ERB stories 581
Day, Bradford M.: *Beyond Thirty* and *The Man-Eater* 63, 311; "Edgar Rice Burroughs: A Bit of His Life" 1035
Dean, Ray (illustrator for "Tarzan and the Lion Man") 626
"Dear Old Eighty Two-Three" (an unpublished ERB poem) 864
"Death Valley Expedition of the Intrepid 33ers" (an unpublished ERB article) 865

273

INDEX

DeCamp, L. Sprague 23, 435; ("Sir Harold of Zodanga") 973
"Dejah Thoris, Martian Princess" (*A Princess of Mars*) 421
Dell (paperback publisher): *Cave Girl* 84; *Tarzan and the Lost Empire* 644
Denkena, Kurt S. (*ERB-Notizen*) *page 5*
The Deputy Sheriff of Comanche County 108–114, 732, 782
des Vignes, Jean (ERB illustrator) 84
"Diana of the Bar Y" (*The Bandit of Hell's Bend*) 33
"Diary of a Confused Old Man, or Buck Burroughs Rides Again" (an unpublished ERB article) 866
"Diary of an Automobile Camping Trip Undertaken by the Burroughs Family in 1916" 867
"Do Boys Make Good Soldiers?" (an unpublished ERB article) 868
Donohue printer's imprint 93, 94, 95, 754, 755, 768, 769
"Don't Let 'Em Kid You, Joe" (ERB newspaper article) 869
Doubleday 21, 101, 155, 183, 202, 260, 282, 325, 431, 508, 515, 814, 835
Dover Publications 15, 96, 154, 255, 256, 292, 318, 347, 348, 394, 414, 429, 430, 525, 809
Dunn, Laurence *page viii*
Durban, Frank (ERB illustrator) 123, 277, 279

Easton Press 23, 435, 730
Edgar Rice Burroughs (Erling B. Holtsmark) 1068
"Edgar Rice Burroughs: A Biographical Sketch" (George T. McWhorter) 1095
"Edgar Rice Burroughs: A Bibliography" (Bradford M. Day) 1037
"Edgar Rice Burroughs: Bibliography and Price Guide" (Pat H. Adkins) 997
"Edgar Rice Burroughs: A Bit of His Life" (Bradford Day) 1035

"Edgar Rice Burroughs: Creator of Tarzan" (Margret Romer) 1120
"Edgar Rice Burroughs: His Life and His Work" (Robert B. Zeuschner) *pages 7–19*
"Edgar Rice Burroughs: Life and Work" (Sol Malkin) 1097
Edgar Rice Burroughs: The Man Who Created Tarzan (Irwin Porges) 1116; *pages 4, 19n, 222, 267*
Edgar Rice Burroughs: Master of Adventure (Richard A. Lupoff) 546, 550, 1089
"Edgar Rice Burroughs: Multimillionaire Author" (Cyril Clemens) 1024
"Edgar Rice Burroughs' Apache Epic" (Robert E. Morsberger) 1103
"Edgar Rice Burroughs Biblio" (Bradford M. Day) 1036
"An Edgar Rice Burroughs Checklist" (Cummings/Peters) 1033
"An Edgar Rice Burroughs Collector's Notebook" (Hal Peters) 1113
"The Edgar Rice Burroughs Collector's Pocket Checklist" (J.G. Huckenpöhler 1996) *page viii*
Edgar Rice Burroughs' Fantastic Worlds (James Van Hise) 1136
"Edgar Rice Burroughs, Inc." (Dolph Sharp) 1126
The Edgar Rice Burroughs Library of Illustration (Russ Cochran) 1148
Edgar Rice Burroughs Memorial Collection: A Catalog (George T. McWhorter) 585, 1096
EDGAR RICE BURROUGHS NEWS DATELINE (Michael Conran) 552; *page 181*
EDGAR RICE BURROUGHS QUARTERLY (magazine published by George McWhorter) *page 185n*
Edgar Rice Burroughs Reference Guide (James Bergen) 1007
"Edgar Rice Burroughs, Rex Maxon and Harold Foster" (Robert Barrett) 1040
"Edgar Rice Burroughs Tells All" 870; *pages 21–24*

INDEX

Editions for the Armed Services, Inc. (Armed Services Editions): *The Return of Tarzan* 453; *Tarzan of the Apes* 706
The Efficiency Expert 115–118
"The Eleven Year Itch" (an unpublished ERB article or story) 871
ELLERY QUEEN'S MYSTERY MAGAZINE: "Tarzan, Jungle Detective" 226
ELLERY QUEEN'S MYSTERY MAGAZINE 1970 ANTHOLOGY: "Tarzan, Jungle Detective" 229
"Elmer" ("The Resurrection of Jimber-Jaw") 436
Elrick, George S. (*Tarzan and the Mark of the Red Hyena*) 974
Ely, Ron (Tarzan actor) 459, 711
Emsh, Ed (illustrator for Ace Books) 346, 350, 352
Endeweldt, Jack (illustrator for Gold Star Tarzan pastiches) 993
Enrich (ERB illustrator for Ace Books) 239, 334
"Entertainment Is Fiction's Purpose" (WRITER'S DIGEST 1930) 872
"ERB and the Heroic Epic" (Tom Slate) 1129
ERB-DOM (Burroughs fan publication edited by Caz Cazedessus) 479, 986, 1112; *pages vii, 97, 132, 222, 234, 260*
ERB, Inc: *Lost on Venus* 288; *Pirates of Venus* 410; *Swords of Mars* 504; *Tarzan and the Leopard Men* 621; *Tarzan and the Lion Man* 631; *Tarzan Triumphant* 787; *Tarzan's Quest* 796
"ERB's Rarest Book": questionable label affixed to *The Lad and the Lion* 237
Escape on Venus 119–133, 649
Eshbach, Lloyd A. 61; "Beyond Thirty" 62; "The Man-Eater" 310
Essays on Mars: Exploring the Red Planet of Edgar Rice Burroughs (William P. Waters) 1139
Essoe, Gabe (*Tarzan of the Movies*) 1042

The Eternal Lover 40, 134–144, 300
"The Eternal Savage" *(The Eternal Lover)* 141–144
"Even Apes Fight for It" (ERB humorous magazine article) 873
EVENING WORLD (newspaper): "Beyond Thirty" 60; "The Man-Eater" 309
Everett, Eldon K. (Wilma edition of "Girl from Farris's") 159

Fairchild, W. C. (ERB illustrator for ALL-STORY WEEKLY) 300; *page 94*
fairy castle (a dollhouse built for movie star Colleen Moore) 680; *page 180*
"Fall of a Democracy" (an unpublished ERB article) 874
"Famous Living Americans and Their Homes" (unpublished ERB article) 875
FANTASTIC ADVENTURES (magazine): "Goddess of Fire" 120; "The Living Dead" 122; "Scientists Revolt" 478; "Slaves of the Fish Men" 119; "War on Venus" 124
FANTASTIC ADVENTURES QUARTERLY: "Goddess of Fire" 121; "The Living Dead" 123; "War on Venus" 125
The Fantastic Pulps 441, 442
The Fantasy Press (Lloyd A. Eshbach) 62, 310
fanzines (fan magazines devoted to Burroughs) 1178–1221; *pages 4–5, 252–254*
Farewell Pellucidar (pastiche by Allan H. Gross) 978
Farmer, Philip José: novels featuring ERB characters 975, 1043–1045; *page 1*
A Fighting Man of Mars 145–157, 204
"The Fighting Prince of Mars" (*The Warlord of Mars*) 828
Fink, Robert (ERB illustrator) 500
Finlay, Virgil (illustrator of "Quest of Tarzan") 545, 552

275

INDEX

"The Fire Goddess" (*Escape on Venus*) 120
First Edition Library (*Tarzan of the Apes*) 731
first editions, their value to collectors see Appendix A
"For the Fool's Mother" (an unpublished ERB film scenario) 876
"For the Victory Loan" (unpublished ERB poem) 877
Forgotten Sea of Mars (Michael P. Resnick) 986
"Fortunino Mantania" by Robert R. Barrett 1149
Foster, Hal 188, 189, 190, 191, 1149; *page 72*
Fowler, George: "The Case Against the Acorn" *page 185n*
Franke, Henry G. (*Snowmen of Jupiter*) 976
Frazetta, Frank (premiere ERB illustrator) 19, 27, 29–31, 51, 57, 64–66, 73–75, 88–89, 101, 116–117, 132, 152, 155, 160, 183, 211, 224, 242–245, 264–266, 291, 294–296, 305–308, 325, 332–333, 353–354, 369–370, 377, 379, 385–386, 399, 431, 466, 473–476, 494, 508, 515, 529, 546–547, 562, 610, 633, 645, 670, 671, 673–676, 737, 789, 814, 835, 1151–1155
Freedman, Alan M. 423, 682, 696; *page 185n*
"The Frozen Men of Mars" (*Llana of Gathol*) 273
Fury, David (*Kings of the Jungle*) 1051

Gardner, Maurice 301
Gaydos, Tim (illustrator for Random House) 718
Gernsback, Hugo (publisher of AMAZING STORIES) 314
"Ghengis Khan" (an unpublished ERB poem) 878
"Ghostly Script" (an unpublished ERB short story) 879

Gianni, Gary (illustrator, *Tarzan: The Lost Adventure*) 743
Gilmour, William (author of pastiches) 977
"The Girl from Farris's" (original title: "The Girl from Harris's") 158–162, 801
The Girl from Hollywood 163–173, 581
"Girl of Pellucidar" (*Savage Pellucidar*) 472
"Go to Pershing" (an unpublished ERB article from WWI) 880
"Goddess of Fire" (*Escape on Venus*) 120, 121
The Gods of Mars 174–185, 443, 694, 828
Gods of Xuma or Barsoom Revisited (David J. Lake) 982
Goodstone, Tony (editor of *The Pulps*) 439
Grant, Donald M.: *Marcia of the Doorstep* 313; *You Lucky Girl!* 846
Grant, Douglas (ERB illustrator for *The Tarzan Twins*) (Volland) 653–656; *page 173*
"The Green Martians" (*A Princess of Mars*) 421
Gregg Publishers: *Apache Devil* 6; *Bandit of Hell's Bend* 38; *Deputy Sheriff of Comanche County* 114; *War Chief* 825
"Gretter" (illustrator for *Tarzan in the Forbidden City*) 470
Grey, Zane 831
"Greystoke Connection: Medievalism in Two Edgar Rice Burroughs Novels" (Stan Galloway) 1052
Gross, Allan H. (*Farewell Pellucidar*) 978
Gross, George (ERB illustrator) 714
"A Guide to Barsoom: The Mars of Edgar Rice Burroughs" (John Flint Roy) 1121
Gustavson, L. R. (ERB illustrator) 543

Habblitz, Harry ("The Wizard of Venus") 840

INDEX

Haining, Peter (editor for *The Fantastic Pulps*) 441, 442
Hall, Quin (ERB illustrator) 249
Hall, W.F.: *Gods of Mars* 175, 176, 177, 178; *Jungle Tales of Tarzan* 214, 215; *A Princess of Mars* 423; *Return of Tarzan* 446; *Son of Tarzan* 485; *Tarzan and the Jewels of Opar* 598; *Tarzan of the Apes* 696, 698; *Warlord of Mars* 829, 830
Hanson, Alan ("A Chrono-log of ERB's Tarzan Series") 1059
"Harold Foster: Artist Adventurer" by Robert R. Barrett 1150
Harrison, Mitchell 42, 698, 1060; *page viii*
Harwood, John 1061, 1062
"Heil Hitler" (ERB film scenario) 881
Heinlein, Robert (*The Number of the Beast*) 979
Heins, Henry 72, 155, 164, 168, 301, 302, 325, 538, 569, 582, 657, 679, 696, 706, 831, 1063–1064; *pages vii, 4, 97, 180, 185, 222, 267; Marcia of the Doorstep page 97*
Herndon, Laurence (ERB illustrator for BLUE BOOK) 145, 204, 732, 782
Herring, Michael (ERB illustrator) 59, 68, 90, 144, 212, 270–272, 336
Hescox, Richard (Ballantine artist) 76, 133, 298, 404, 420, 845, 1156
Hildebrandt, Greg (ERB illustrator) 7, 827
Hildebrandt, Tim (ERB illustrator) 7, 827
Hill, Edwin (author of *The Iron Horse* which has an ERB copyright) 585
Hill, Roger (*The Fantastic Worlds of P.J. Monahan*) 1066
Hirschman, Edward (author of two Burroughs pastiches) 980
"His Majesty, the Janitor" (ERB film scenario) 882
Hoban, Frank (ERB illustrator) 145, 204, 519, 617, 637, 664, 681, 732, 782, 793
"Hodon and O-aa" (*Savage Pellucidar*) 467

Hogarth, Burne (great Tarzan illustrator) 1146, 1157
Hollow, John ("Rereading *Tarzan of the Apes*") 1067
"Hollywood" (unpublished poem by ERB) 883
"Hollywood and Vines: Edgar Rice Burroughs Climbed to the Top Building His Own Empire State" (Joel H. Cohen) 1027
Holmes, John Eric (*Mahars of Pellucidar, Red Axe of Pellucidar*) 981
Holtsmark, Erling B. 1068, 1069
Hope, Anthony (*Prisoner of Zenda*) 299
Horvath, Robert (*Amtorian Dictionary*) 1071
House of Greystoke publications 612, 662; *see also* Appendix F
"How Burroughs Wrote the Tarzan Tales" (an appendix to *Tarzan and the Ant Men* by Robert H. Davis) 532–533, 534
"How I Wrote the Tarzan Books" (ERB newspaper article) 884
"H.R.H. the Rider" (*The Oakdale Affair and the Rider*) 358, 372, 462, 597
Huckenpöhler, J. G. (author of "The Edgar Rice Burroughs Collector's Pocket Checklist," 1996) *page viii*
Hutton, Hugh (ERB illustrator) 146, 150, 429, 452
Hyde, C.B. (Burroughs scholar, collector and president of the Burroughs Bibliophiles literary organization) 192, 569; *page viii*

I Am a Barbarian 186–187
IDLE HOUR MAGAZINE: "The Eternal Lover" 136
The Illustrated Tarzan Book No. 1 188–191
"The Illustrator and the Author" (ERB magazine article) 886
"In the Shadow of the Sun: Fred J. Arting and Clinton Pettee" (Robert Barrett) 1145

277

INDEX

"An Index to the Magazines and Newspaper Stories of Edgar Rice Burroughs" (John F. Cook) 1028
"The Inner World" (*At the Earth's Core*) 8
The Iron Horse (book by Edwin C. Hill with an ERB copyright page) 585
"It's Ants" (an unpublished ERB poem) 887
Ivie, Larry (ERB illustrator) 68, 471

Jackson, Jay (ERB illustrator) 123
Janus (god of Greek mythology) 627
"Jetan, or Martian Chess" (Edgar Rice Burroughs) 92
"John Carter and the Giant of Mars" (*John Carter of Mars*) 192–193, 198
"John Carter and the Pits of Horz" (*Llana of Gathol*) 273
John Carter of Mars 192–203
John Carter of Mars (Better Little Book) 949, 968
Johnson, Kevin (ERB illustrator) 105, 818
Jones, Jeff (illustrator for *I Am a Barbarian*) 186
Juhré, William (illustrator for "Tarzan Under Fire" aka *The Tarzan Twins*) 662
Julius, Kevin C. 1075
Jungle Girl 145, 204–212, 732
Jungle of Dreams: The Tarzan Mythos of Edgar Rice Burroughs (William P. Waters) 1140
"The Jungle Secret of Lost Atlantis" (*Tarzan and the Jewels of Opar*, Ace paperback) 610
Jungle Tales of Tarzan 213–232, 371, 768

Kaluta, Michael W. (illustrator for *Tarzan: The Lost Adventure*) 744
Kane, Gilbert (illustrator for *Beyond Thirty* and *The Man-Eater*) 63, 311

Kiko (illustrator for *A Princess of Mars*) 434
Kings of the Jungle (David Fury) 1051
Kirby, Brian 444; *page viii*
Kline, Robert (ERB illustrator for paperback of *The Man Eater*) 312
Knibbs, H.H., poet 358
Krenkel, Roy G. (premiere ERB illustrator) 13, 17–18, 27, 29–30, 56, 85–87, 98, 128, 130–132, 141–142, 143, 152, 209–210, 241, 257–259, 261–263, 320, 345–346, 349–352, 354, 384, 392, 397, 398, 401–402, 413, 416–418, 437, 517, 524, 527–528, 658, 789, 810, 839, 841–842, 1147, 1158–1159
Krupa, Julian S. (ERB illustrator) 125, 194–195, 277–279, 470, 478, 481
Kure, Henning ("A Tarzan Chronology") 744

Laager, Kenneth E. (ERB illustrator) 727
The Lad and the Lion 233–239; *page 82*
Lake, David J. (*Gods of Xuma or Barsoom Revisited*) 982
"Land of Hidden Men" 204, 209–212
Land of Terror 240–246
The Land That Time Forgot 11, 247–272, 347–348, 371
Lansdale, Joe (coauthor of *Tarzan: The Lost Adventure*, published by Dark Horse) 578, 745; *page 196*
"Laughs at Sea" (ERB newspaper article) 888
Lavin, Dom J. (ERB illustrator) 371
Leiber, Fritz (*Tarzan and the Valley of Gold*) 984
Leist, Frank (Methuen dust jacket illustrator) 361, 363–365
Lessor, Ronnie M. (ERB illustrator) 5, 824
Lewis, Alex (*Mars in Her Ashen Glory*) 983
LIBERTY MAGAZINE: "Tarzan and the Lion Man" 626

INDEX

"The Lion Hunter" (an ERB outline for a comedy) 889
"The Little Door" (an unpublished ERB story) 890
"Little Lessons for Little Learners" (ERB Sunday School story) 891
"Little Ol' Buck Private" (an unpublished ERB poem) 892
"The Living Dead" (*Escape on Venus*) 122–123
Llana of Gathol 273–284, 467
London, Jack 831
Lord Tyger (Philip José Farmer) 975
Los Angeles 840
"The Lost Continent" (*Beyond Thirty*) 64–68
"Lost Inside the Earth" (*At the Earth's Core*) 11
Lost on Jupiter (William Gilmour) 977
Lost on Venus 115, 285–298, 626
"The Lost U-Boat" (*The Land That Time Forgot*) 247
Love Stories ("**Tarzan's First Love**" aka "**The Battle for Teeka**") 231
Lowery, Larry (*A Guide to the Tarzan Big Little Books*) 1087
Lukes, Joe *page viii*
Lupoff, Richard A. 198, 200–203, 517, 546, 547, 550, 839, 1088–1091

Macaulay Company 164–171; *page 258*
McCall (ERB illustrator) 125
McCann, Gerald (ERB illustrator) 708, 712
McCarthy, Frank (ERB illustrator) 826
McCauley, H.W. (coillustrator for "Goddess of Fire") 120
McClure, Doug (star of the film *At the Earth's Core*) 21
McClurg, publishers 381, 453; *At the Earth's Core* 9; *The Bandit of Hell's Bend* 34; *The Beasts of Tarzan* 41–43; *The Cave Girl* 79–80; *The Chessmen of Mars* 92; *The Eternal Lover* 137–138; *The Gods of Mars* 175–176; *Jungle Tales of Tarzan* 214–217; *The Land That Time Forgot* 250; *The Mad King* 301–302; *The Master Mind of Mars* 315; *The Monster Men* 329; *The Moon Maid* 340; *The Outlaw of Torn* 359–360; *Pellucidar* 381–382, 388; *A Princess of Mars* 422–423; *The Return of Tarzan* 444–447; *The Son of Tarzan* 483–488; *Tarzan and the Ant Men* 532; *Tarzan and the Golden Lion* 582; *Tarzan and the Jewels of Opar* 598–599; *Tarzan, Lord of the Jungle* 682–683; *Tarzan of the Apes* 695–698, 724; *Tarzan the Terrible* 754–755; *Tarzan the Untamed* 768–769; *Thuvia, Maid of Mars* 802–803; *The War Chief* 822; *Warlord of Mars* 829–830; *see also* Appendix C and Appendix E
McCullouch, John Tyler (ERB penname) 401, 478, 480; *page 115*
McCutcheon, George Barr (*Graustark*) 299
MacDonald, Neal (ERB illustrator) 479
McGeehan, John (*Adventures of Lord Blackstroke*) 985
McGeehan, Thomas (*Adventures of Lord Blackstroke*) 985
McLoughlin, Don (ERB illustrator) 560–561, 564, 572, 575
McWhorter, George (curator, Burroughs Memorial Collection, Ekstrom Library, University of Louisville) 14, 51, 489, 585, 730, 745, 746, 1084, 1094–1096; *pages vii, viii, 4, 185, 252*
The Mad King 299–308
"The Mad King of Lutha" (*The Mad King*) 299
Madison Square Garden editions 50, 222, 454, 493, 536, 590, 608, 687, 707, 760, 775
Mahars of Pellucidar (John Eric Holmes) 981
The Man-Eater 309–312, 482
"Man-Eaters" (newspaper article) 893

INDEX

"A Man Without a Soul" (*The Monster Men*) 328
"The Man Without a Soul" (*The Mucker* [Part 2]) 361, 363–365
Manning, Russ (ERB illustrator) 1161, 1162
Marcia of the Doorstep 313, 314, 546
Maroto, Esteban (ERB illustrator) 297, 403, 419, 499, 724, 844
Mars in Her Ashen Glory (Alex Lewis) 983
Marsh, Jesse (ERB illustrator) 560, 572, 643, 710
"Marvelous Voyages—II: The Scientific Romances of Edgar Rice Burroughs" (Laurence LaFleur) 1080
The Master Mind of Mars 155, 314–327, 586, 821
Masterpieces of Science Fiction (Sam Moskowitz, editor) 438, 440
"Masterpieces of Science Fiction" (series by Easton Press) 23, 435, 730
Matania, Fortunino (ERB illustrator) 292, 414, 1148
Mattingly, David (ERB illustrator) 22, 32, 246, 400, 477, 530, 1163
Maxon, Rex (Big Little Books illustrator) 48, 452, 491, 537, 591, 606, 643, 688, 759, 774; *see also* 932–968 (Big Little Books)
"Meet the Authors: Edgar Rice Burroughs" (AMAZING STORIES biography) 895
"Men and Beasts" (*Lad and the Lion*) 233
"Men of the Bronze Age" 468
"Men Who Make the Argosy" (ARGOSY biography) 896
Metcalf, Thomas (editor at ALL-STORY magazine) 421, 443
Methuen, Sir Algernon 33
Methuen Press 328, 361, 363–365
Metropolitan Books, Inc. 46, 147, 520, 638–639, 665, 660; *pages 258, 259*
Michel, Jacques 1101
Miller, John A. *page viii*
Miller, Ron (ERB illustrator) 23, 435

"Minidoka 937th Earl of One Mile Series M" (an unpublished ERB story) 897
"Misogynists Preferred" (unpublished ERB story) 898
Mitchell, Arthur (illustrator for "The Terrible Tenderfoot") 108
Mitchell, Burroughs 568
Mitchell, Edward Page 568
mixed editions (combining first edition and reprint editions) 26, 147, 374, 464, 533, 604, 628, 639, 666, 784, 804
MODERN MECHANICS AND INVENTION MAGAZINE: "Carter of the Red Planet" 11, 425; "Conquest of the Moon" 342; "Lost Inside the Earth" 11
Monahan, Patrick John Sullivan (ERB illustrator) 91, 135, 164–168, 328, 337, 357–358, 482, 581, 597, 639, 753, 767, 801–808, 1164; *pages 56, 65, 101, 134, 160, 204*
Monroe, C. Edmund, Jr. (ERB illustrator for 1950s G&D editions) 223, 227, 455, 457, 538, 592, 594, 609, 613, 689, 691, 761, 763, 767, 776, 778, 1165
"Monsieur Tarzan" (*The Return of Tarzan*) 443
The Monster Men 328–336, 361, 828
The Moon Maid 11, 255, 256, 337–356, 581
The Moon Men (*The Moon Maid*) 338–340, 344, 346, 350, 352, 354, 356
Moore, Coleen ("Tarzan, Jr.") 680; *page 180*
Moore, Sparky (ERB illustrator) 458
"More Fun! More People Killed!" (unpublished ERB short story) 899
Mori *see* Morrison, Roger B.
Morrison, Roger B. (ERB illustrator) 1, 33, 91, 115–117, 161, 338–339, 531, 821
Morse, William *page viii*
Moskowitz, Sam 438, 440, 1104–1106
The Mucker 299, 357–370

INDEX

Mulford, Stockton (ERB illustrator) 115, 338, 531, 1166
Munro, Caroline (star of the film *At the Earth's Core*) 21
MUNSEY'S MAGAZINE: "The Girl from Hollywood" 163
"Murder: A Collection of Short Murder Mystery Puzzles" (by Burroughs, some unpublished) 900
"Murder in the Jungle" 544
Murphy, C. A. (ERB illustrator) 108, 544
Museum of Science & Industry, Chicago *page 180*
"My First Adventure on Mars" (*A Princess of Mars*) 421

Napier, Carson (friend of Edgar Rice Burroughs) 405
"A National Reserve Army" (published newspaper article from 1918) 901
Neely, Hugh Munro *page 220*
Nelson, Ben 568
New Adventures of Tarzan (Big Little Book) 940
New American Library (Signet Classics) 725
"New Stories of 'Tarzan'" (*Jungle Tales of Tarzan*) 213
NEW STORY MAGAZINE: "The Outlaw of Torn" 380; "The Return of Tarzan" 443
NEW YORK EVENING WORLD (newspaper): "Beyond Thirty" 60; "The Man-Eater" 309
"Night of Terror" (an unpublished ERB short story) 902
"Nu of the Niocene" (*The Eternal Lover*) 134
Number of the Beast (Robert Heinlein) 979
"Number Thirteen" (*The Monster Men*) 328

"Oahu: Singapore or Wake" (published ERB newspaper article) 903
The Oakdale Affair 247, 371–379, 463

The Oakdale Affair and the Rider 373–376, 463–465
Ogden, D. Peter (editor of ERBANIA) *page 4*
Orth, Michael ("The Vaults of Opar") 1112
O'Sullivan, Maureen (movie "Jane") *page 180*
"Our Japanese Problem" (published ERB newspaper article) 904
"Out of Time's Abyss" (article for the Urban Military Academy) 905
Out of Time's Abyss (*The Land That Time Forgot*) 249, 259, 263, 266, 269, 272, 766
"Out There Somewhere" (poem by H. H. Knibbs) 358
The Outlaw of Torn 380–386, 421

Palacios, Rafael (ERB illustrator) 223, 455, 538, 540, 592, 609, 689, 691, 761, 776
Palmer, Raymond 193, 478–481; "Tarzan on Mars" 969
Parker, Frank (illustrator for "Tarzan and the Jewels of Opar") 603, 612
THE PASSING SHOW (magazine) 292
"Patriotism by Proxy" (published ERB article) 906
Paul, Frank R. (ERB illustrator) 252, 314, 323, 326, 441
"Peace and the Militia" (published ERB article) 907
Peeples, Samuel A. *page 187n*
Pellucidar 15–16, 387–400, 482
Penguin Books 726
"The Penningtons" (*The Girl from Hollywood*) 163
The People That Time Forgot (*The Land That Time Forgot*) 248, 262, 265, 268, 271
Pettee, Clinton 77; as illustrator of *Tarzan of the Apes* 694, 1145; *pages 44, 185*
Pflueger, Mary Lucas 110
A Pictorial History of the Tarzan Movies (Lee and Coriell) 1081

281

INDEX

Pierce, James (actor and ERB's son-in-law) 373, 585, 846
Pierce, Joan Burroughs II (ERB's granddaughter) 520
Pilgrims Through Space and Time 1005
Pirate Blood 285, 401–404, 553
Pirates of Venus 292, 405–420, 553, 617, 627
Porges, Irwin: *Edgar Rice Burroughs: The Man Who Created Tarzan* 1116; pages 4, 19n, 222, 267
Powers, Richard (ERB illustrator) 52, 225, 456, 495, 539, 563, 574, 579, 593, 611, 623, 634, 646, 672, 690, 709, 738, 751, 762, 777, 790, 799
prepublication paperbacks: *Beasts of Tarzan* 41; *A Princess of Mars* 422; *Return of Tarzan* 445; *The Son of Tarzan* 483; *Tarzan of the Apes* 695
Price and Reference Guide to Books Written by Edgar Rice Burroughs (James A. Bergen, Jr.) 1008
"The Prince of Helium" (*Warlord of Mars*) 828
A Princess of Mars 23, 342, 421–435, 741–744, 828
printer's "dummy": *The Beasts of Tarzan* 42; *Cave Girl* 79; *Deputy Sheriff of Comanche County* 109; *The Eternal Lover* 137; *Jungle Girl* 205; *Lad and the Lion* 234; *A Princess of Mars* 11, 421, 425; *The Return of Tarzan* 444; *Son of Tarzan* 484; *Tarzan Twins* 653
"The Prospector" (an unpublished ERB film scenario) 908
The Pulps (edited by Tony Goodstone) 439

"The Quest of Tarzan" (Michael Conran reprinting of ARGOSY pulp edition) 552
"Quiet Please!" (unpublished ERB newspaper articles) 909

Random House 718–721, 727
Raymond, Alex 968
The Reader's Guide to Barsoom and Amtor (Dave Van Arnam) 1134
Red Axe of Pellucidar (John Eric Holmes) 981
RED BOOK (magazine): "Tarzan the Untamed" 766
"The Red Hawk" (*The Moon Maid*) 314, 339
"Red Star of Tarzan" (*Tarzan and the Forbidden City*) 569
Ren, Charles (illustrator for Random House) 720, 722
Resnick, Michael D. (*Forgotten Sea of Mars*) 986
"The Resurrection of Jimber-Jaw" 56, 436–442, 517–518, 748, 839, 843; *page 141*
Return of Tarzan 8, 443–461, 484; Armed Services Edition 453; Big Little Book 452, 942; "The Gods of Mars" 174
"Return of the Mucker" 213, 328, 358, 370
"Return to Pellucidar" 467
Richardson, Darrell C.: "Beyond Thirty" reprint 61; *J. Allen St. John: An Illustrated Bibliography* 1169
The Rider 462–466
Rogers, Hubert (ERB illustrator for ARGOSY) 747
Ross, Bill 164, 166, 192, 493, 628; *pages vii, 4*
Rothmund, Cyril Ralph (personal secretary to Burroughs) 749; *page 179*
Roy, John Flint (*A Guide to Barsoom*) 1121
Royer, Mike ("The Wizard of Venus") 840
Rubanowice, Robert J. 1122
Rubimor (Tarzan comic strip illustrator) 1167
Rupert, Conrad H. (*Vikings in Pellucidar*) 987
Rush, John (ERB illustrator) 118, 162

INDEX

"Saddle Horse in Southern California" (published ERB newspaper article) 910

St. John, J. Allen (premiere Burroughs artist) 9–10, 12, 15, 41–46, 49–51, 80–82, 92–97, 99, 104, 107, 119–125, 137–140, 192–197, 214–223, 227, 250–253, 255–256, 273–278, 286–290, 293, 301–304, 315–319, 320, 323, 326, 329–330, 340–341, 347–348, 359–360, 362, 366–367, 371, 381–383, 388–391, 394–396, 406–412, 446, 449–451, 454, 467–470, 472, 483–490, 492–493, 499, 501–505, 525, 532–536, 554–559, 582–590, 598–602, 604–605, 607–608, 612, 618–622, 627–632, 665–669, 679, 681–687, 707, 724, 743, 754–758, 760, 768–773, 775, 794–798, 802–806, 808–809, 811, 817, 820, 829–833, 1168–1169; *pages 25, 36, 58, 145, 164, 177, 182, 200, 240, 250*

St. Martin's Press 441

Samuel, Michael (ERB dust jacket for Book-of-the-Month-Club) 728, 729

Sanjulian (ERB illustrator) 67

Saunders, C. (ERB illustrator) 342, 425

"The Savage Breast" (unpublished ERB film scenario) 911

Savage Pellucidar 467–477

Schoonover, Frank (ERB illustrator) 155, 175–180, 422–424, 426–427, 429–430, 1170; *page 120*

Schwinger, Lawrence (ERB illustrator) 355–356

Science Fiction: The Early Years (Ev Bleiler) 1010

Science-Fiction and Fantasy Publications 63, 311

Science Fiction Book Club editions 21, 101, 155, 183, 202, 260, 282, 325, 431, 508, 515, 814, 835

Science Fiction Classics by Edgar Rice Burroughs 104–106, 396, 817–819

The Scientists Revolt 478–481

Seelye, John (author of introduction to 1990 Penguin *Tarzan of the Apes*) 726

Segrelles (ERB illustrator) 267, 269

"Selling Satisfaction: An Anecdote by Normal Bean" (unpublished ERB article) 912

"Seven Worlds to Conquer" (*Back to the Stone Age*) 24

"The 75th Anniversary Dinner Celebrating the First Publication of a Hardcover Novel by Edgar Rice Burroughs" *pages 186–187n*

Sgroi, Tony (ERB illustrator for Whitman) 561, 564, 573, 575

Shaw, Barclay (ERB illustrator) 232, 616, 1171

Sheldon, Monty 745

Shonfeld, Frank P. (*Bridge of Life; Tarzan's Tribute*) 988

Sigaloff, Sam (ERB illustrator) 28, 72, 127, 129, 412

Signet Classics (New American Library) 725

"Skeleton Men of Jupiter" (*John Carter of Mars*) 186, 194

"Slaves of the Fish Men" (*Escape on Venus*) 119

Sleuthing in the Stacks (Rudolph Altrocchi) 999

Small, Fred W. (ERB illustrator) 40, 77–78, 134, 174, 299, 328, 421, 694, 828; *pages 93, 215*

Smith, Malcolm (ERB illustrator) 195

Smith, Peter (publisher) 16, 99, 319, 395, 526, 811

Snowmen of Jupiter (Henry G. Franke III) 976

Son of Tarzan 311, 482–499, 724; Big Little Book 491, 947

Sorel, Stephen (*Tarzan de Deutschenfresser*) 1130

Soulen, Henry (ERB illustrator) 500

Sperry, A.W. (ERB illustrator) 638–642, 1172; *page 169*

Stahr, Paul (ERB illustrator) 1, 285, 405, 553, 701, 821–823, 825, 1173

Stanley, Robert (ERB illustrator for Dell) 644

283

INDEX

Stein, Modest (ERB illustrator) 8, 33–36, 134, 233, 299, 339, 387; *pages 30, 112*
Stoops, Herbert M. (ERB illustrator) 213, 748, 793
"Stout" (ERB illustrator for the ARGOSY pulp magazine) 337, 581
Stout, William (ERB illustrator) 1174; *pages 223, 233, 236*
"Strange Adventure of Mr. Dinwiddie" (an unpublished ERB story) 913
Stubbersfield, Barry E. (author of numerous Burroughs pastiches) 989
Suydam, Arthur (cover illustrations for Dark Horse Tarzan publications) 741–744
Swords of Mars 500–509, 626, 793
"Symbol of a New Day" (published ERB magazine article) 914
Synthetic Men of Mars 240, 510–516

TACOMA TRIBUNE 160–161
Tales of Three Planets 56, 437, 517–518, 839, 843
Tanar of Pellucidar 15–16, 519–530, 637, 664
"Tangor Returns" 56, 437, 517–518, 839, 843
Tarzan (ice cream cup give-away) 960
"Tarzan: Hollywood's Greatest Jungle Hero" (Behlmer) 1006
Tarzan: In Color (reproductions of the Tarzan Sunday comic strips) 1146
Tarzan: The Lost Adventure 741–746
Tarzan: The Mark of the Red Hyena (Big Little Book) 959
Tarzan Alive (Philip José Farmer) 975
Tarzan and a Daring Rescue (Pam-Am Oil give-away) 962, 963
Tarzan and His Jungle Friends (ice cream cup give-away) 961
"Tarzan and Jane" (*Tarzan's Quest*) 793
Tarzan and Jane in The Collector (Dennis Wilcutt) 994
"Tarzan and Literature" (E. H. Lacon-Watson) 1079, 1141

"Tarzan and Pellucidar" (*Tarzan at the Earth's Core*) 664
Tarzan and the Ant Men 33, 339, 531–542; Better Little Book 537, 953, 954
Tarzan and the Castaways 543–552
"Tarzan and the Champion" (*Tarzan and the Castaways*) 543
Tarzan and the City of Gold 115, 405, 553–567
"Tarzan and the Diamond of Asher" (1934 Tarzan radio series) 568
"Tarzan and the Elephant Men" (*Tarzan the Magnificent*) 748
Tarzan and the Forbidden City 510, 568–577
Tarzan and "The Foreign Legion" 186, 578–580
Tarzan and the Golden Lion 163, 581–596; Better Little Book 591, 952; Photoplay edition 585–588
"Tarzan and the Huns" (*Tarzan the Untamed*) 766
"Tarzan and the Immortal Men" (*Tarzan's Quest*) 793
Tarzan and the Jewels of Opar 11, 462, 597–616; Better Little Book 606, 948
Tarzan and the Journey of Terror (New Better Little Book) 958
Tarzan and the Land of Giant Apes (Better Little Book) 957
Tarzan and the Leopard Men 405, 504, 505, 617–625
Tarzan and the Lightning Man (William Gilmour) 977
Tarzan and the Lion Man 500, 626–636
Tarzan and the Lost Empire 519, 587, 588, 637–648; Better Little Book 643, 956
Tarzan and the Lost Safari 971
"Tarzan and the Lost Tribe" (*Tarzan and the Lost Empire*) 637
Tarzan and the Madman 119, 649–652
"Tarzan and the Magic Men" (*Tarzan the Magnificent*) 436, 747

284

INDEX

"Tarzan and the Man Things" (*Tarzan the Invincible*) 732
Tarzan and the Mark of the Red Hyena (Big Little Book) 974
"Tarzan and the Raiders" (*Tarzan Triumphant*) 782
Tarzan and the Tarzan Twins 653–663; Big Little Books 659–662, 937–939, 966
"Tarzan and the Valley of Luna" (*Tarzan the Untamed*) 767
Tarzan and Tradition: Classical Myth in Popular Literature (Erling Holtsmark) 1068
Tarzan at Mar's Core (Edward Hirschman) 980
Tarzan at the Earth's Core 145, 519, 664–678; Avenel edition 499, 724
"A Tarzan Chronology" (Henning Kure) 744
Tarzan Clans of America 679
Tarzan Escapes (Big Little Book) 941
"The Tarzan Films" (Derral Cheatwood) 1023
Tarzan Finds a Son (MGM film) *page 179*
"Tarzan, Guard of the Jungle" (*Tarzan the Invincible*) 732
Tarzan in the Forbidden City (first ERB paperback book [1940]) 570
Tarzan in the Golden City (Whitman Premium give-away) 964, 965
Tarzan, Jane and Jungle Lust (Edward Hirschman) 980
"Tarzan, John Carter, Mr. Burroughs, and the Long Mad Summer of 1930" (Ray Bradbury) 1013
"Tarzan Jr." (fairy tale written for Colleen Moore) 680
"Tarzan Jungle Detective" 226, 229
Tarzan, King of the Apes (*Tarzan of the Apes*) 721
Tarzan, Lord of the Jungle 1, 586–588, 681–693; Better Little Book 688, 955
"The Tarzan Myth and Jung's Genesis of the Self" (David Cowart) 1030
Tarzan of the Apes 11, 174, 252, 380, 422, 443, 619, 657, 694–731; Acorn edition 696; Armed Services Edition 706; Avenel edition 499, 724; Ballantine reprint 709; Big Little Books 703–704, 932–934; Buccaneer Books 717
Tarzan of the Apes and Little Konga 970
Tarzan of the Grapes (Gene Wolf) 995
Tarzan of the Movies (Gabe Essoe) 1042
Tarzan of the Screen (Big Little Book) 936
Tarzan on Mars (Stuart J. Byrne aka "John Bloodstone") 969
"Tarzan Returns" (*The Beasts of Tarzan*) 47
"The Tarzan Series: A Twentieth Century Case Against Civilization" (Robert J. Rubanowice) 1122
Tarzan the Ape Man (Johnny Weissmuller film from 1932) *page 180*
Tarzan the Avenger (Dell Fast Action book) 967
Tarzan the Fearless (Big Little Book) 935
Tarzan the Invincible 204, 315, 681, 732–740
Tarzan the Magnificent 436, 747–752
Tarzan the Terrible 753–765; Better Little Book 750, 951
Tarzan the Untamed 338, 766–781; Better Little Book 774, 950
"The Tarzan Theme" (ERB article from WRITER'S DIGEST 1932) 916
Tarzan Triumphant 782–792; Avenel edition 499, 724
Tarzan Twins 637, 653–663, 681, 821; Big Little Books 937–939, 966
"Tarzan Under Fire" (newspaper strip of *Tarzan Twins*) 662
Tarzan's Quest 24, 500, 793–800
Tarzan's Revenge (Big Little Book) 945, 946
"Tarzan's Seven Lives" (unpublished Tarzan screenplay) 915
"Tarzan's Tribute" (Frank P. Shonfeld) 988

"The Terrible Tenderfoot" (*The Deputy Sheriff of Comanche County*) 108
"That Damn Dude" (*The Deputy Sheriff of Comanche County*) 108
"Them Thar Papers" (an unpublished ERB script for a home movie) 917
Thompson, Rob (scriptwriter for "Tarzan and the Diamond of Asher" radio series) 568
Three Martian Novels (Dover) 97, 99, 107, 318, 319, 811, 809, 811, 820
Three Science Fiction Novels by Edgar Rice Burroughs 15, 16, 394, 525–526
THRILLING ADVENTURES (magazine): "Tarzan and the Jungle Murders" 544; "The Terrible Tenderfoot" (*The Deputy Sheriff of Comanche County*) 108
Thuvia, Maid of Mars 801–820
Time's Last Gift (Philip José Farmer) 975
"Tiger Girl" 469, 470
Triolo, Jean-Luc (*Les Insurgés de Mars*) 990
TRIPLE-X MAGAZINE 47
"Two-Gun Doak Flies South" (unpublished story by Edgar Rice Burroughs) 918
Two Martian Novels by Edgar Rice Burroughs (Dover Publications) 154, 429–430
Two Venus Novels by Edgar Rice Burroughs (Dover Publications) 292, 414

"Uncle Bill" (an unpublished ERB story) 919
"Uncle Miner and Other Relatives" (an unpublished ERB story) 920
"Under the Moons of Mars" (*A Princess of Mars*) 380, 421
"Under the Red Flag" (*The Moon Maid*) 338
"Unique Salesman's Copy" *see* printer's "dummy"

"Vad Varo of Barsoom" (*The Master Mind of Mars*) 314
Vallejo, Boris (ERB illustrator) 37, 39, 112–113, 172–173, 187, 308, 335, 542, 551, 577, 580, 596, 648, 652, 693, 752, 765, 780–781, 800
Vallely, Henry (Big Little Book illustrator) 491
Van der Merwe, J. D. (*Tarzan*) 991
Van Hise, James 1135, 1136
"Vaults of Opar" (Michael Orth) 1112
Vess, Charles (illustrator for *Tarzan: The Lost Adventure*) 742
Vidal, Gore 725, 1137–1138
Vikings in Pellucidar (Conrad H. Rupert) 987
Vinge, Joan D. (adapter of "Tarzan of the Apes") 720
"The Violet Veil: A Treely True Story" (unpublished very early story) 921
VIRGINIA LEADER (magazine): "Tarzan and the Jewels of Opar" 603, 612
Volland (*The Tarzan Twins*) 653–655; *page 259*

"Wanted—Good Citizens" (an ERB piece from 1918) 922
The War Chief 1, 821–827
The Warlord of Mars 357, 828–838
Waters, William P. (*Essays on Mars: Exploring the Red Planet of Edgar Rice Burroughs*) 1139
Watson, Emmett (ERB illustrator) 24, 436
"Wax Recording by Creator of Tarzan Discovered" 1142
Weiner, Gina Ingoglia (author of *Tarzan*, Whitman Little Golden Book) 992
"A Weird Adventure on Mars" (*The Master Mind of Mars*) 314
Weisman, Robert (Big Little Book illustrator) 606
Weissmuller, Johnny (movie "Tarzan") 1111, 568; *pages 179, 180*
"Welcome to Barsoom" (poster by Gino d'Achille) 815

INDEX

Werper, Barton (pseudonym for author of Gold Star Tarzan pastiches) 993
Westwood, Frank 361, 363, 1206; *page 5*
"What Every Young Couple Should Know" (an unpublished ERB article) 923
"What Is the Matter with the U.S. Army" (an unpublished ERB article) 924
Whelan, Michael (ERB illustrator) 103, 157, 185, 203, 284, 327, 433, 509, 516, 816, 837, 1175
Whipple, Chandler 568
Wilcutt, Dennis (*Tarzan and Jane in The Collector*) 994
Williams, C. D. (ERB illustrator for ALL-STORY) 158
Williams, Dean (ERB illustrator) 745, 746
Williamson, Arlene (map illustrator for Canaveral) 437, 517, 839
Wilma Company, publisher (**"The Girl from Farris's"**) 159
The Wizard of Venus 56, 401–404, 437, 517–518, 839–845, *page 115*

Wolfe, Gene (*Tarzan of the Grapes*) 995
Wolheim, Donald A. (editor of DAW Books) 401
Wyeth, N. C. (artist for *Return of Tarzan*) 443–446, 448–451, 1176–1177; *page 125*

Yeates, Thomas (illustrator for *Tarzan: The Lost Adventure*, published by Dark Horse) 741; *pages v, 71, 129, 157, 221, 243*
"Yellow Men of Barsoom" (*Warlord of Mars*) 828
You Lucky Girl! 546, 846
Young, Robert F. ("The Blonde from Barsoom") 996

Zaula, Ondrek (BLUE BOOK illustrator) 500
"The Zealots" (an unpublished ERB article or story) 926

287

www.ingramcontent.com/pod-product-compliance
Ingram Content Group UK Ltd.
Pitfield, Milton Keynes, MK11 3LW, UK
UKHW041927140426
5217IPUK00014B/346